An Essential Guide to
Business Statistics

An Essential Guide to Business Statistics

Dawn Willoughby

Registered office
John Wiley & Sons Ltd, The Atrium, Southern Gate, Chichester, West Sussex, PO19 8SQ, United Kingdom

For details of our global editorial offices, for customer services and for information about how to apply for permission to reuse the copyright material in this book please see our website at www.wiley.com.

The right of Dawn Willoughby to be identified as the author of this work has been asserted in accordance with the Copyright, Designs and Patents Act 1988.

Library of Congress Cataloging-in-Publication Data

Willoughby, Dawn.
  An essential guide to business statistics / Dawn Willoughby.
      pages cm
  Includes index.
  ISBN 978-1-118-71563-5 (pbk.) – (ebk) – ISBN
978-1-119-06604-0 (ebk) 1. Commercial statistics. I. Title.
  HF1017.W55 2015
  650.01'5195–dc23

                  2014048324

ISBN 978-1-118-71563-5 (pbk)
ISBN 978-1-119-06604-0 (ebk)
ISBN 978-1-119-11854-1 (ebk)

A catalogue record for this book is available from the British Library

Set in 10/12pt, TimesLTStd-Roman by Thomson Digital, Noida, India

Printed in Great Britain by Bell and Bain Ltd, Glasgow

Contents

Preface

Overview

In writing this book for first-year undergraduates who are studying a business-related degree, there have always been three main objectives:

1. To use business-based data and scenarios which are directly related to the subject areas included in the students' chosen degree courses. This helps with engagement, understanding and motivation.
2. To write in a clearly expressed, concise style with sufficient explanation to aid comprehension but without lengthy discussions of statistical concepts that non-mathematicians would find overwhelming.
3. To focus on providing a sufficient quantity of practice exercises so that students have the opportunity to rigorously test their understanding of each topic.

This book will help students to become proficient in the collection, analysis, interpretation and presentation of data. But more than this, it is hoped that they will achieve a deeper appreciation of the importance of statistics in a business context, for understanding customers, making decisions, and planning for the future.

Intended Audience

The intended audience for this book is undergraduate students in their first year at university. The students who will benefit the most will be enrolled on a business-related degree course that requires them to complete an introductory module in business statistics or quantitative methods.

Throughout the UK and Europe, university business schools have been expanding. Student numbers are rising, for both undergraduate and postgraduate courses, and many schools have embarked on ambitious building programmes and extensive partnerships with private enterprises.

Undergraduate degree courses in business schools often include a compulsory module in business statistics, quantitative methods, or similar, in the first year of study.

For example, the following degree courses usually include such a module:

- Accounting and Business
- Accounting and Management
- Finance and Investment Banking
- Business and Management
- Management with Information Technology

Throughout the book, the use of business-based scenarios and associated relevant data will ensure that students are motivated to study and engaged in the material, even if they do not feel a natural affinity with numerical-based subjects.

The book can be used in weekly tutorial classes or for homework exercises, giving students the opportunity to practice applying statistical techniques to business-related data. It can be used as a revision guide in preparation for examinations, or as a resource during classroom teaching.

Key Benefits

This book will benefit students in a variety of ways:

- The learning points of each topic are concisely summarised, providing an essential resource for enhancing understanding and supporting revision.
- Clearly laid-out examples help students to understand the use of statistical formulae and to apply their knowledge to business-related problems which will reinforce their learning.
- Forty practice exercises are available for each chapter in the book, all of which use realistic business-related data. Full worked solutions are provided for every exercise, including tables, graphs and charts.
- Every chapter includes a hints and tips section which will help students to maximise their learning potential and avoid making common mistakes in their calculations and when interpreting their results.
- With reference to examples in the chapter text, screen shots and associated instructions are provided to explain how to use Microsoft Excel 2010 to implement many of the statistical techniques.
- The writing is presented in a clear, readable style with supporting diagrams and examples to ensure that the material is accessible to all students, including those who do not feel that numeracy is their strongest skill.

Acknowledgements

With grateful thanks to all the team at Wiley for their help and support, especially Steve Hardman, Georgia King, Joyce Poh and Juliet Booker.

About the Author

Dawn Willoughby is an award-winning writer and lecturer in statistics who has spent the past ten years working at the University of Reading. She is a qualified mathematics teacher with a degree in Statistics and Computer Science, and currently teaches students on a wide range of undergraduate programmes in areas including business management, statistics, mathematics, psychology, information systems and computer science.

Outside the lecture theatre, Dawn is involved in a variety of projects linked to teaching and learning. She is particularly interested in using technology to enhance student engagement, and also in facilitating a smooth transition for students as they move through the stages of their journey in education.

Her principal mission is to make statistics accessible to students and a wider audience who do not feel a natural affinity with numerical subjects. She firmly believes that everyone should learn to assess the value and quality of figures that are presented to them. With this in mind, she co-authored her first book, *Numbers: Data and statistics for the non-specialist*, which was part of the Academic Skills Series winning the award for Innovation in Learner Resources at the British Council ELTons 2014. Dawn has recently achieved professional recognition as a Fellow of the Higher Education Academy and she is currently working on a master's degree in Education.

Outside education, Dawn is a keen photographer and spends any remaining free time with a good book.

Introduction

In a business context, we frequently collect information with a variety of different objectives in mind. Some examples are:

- To understand our customers better – which products do they prefer to purchase?
- To make decisions about the size of our business – should we expand our sales team?
- To analyse financial information – by how much did our market share increase last year?
- To plan for the future – which location would be suitable for our new manufacturing facility?

However, business-related information, also referred to as data, has no practical use unless it can be properly processed and understood. We need statistics to help us achieve this understanding: statistics is a mathematical science that involves the collection, analysis, interpretation and presentation of data.

KEY TERMS

data	continuous	quantitative data
data set	inferential statistics	variable
descriptive statistics	observation	
discrete	qualitative data	

Collection

In collecting information, we need to ensure that the methods used are efficient in terms of both time and expense. If we choose to focus on a small selection of people or objects then it is important that this group is representative of the entire set of people or objects that we could investigate.

Chapter 2 describes some data collection techniques that can be used when people are involved in an investigation. It also provides a comparison of sampling methods to help us choose people to be included in our group of interest, and it explains how bias can occur when we ask people for information.

Analysis

Throughout the next six chapters, we develop a wide variety of processes that allow us to analyse our information more effectively using three main forms: tabular, graphical and numerical. As data are often collected in large quantities, it is necessary to condense and summarise the detail so that we can begin to understand its meaning. Collectively, these processes are called descriptive statistics.

Chapters 3 and 4 provide examples to illustrate the use of a range of tables, charts and graphs for summarising many different types of information. In Chapters 5 and 6 we focus on numerical methods, describing a 'typical value' and a measure of the variation within our data. When we are especially interested in analysing potential relationships between two data sets, correlation and regression techniques are used, as described in Chapters 7 and 8.

Interpretation

In the final two chapters of this book, we start to introduce some of the theory and techniques known as inferential statistics. Here we attempt to reach conclusions about the entire set of people or objects that we could investigate based on a smaller, representative group.

Covering the basics of probability, Chapter 9 lays the foundation of learning that is needed to understand inferential statistical methods. It explains techniques that can be applied in situations where there is uncertainty and allows us to assign a numerical value to the likelihood of something occurring. Chapter 10 extends our knowledge, providing instructions in using statistical tables to estimate numerical values that describe our collected data.

Presentation

When we have investigated our information thoroughly and discovered new facts, we often need to present these ideas to other people; this might involve writing a report, developing a website or giving a verbal presentation. It is important that we justify our choice of techniques and fully explain the way in which our conclusions have been reached.

Throughout this book, each chapter provides advice on how to present your information. For example, Chapter 4 lists some straightforward guidelines to ensure that graphs and charts are always well presented. Chapters 5 and 6 explain when it is appropriate to use each numerical measure, and Chapter 7 describes the limitations that should be considered before reaching your final conclusions.

Terminology

Before we can apply any of the techniques involved in descriptive and inferential statistics, we need to understand the meaning of some basic terminology.

Variable

A variable is a characteristic or an attribute that can have different values. When you are collecting information, each person or object might provide a different value for each variable.

Observation

The value of a variable for a specific person or object in the group that is of interest is known as an observation. When we have collected many observations for a range of variables, we describe this collection as a data set.

Quantitative and qualitative

Every variable, and therefore each observation, can be classified as quantitative or qualitative depending on the nature of the information. Quantitative data are information that can be counted or measured on a numerical scale. We say that quantitative data can be expressed numerically. Qualitative data represent a characteristic or an attribute that cannot be described using a numerical value. We use words or a single letter for qualitative data.

Discrete and continuous

For quantitative variables only, we can make a further distinction between discrete and continuous data. A discrete variable can assume only specific numerical values, whereas if a variable can assume any numerical value within a specific range, then it is known as continuous. Discrete data can be counted but continuous data are usually measured.

The table below demonstrates how to classify information using this terminology.

Variable	Examples of observations	Quantitative or qualitative	Discrete or continuous
number of employees working for a company	2350; 31; 175,000	quantitative	discrete
reason for customers making their purchase choice	brand; colour; functionality	qualitative	n/a
weight of a cereal packet in a production facility	500.5 g; 499.2 g; 502.3 g	quantitative	continuous

Whenever you collect data for an investigation, they should be classified immediately before the application of any statistical techniques. Deciding whether your data are quantitative or qualitative is an important, but often overlooked, first step: the nature of your information will determine which techniques are appropriate for use, and any conclusions reached at the end of your investigation will depend on correct classification.

Using Excel

Although Microsoft Excel is a general-purpose spreadsheet package, it provides a range of features that we can use to analyse and present our data.

In particular, Excel allows us to:

- construct formulae for performing calculations;
- use built-in functions;
- create graphs and charts to display data.

In this section, we will explain how to construct basic formulae and introduce some simple built-in mathematical functions. The use of statistical functions for measures of central tendency and dispersion, correlation and regression, and for graphical displays will be described at the end of each appropriate chapter.

The screen shots and instructions are associated with the use of MS Excel 2010. Earlier and more recent versions of the software package may have different menu options and may refer to different function names in comparison to the examples provided.

CONSTRUCTING BASIC FORMULAE

To construct a basic formula in Excel, click in the cell in which you want the result to appear and then start your formula with an equals sign (=); this indicates that the subsequent typed information should be regarded by the software package as a formula rather than ordinary text.

Once you have typed an equals sign, you will need to use an appropriate combination of numbers, cell references and operators to produce the calculation in which you are interested. Cell references can be typed, or alternatively you can click in the appropriate cell. When your formula is complete, press **<enter>** to see the result of the calculation.

The following tables show screenshots of the most common operators being used.

Operator	Description	Example: formula	Example: result
*	multiplication		A
1	=3*4
2				A	B
1	12	
2		

Operator	Description	Example: formula	Example: result
			A
1	4
2	5
3	=A1*A2			A	B
1	4	
2	5	
3	20	

To view a completed formula, click in the cell which contains the result and the formula will be displayed in the **formula bar** at the top of the spreadsheet, as follows:

A3	▼		f_x	=A1*A2

	A	B	C	D	E
1	4				
2	5				
3	20				
4					

Operator	Description	Example: formula	Example: result
/	division		

◢	A
1	=18/6
2	

◢	A	B
1	3	
2		

◢	A
1	50
2	10
3	=A1/A2

◢	A	B
1	50	
2	10	
3	5	

Operator	Description	Example: formula	Example: result
+	addition		

◢	A
1	=9+14
2	

◢	A	B
1	23	
2		

◢	A
1	17
2	8
3	=A1+A2

◢	A	B
1	17	
2	8	
3	25	

Operator	Description	Example: formula	Example: result
–	subtraction		

◢	A
1	=19-3
2	

◢	A	B
1	16	
2		

◢	A
1	4
2	15
3	=A1-A2

◢	A	B
1	4	
2	15	
3	-11	

When you are constructing a formula, it is important to consider the order of precedence for the operators that you are using. Excel applies the usual order of precedence so that multiplication and division are performed before addition and subtraction. You will need to use brackets if a change to the order of precedence is required.

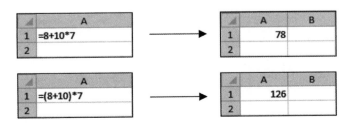

USING BUILT-IN FUNCTIONS

Excel provides a variety of built-in mathematical functions which can be used in addition to creating your own formulae using operators such as multiplication, division, addition and subtraction.

Using the **Formulas** tab on the ribbon, you can access built-in functions in two different ways, as described below.

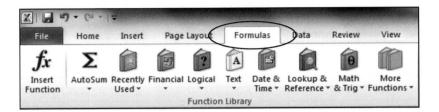

- Click the cell in which you wish the result to appear and then click on **Math & Trig**. Scroll down the list until you find the function required.

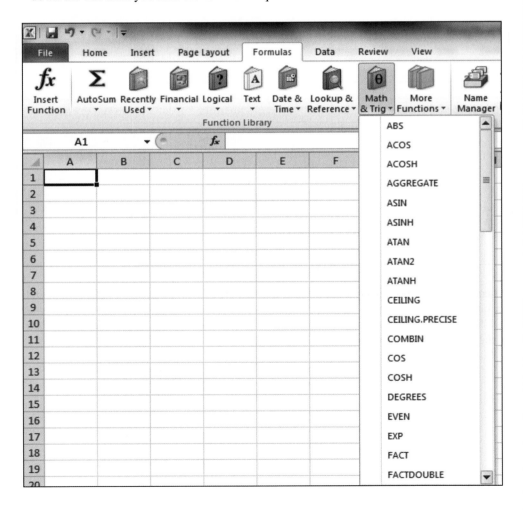

- Alternatively, click in the cell in which you wish the result to appear and then click on **Insert Function**. Select the **Math & Trig** category. Either type some search text in the **Search for a function** box or use the **Select a function** box to find the function you require and click **OK**.

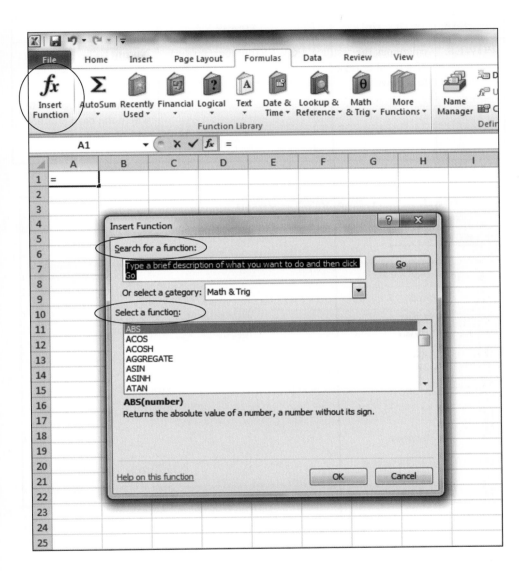

When you have selected the required function from the list, the **Function Arguments** dialog box will be displayed. This provides basic information, including a description of the value that the function will return and details of the arguments required for its operation.

Arguments in bold type must be entered; other arguments are optional and may contain assumed values. Once you have entered a combination of numbers and/or cell references as arguments, the dialog box will show you the result of the function. Finally, press **<enter>** or click **OK** to see the result of the calculation in the spreadsheet cell.

When constructing statistical formulae that include built-in functions, it is most likely that you will use **POWER, SQRT** and **SUM**. A description, screenshots of the **Function Arguments** dialog box and examples of use are shown below for each function each of these functions.

Function	Description	Syntax	Arguments
POWER	calculates the result of a number raised to a power	POWER(number, power)	**Number**: the base number which will be raised to the power **Power**: the exponent to which the base number will be raised

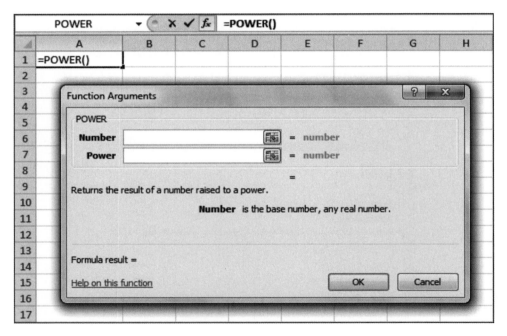

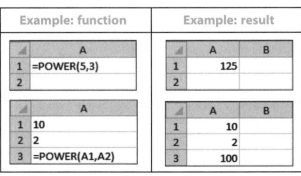

Example: function		Example: result		

	A
1	=POWER(5,3)
2	

	A	B
1	125	
2		

	A
1	10
2	2
3	=POWER(A1,A2)

	A	B
1	10	
2	2	
3	100	

Function	Description	Syntax	Arguments
SQRT	calculates the square root of a number; an error will be returned **#NUM!** if a negative number is used	SQRT(number)	**Number**: the number for which the square root will be calculated

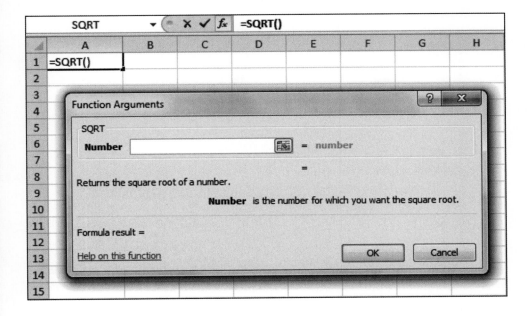

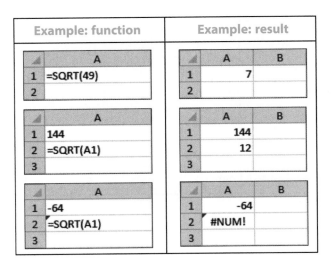

Function	Description	Syntax
SUM	calculates the total of all the numbers used as arguments	SUM(number1, number2 . . .)

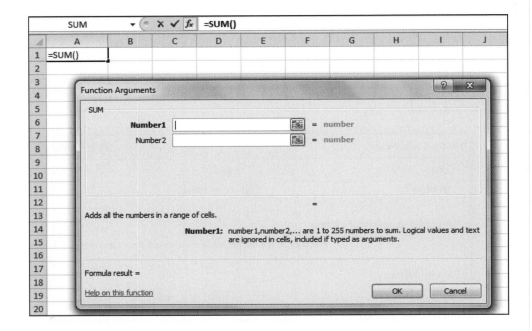

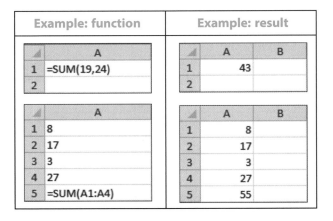

STATISTICAL FUNCTIONS

You can also use the **Formulas** tab to access a selection of statistical functions. As before, there are two methods:

- Click the cell in which you wish the result to appear and then click on **Insert Function**. Select the **Statistical** category. Either type some search text in the **Search for a function** box or use the **Select a function** box to find the function you require, and click **OK**.

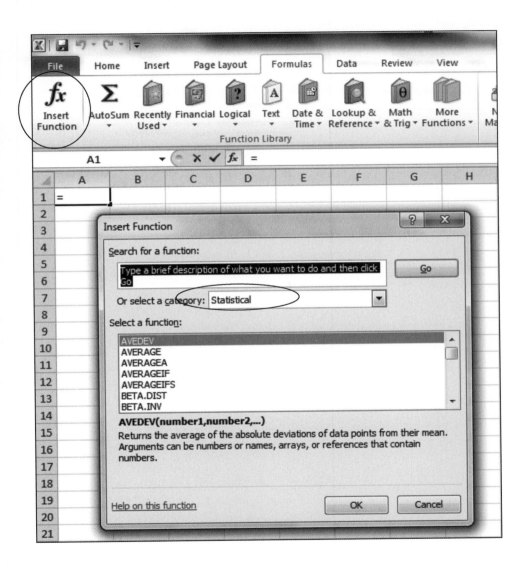

- Alternatively, click the cell in which you wish the result to appear and then click on **More Functions**, and select **Statistical** from the drop-down menu. Scroll down the list until you find the function required.

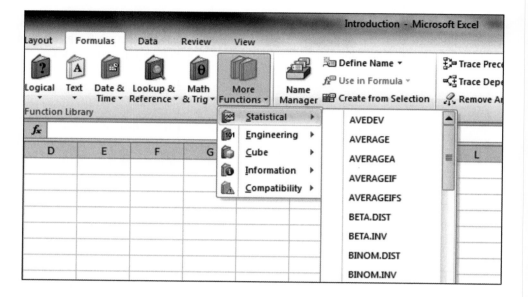

CHAPTER 2

Data Collection

OBJECTIVES

This chapter explains how to:

- distinguish between
  - a population and a sample
  - primary and secondary data
- carry out and compare different sampling methods
- conduct interviews and use questionnaires for data collection
- understand how bias can occur when collecting data

KEY TERMS

census	pilot study	response bias
closed question	population	sample
cluster sampling	primary data	sampling frame
convenience sampling	proportional allocation	secondary data
interview	questionnaire	simple random sampling
interviewee	quota sampling	stratified sampling
non-response bias	representative	systematic sampling
open question	respondent	

Introduction

Many research projects and studies with a business-related focus include collecting data about people. We begin this chapter by introducing some basic terminology that is common to all investigations involving data. We will also explore some of the ways in which we can select a smaller group of people for analysis when it is impractical to collect data about everyone.

We will compare two different techniques for data collection, interviews and questionnaires. Finally, we will discuss how bias can occur.

Throughout the chapter, we will use the same scenario as an example for an investigation. This will give context to the method descriptions and demonstrate some of their associated problems and benefits. The scenario involves investigating the mode of transport used for travelling to work by the 20,000 employees of a large insurance company with offices located in 30 different countries; we are interested in whether employees walk or cycle to work, or use a car, train or bus.

Terminology

Population

When carrying out an investigation to find out information about a group of people, this group is known as the **population**. It is the collection of all the people in whom we are interested.

Sampling frame

A **sampling frame** is a list that includes information about every member of the population. It should contain accurate and up-to-date information and each individual person should only be included in the list once.

Census

If you wanted to find out information about every member of a population then you would carry out a **census**. This is possible if the population of interest contains a reasonably small number of identifiable people. However, when the population is very large, it can become impractical because of the resources required in terms of time and money.

Sample

Rather than carrying out a census of the whole population, you could decide to collect data from a smaller group of members. This smaller group is known as a **sample** – it is the part of the population from which we gather information. Using a sample is often less expensive, quicker and much easier than questioning or observing every member of a population.

EXAMPLE

For our scenario, the population is every person who is employed by the company and the sampling frame is the list of all of those people. To carry out a census of the population in this scenario, we would use the information in the sampling frame to contact every employee of the company and ask them how they travel to work. If we wished to select a sample from the population instead, we may decide to question:

- the employees who work at the insurance office in Brazil, or
- the employees who are aged 25–34, or
- the female employees in the company, or
- the employees who work full-time.

Primary and Secondary Data

In statistics, we also make a distinction between primary and secondary data. **Primary data** are data that you collect yourself as part of your study or investigation, usually using interviews or questionnaires. **Secondary data** are data that have already been collected by someone else, typically found in newspapers and reports, government and business publications, and historical records.

Some advantages and disadvantages of using each type of data are given in the following table:

Primary data	Secondary data
When collecting your own data, they can be processed and presented in ways which best suit your research and results	It is likely that secondary data have already been processed and so they may not be presented in the way you would prefer
Primary data are likely to be • directly related to your investigation • collected in the geographical areas in which you are interested • up to date	Secondary data might have been collected • for a different reason, not directly related to your investigation • in a different geographical area • some time ago and may be out of date
It is difficult and time-consuming to use data collection methods to gather information from large samples of the population	You could have easy and quick access to a large database of information that has been collected over a long period of time
Use of interviews or questionnaires to collect primary data can be expensive	Access to secondary data is often free of charge
You have control over how a sample is chosen and the methods used for data collection	It is often difficult to find out details about how secondary data have been collected

Sampling Methods

If you decide to collect primary data for your investigation, there are many different methods that can be used when selecting a sample from a population of interest, including: simple random, convenience, quota, systematic, cluster and stratified sampling.

The main aim in selecting a sample should be to ensure as far as possible that the sample is **representative** of the entire population. This means that the characteristics of the sample members should reflect as closely as possible the characteristics of the population members.

SIMPLE RANDOM SAMPLING

In simple random sampling, every possible sample of a specified size has an equal chance of being selected. There are three basic steps to creating a simple random sample. Firstly, a unique number is given to each member of the population. Then a computer program is used to randomly generate a subset of the allocated numbers according to the size of sample required. Finally, the sample is created by choosing the members of the population whose numbers match the set of generated random numbers, without replacement, so that if someone is chosen once, they cannot be chosen again.

The main advantage with this method is that every member of the population has an equal chance of being chosen for the sample, rather than leaving selection to the judgement of the researcher. The resulting sample may be representative of the entire population, but this would depend on the characteristics of the members that were randomly selected. However, it is only possible to use simple random sampling if a reliable sampling frame is available, listing all the population members. Sometimes it can be expensive and time-consuming to produce the sample, particularly if the population members are geographically dispersed.

EXAMPLE

Suppose we decide to select a sample of 500 employees from the insurance company so that we can ask them about their transport for travelling to work. Starting with the sampling frame, each of the 20,000 employees would be given a unique number from 1 to 20,000. A section of the list might look like this:

Number	Surname	First name	Gender	Age
. . .	. . .	. . .	. . .	. . .
15235	Smith	Alison	f	< 25
15236	Fields	George	m	> 54
15237	Whitman	Sally	f	< 25
15238	Green	Samantha	f	25–34
15239	Hall	Jim	m	< 25
15240	Pearce	Susan	f	25–34
15241	Thomas	Amanda	f	45–54
15242	Jones	Adrian	m	35–44
15243	Taylor	Peter	m	35–44
15244	Davies	Julia	f	25–34
. . .	. . .	. . .	. . .	

The next step would involve using a computer program to randomly generate numbers, between 1 and 20,000. We would identify the person represented by each randomly generated number and then select that person for the sample. For example, if the number 15238 was included in the generated list, then Samantha Green would be selected for the sample and we would contact her to find out whether she walks or cycles to work, or uses a car, train or bus.

Number	Surname	First name	Gender	Age
. . .	. . .	. . .	. . .	. . .
15237	Whitman	Sally	f	< 25
15238	Green	Samantha	f	25–34
15239	Hall	Jim	m	< 25
. . .	. . .	. . .	. . .	

Using this method of sampling, it is possible that the selected 500 employees might work in 25 of the 30 countries in which the insurance company has offices. If we needed to physically travel to meet each member of the sample in person, this would be a very time-consuming investigation. However, if we decided to email each member of the sample, then clearly the investigation would require fewer resources.

The sample may be representative of the population with respect to characteristics such as gender and age, but this will not necessarily happen with a simple random sampling method. It is possible that every randomly generated number will be associated with an employee who is aged under 25. In this situation, any analysis of the data collected will be biased towards the younger employees in the company who may find car insurance too expensive and therefore use an alternative mode of transport rather than driving.

CONVENIENCE SAMPLING

Convenience sampling simply involves choosing people who are conveniently available to be questioned.

On the positive side, this method can be carried out very quickly. It is also inexpensive and a sampling frame containing information about every population member is not required. However, the resulting sample is not likely to be representative of the entire population – for example, it will probably only involve people in the local area or perhaps the friends, family and colleagues of the researcher.

EXAMPLE

To use convenience sampling for our insurance company scenario, we could simply stand outside the main entrance of the London office at 9am on a Monday morning and ask the next 500 people who enter the building whether they travelled by car, bus, train, or bicycle, or whether they walked.

Although this method would be fast and inexpensive, it is likely that our sample would not be representative of all the employees in the company for some of the following reasons:

- The main door may be situated directly opposite a train station, whereas the large car park for employees might have a covered walkway leading directly into an alternative entrance.
- We have selected 9am to conduct our survey, which limits the sample to people who enter the building at that time; some employees may work in shift patterns depending on their role within the company.
- By choosing to be located in London, we are eliminating all of the people who work at the other offices around the world.

QUOTA SAMPLING

With **quota sampling**, we choose a characteristic of the population, and then use that characteristic to choose specified numbers of people who are conveniently available. For example, we may decide to split the population by gender, and then question 20 women and 20 men to collect data for an investigation.

Quota sampling is similar to convenience sampling, but the resulting sample is likely to be more representative of the population because it takes into account the characteristics of population members. It does not require a sampling frame and is a fairly quick and inexpensive method of sampling.

EXAMPLE

Considering our investigation into the mode of transport used for commuting to work, we could make use of the fact that our population of employees is divided into different age groups: under 25, 25–34, 35–44, 45–54, and over 54. We could then stand outside the main entrance of the London office at 9am on a Monday morning and question the next 100 people from each age group who enter the building.

Clearly our sample would not be entirely representative of all the employees in the company for the same set of reasons that we highlighted with respect to convenience sampling, but at least each age group would be represented in this sample.

SYSTEMATIC SAMPLING

For **systematic sampling**, you would choose a starting point at random in a list of all members of the population, and then systematically select each person occurring in the list at a specific interval. For example, if the population contained 200 people and you wanted to create a sample of 20, then you would select every 10th person from the random starting point in the list.

This method is a good approximation of simple random sampling in terms of creating a representative sample, but it is likely to be easier to administer. Once again, it is only possible to use systematic sampling if a reliable sampling frame is available, listing all the population members. If the population members are geographically dispersed, it can be expensive and time-consuming to produce the sample. The sample may not be representative if there is a pattern in the population where people with similar characteristics occur at regular intervals.

EXAMPLE

For our insurance company scenario, we would begin with the sampling frame for the population and use a computer program to randomly generate a single number between 1 and 40 to use as a starting point in the list. We would then include the person represented by the starting number, and every subsequent 40th person from the list until 500 employees had been selected in total for the sample. Suppose our randomly generated number was 26. Then we would choose employees from the sampling frame as follows:

Number	Surname	First name	Gender	Age
. . .	. . .	. . .	. . .	. . .
00026	Price	John	m	45–54
. . .	. . .	. . .	. . .	. . .
. . .	. . .	. . .	. . .	. . .
00066	Brown	Stephanie	f	>54
. . .	. . .	. . .	. . .	. . .
. . .	. . .	. . .	. . .	. . .
00106	Fisher	Molly	f	>54
. . .	. . .	. . .	. . .	. . .
. . .	. . .	. . .	. . .	. . .
00146	Young	Patrick	m	45–54
. . .	. . .	. . .	. . .	

For simple random sampling, we highlighted the problems of increased resources if our selected 500 employees worked in 25 of the 30 countries in which the insurance company has offices, and also the possibility that every member selected for the sample would be aged under 25. Both of these issues apply equally to systematic sampling.

CLUSTER SAMPLING

In **cluster sampling**, it is necessary to divide the population members into groups or clusters. A random sample of clusters is chosen and then the sample is created from all of the people contained in each chosen cluster.

Cluster sampling can be a very convenient and practical way of producing a sample – it can reduce the time and money involved if the members of the population are spread throughout a wide geographical area. Unlike some of the other sampling methods, cluster sampling does not require us to obtain a sampling frame to provide information about the whole population. However, if the people in each cluster have very similar characteristics then the sample may not be fully representative of the population – this can be improved by ensuring that the members of each cluster are as representative as possible.

EXAMPLE

Using cluster sampling to produce a sample of employees from the insurance company, it would be sensible to view the employees working at the office in each of the 30 countries as a group, or cluster.

If we decided to choose six clusters for sampling, we would number each cluster 1–30 and use a computer package to randomly generate numbers within this range, as follows:

1	2	3	4	5	6
Canada	Mexico	Latvia	China	Brazil	Spain

7	8	9	10	11	12
Poland	England	Uruguay	Belgium	Chile	Singapore

13	14	15	16	17	18
Sweden	Germany	Argentina	Finland	Oman	Estonia

19	20	21	22	23	24
Saudi Arabia	Columbia	France	Lithuania	Bahrain	Italy

25	26	27	28	29	30
India	Norway	Ireland	Croatia	Malaysia	Switzerland

To produce our sample data, we would contact every employee in the offices located in Mexico, Chile, Sweden, Estonia, Columbia and Malaysia to ask their mode of transport for travelling to work.

Now if we needed to physically travel to meet each member of the sample in person, we have considerably reduced the time and money resources required compared to our simple random sampling method because we will only travel to six countries. However, if each of our chosen offices shares a common characteristic then our sample may not necessarily be representative of the entire population. Suppose these six offices are situated in city-centre locations where parking for cars is limited and expensive. Our sample data may show that very few employees drive to work, but this might not be a good representation of the number of drivers in the entire population.

STRATIFIED SAMPLING

Stratified sampling is similar to cluster sampling, but this time the population is divided into groups or strata chosen specifically to represent different characteristics within the population. The choice of characteristic will probably be influenced by the interests of the researcher, but each member of the population must belong to one, and only one, of the strata. A simple random sample of members is then selected from every stratum. Sometimes the sample size taken from each stratum is in proportion to the relative size of the group in the whole population; this is known as proportional allocation. For example, if the population contained 1000 women and 500 men, the sample of women would be twice the size of the sample of men.

Using stratified sampling can be a rather complex and time-consuming process, but the resulting sample is likely to be representative, particularly if randomly generated numbers are used to select members from each stratum. Before beginning the process, a very detailed sampling frame is required so that the information can be used to divide up the population effectively.

EXAMPLE

Considering our insurance company scenario, we may be interested in whether the mode of transport that employees use to travel to work is somehow linked to their age.

In this situation, it would be appropriate to divide the members of the population into groups, or strata, according to their age. Each member of each stratum would be given a unique number within that stratum.

Age: <25			
Number	Surname	First name	Gender
. . .	. . .	. . .	...
0346	Smith	Alison	f
0347	Whitman	Sally	f
0348	Hall	Jim	m
. . .	. . .	. . .	. . .

Age: 25–34			
Number	Surname	First name	Gender
. . .	. . .	. . .	. . .
1002	Green	Samantha	f
1003	Pearce	Susan	f
1004	Davies	Julia	f
. . .	. . .	. . .	. . .

Age: 35–44			
Number	Surname	First name	Gender
. . .	. . .	. . .	. . .
1025	Jones	Adrian	m
1026	Taylor	Peter	m
1027	Piper	Jack	m
. . .	. . .	. . .	. . .

Age: 45–54			
Number	Surname	First name	Gender
. . .	. . .	. . .	. . .
0650	Thomas	Amanda	f
0651	Price	John	m
0652	Young	Patrick	m
. . .	. . .	. . .	. . .

Age: >54			
Number	Surname	First name	Gender
. . .	. . .	. . .	. . .
0098	Fields	George	m
0099	Brown	Stephanie	f
0100	Fisher	Molly	f
. . .	. . .	. . .	. . .

Using simple random sampling, a selection of employees would then be chosen from each stratum corresponding to the numbers generated randomly by a computer program. As there are five strata, we would choose 100 members from each stratum to provide us with a sample of 500 employees.

Stratified sampling with proportional allocation affects the number of members we would choose from each stratum. Suppose 10% of our employees were under 25, 40% were aged 25–34, 30% were aged 35–44, 15% were aged 45–54 and 5% were over 54.

We would choose our sample sizes from the strata relative to these percentages in the population as follows:

10% of 500 = 50 employees under 25
40% of 500 = 200 employees aged 25–34
30% of 500 = 150 employees aged 35–44
15% of 500 = 75 employees aged 45–54
5% of 500 = 25 employees over 54

Using stratified sampling ensures that all of the age groups in the population are represented in the sample of employees. This is important if we are interested in linking mode of transport for travelling to work with age. The method is quite complex to administer and a detailed list of all the employees, including their age, is required before we can start the process. However, the resulting sample should be highly representative of the population, especially if proportional allocation is also used to take account of the number of employees in each age group working for the company.

COMPARING SAMPLING METHODS

The method chosen for sampling depends on the nature of the population and resources available in terms of both time and money. The main aim is to produce a sample that is as representative of the entire population as possible given our (usually limited) resources, so that any observations made about the sample can be generalised to draw conclusions about the population.

	Sample frame needed	Easy to carry out	Representative
Simple random	yes	✓	✓✓
Convenience	no	✓✓✓	✗
Quota	no	✓✓✓	✓
Systematic	yes	✓✓	✓✓
Cluster	no	✓✓✓	✓✓
Stratified	yes	✓	✓✓✓

Each sampling method described in this chapter has been considered in the context of an investigation which involves collecting data about people. However, these five methods could also be used if we are interested in making observations about objects. Examples might include:

- type of houses built in Hampshire;
- colour of cars purchased in the UK in July;
- genre of film shown at cinemas last year;
- exam results in the 10 best schools in Manchester.

Data Collection Techniques

Once you have decided how to select a sample from the population of interest, the next stage in your investigation will involve considering how to collect data from the people in the sample. There are two main techniques: interviews and questionnaires.

INTERVIEWS

Interviews involve speaking to each person in your sample individually to ask them questions and gather information about their opinions. The person being interviewed is known as an interviewee. Conducting interviews might be time-consuming, but the researcher is likely to be able to gather rich and varied information from the sample members.

Interviews can be either structured or informal. For a structured interview, the researcher prepares a set of questions in advance and asks only those questions during the interview. The data collected from different interviewees can be compared and analysed easily because each interview consists of the same questions. The prepared set of questions makes structured interviews quicker to conduct than informal interviews. However, they limit the amount of rich data that can be gathered because the researcher is not able to pursue an unexpected direction in the interview leading from an interesting response from an interviewee.

During an informal interview, the researcher is allowed to ask any questions that they feel would be relevant, based on the interviewee's responses. The researcher is not restricted by a prepared set of questions but care must be taken to remain in sight of the investigation objectives, otherwise time will be wasted on collecting irrelevant information. Although this method may result in the collection of very rich data, it is likely to be so varied that making comparisons and analysing responses from different interviewees will be difficult for the researcher; drawing conclusions from the sample data will be a complex process.

Interviews can be conducted face-to-face or by telephone. It can be less expensive, more convenient and quicker to interview sample members by telephone rather than in person, particularly if the sample consists of a large group of people who are geographically dispersed. However, the researcher must give consideration to the time of day at which the telephone call is made: calling in the daytime may result in an over-representation of people who have preschool-aged children, whereas making calls in the evening may under-represent people who attend evening activities.

QUESTIONNAIRES

Using written questionnaires can provide a quicker and less expensive way of collecting data compared to conducting interviews. The person who completes a written questionnaire is known as the **respondent**. The preparation of the questionnaire can be time-consuming because it is important to produce questions that are easy for people to understand and straightforward for them to answer. Questions should also be carefully designed so that the researcher is effectively able to analyse the answers received and use them to draw conclusions for their investigation.

As an alternative to using postal services for distribution, online questionnaires are becoming increasingly popular.

Using an electronic system has many advantages. It will reduce the resources required, in terms of money and time, for distribution and collection because there is no printing or posting involved in this method. Software packages for creating questionnaires are user-friendly and efficient; they are often free of charge and also handle distribution automatically via email and social media. You can design a questionnaire that looks attractive and interesting, using features such as pop-up images and drop-down menus to encourage people to participate. More people may respond to an online request for information because participating is perceived to be quicker than completing a written questionnaire. Responses received can be processed electronically by the researcher; results can be input directly into a spreadsheet or other type of computer program for analysis, which reduces mistakes and saves time.

However, there are some problems associated with online questionnaires. As the use of online distribution increases, people may become overloaded with electronic requests for information and so become more likely to delete or ignore the request. Also, you are restricting your sample members to those who have regular access to the Internet; this may result in under-representation of part of the population such as older people. Even though a request for information via email or social media may be successfully received by a person, software incompatibility or other technical problems may mean that they are unable to access the questionnaire or return it to the researcher.

OPEN AND CLOSED QUESTIONS

In designing a written questionnaire or preparing for a structured interview, there should be a range of open and closed questions presented by the researcher. **Open questions** allow a respondent or an interviewee to give any answer, so that they can express their opinion using their own words. These questions can take a long time to answer, but they provide the researcher with detailed information about the topic under investigation. **Closed questions** have a fixed number of possible answers from which the participant must choose. They can be answered much more quickly than open questions, and the researcher will find that the responses are easier to analyse. However, closed questions will not provide such rich data because there are limited options available for responses.

EXAMPLE

For our scenario involving an investigation into the way in which employees travel to work, we could use the following closed and open questions in a structured interview or a written questionnaire:

CLOSED

What is your age?

under 25 ☐   25–34 ☐   35–44 ☐   45–54 ☐   over 54 ☐

How do you usually commute to work?

walk ☐   cycle ☐   use a car ☐   travel by train ☐   take a bus ☐   other ☐

OPEN

Explain the reasons why you have chosen your method of commuting to work.

Give your opinion on whether you think that the employee or the employer should be responsible for any costs associated with travelling to work.

GOOD QUESTION DESIGN

1. **Avoid giving biased or leading questions**

   Leading or biased questions are ones which strongly suggest the answer that is required by the researcher to support a specific conclusion to their investigation. The questions make the interviewee or respondent feel pressurised into agreeing with an idea or statement even though this may not reflect their real opinion. When answering these questions, participants often take the easiest 'path' of agreement that requires the least amount of time and consideration.

   ## EXAMPLE

   Research has shown that walking to work is associated with a longer life expectancy. Do you think walking to work is better for your health than driving a car?

   The researcher who wrote this question is giving a clear indication of their viewpoint – that walking to work is healthier than driving. It is likely that employees will agree with the strongly worded statement about life expectancy rather than considering their own opinion.

2. **Questions should be unambiguous**

   Questions that are ambiguous are likely to be interpreted in different ways by different people; they are subjective because people can give a different meaning to the same word. The responses are not always useful to the researcher because they do not know whether the question has been correctly understood.

   ## EXAMPLE

   Does it take a long time to travel from your home to the office location where you usually work?

   This question is subjective because different people will interpret the phrase 'a long time' in different ways. Some employees may consider a commuting time of more than 30 minutes to be 'long', whereas others may think that taking less than two hours to travel is reasonable.

3. **Do not use overlapping intervals**

   Any numerical intervals that you provide as answers should not overlap with each other so that there is only one interval that each respondent or interviewee can choose. If you use overlapping intervals, the participant will not know which interval applies to them and therefore may decide not to answer the question.

EXAMPLE

What is the distance between your home and the office location where you usually work?

less than 1 mile ☐   1–3 miles ☐   4–10 miles ☐

11–20 miles ☐   20 miles or more ☐

If an employee lived exactly 20 miles from their office, they would not know whether to tick the box labelled '11–20 miles', or '20 miles or more'.

4. **Avoid compound questions**

Compound questions ask more than one question at the same time so that it is difficult for the participant to know how to interpret and answer the question correctly. It may be possible for the researcher to misinterpret the results of these questions because they cannot be sure about the meaning of the answers received.

EXAMPLE

Do you use travelling to work as part of your weekly fitness routine, or do you exercise in other ways such as playing a team game?   Yes/No

If an employee answers 'no' to this question, they could be saying 'no, I do not use travelling to work as part of my weekly fitness routine' or 'no, I do not exercise in other ways' or 'no, I do not play a team game'. It is not clear how an employee would respond if they walk to work as part of their weekly fitness routine but do not exercise in other ways.

5. **Allow for all possible answers**

You should ensure that every person is able provide an answer to each question. For closed questions, this often means including an 'other' category so that participants can choose an alternative answer if the ones you have provided do not apply to their situation or viewpoint.

EXAMPLE

What is the location of the office where you usually work?

China ☐   Belgium ☐   India ☐   Croatia ☐   Canada ☐   Bahrain ☐

The insurance company has offices in 30 countries but only six choices are given in this question. An employee working in the office in Mexico would not be able to give a response.

6. **Make sure questions can be answered**

A common mistake is to ask people questions to which they cannot remember the answer, often because it is a long time ago or because you are asking them to measure or count something that they would not normally calculate. Many responses will be guesses rather than the true answer, and participants may become frustrated with this type of question.

EXAMPLE

> How much money did you spend on travelling to work last year?

Not every employee will be able to remember or calculate the total cost of travelling to work over the period of a whole year; it is unlikely that car drivers would know their petrol costs because they probably use their car for many other reasons in addition to commuting.

COMPARING TECHNIQUES

When collecting data, there are many benefits but also some difficulties associated with interviewing in comparison to using a questionnaire. Figure 2.1 shows some positive and negative aspects for each technique.

positive ↑ negative

interviews · questionnaires

It is possible to ask more complex questions in an interview because the researcher is available to explain them more fully if the interviewee does not understand the meaning.

Only straightforward questions can be used in a questionnaire; the researcher must make sure that they can easily be understood because no further clarification can be given.

Interviews usually have a higher response rate because people will generally find it harder to refuse a request for information when they are approached directly.

Members of the sample who receive a written questionnaire are more likely to ignore it, particularly if they do not have a strong opinion on the topic under investigation.

In an informal interview, the researcher has the opportunity to ask additional questions if they need more explanation about a response from the interviewee.

If the researcher does not understand an answer given by a respondent, there is no opportunity to ask for more details and the collected data might not be usable.

When conducting your own interviews to collect primary data, you know that the interviewees are the people you have chosen to answer the questions.

When you receive completed questionnaires that have been distributed by post or email, it is not possible to know if the intended sample member has actually answered the questions.

Interviews are time-consuming because the researcher can only talk to one person at a time; data collection will be expensive if the researcher employs several interviewers.

Questionnaires are a time-efficient method of collecting data from a large sample of people; any postage costs incurred are likely to be less than telephone charges or interviewer fees.

If the members of the sample are dispersed geographically then the researcher will have to spend more time and more expense travelling to each location.

Questionnaires can easily be sent to sample members when they are located across a wide geographical area; this allows the researcher to gather data from a wider variety of places.

An interviewee is more likely to give an untruthful or exaggerated answer when the researcher asks a direct question which is sensitive.

Respondents are more likely to give truthful answers to sensitive questions because they will be completing the questionnaire anonymously.

negative ↓ positive

FIGURE 2.1 Positive and negative aspects of interviewing and using questionnaires for data collection

Understanding Bias

If the responses obtained from interviews or written questionnaires are biased, then the data collected might be irrelevant to your investigation or not sufficiently accurate and representative to allow conclusions to be generalised to the population of interest. There are two main types of bias – response and non-response.

When **response bias** occurs, it means that the answers given in an interview or a questionnaire do not reflect the true facts and opinions of the participant. Sometimes people choose to exaggerate or misrepresent facts so that they present themselves more favourably. Particularly with respect to sensitive topics such as their financial situation or health-related issues, they may over-estimate or under-estimate true values, reporting perhaps a higher salary or a lower weekly consumption of alcohol. The way in which questions are asked or worded can also lead to response bias. A participant may feel pressurised into giving an answer which they know is expected rather than an answer which accurately reflects their own viewpoint. In this situation, the collected data in the investigation will be more representative of the researcher's opinion than the sample members' views.

Often people will choose not to participate when you ask them to provide data for your investigation. **Non-response bias** can occur when these non-responders have different characteristics and opinions from the people who do participate, resulting in data being collected that are not representative of the entire population. For example, suppose your sample includes both men and women, but all of the men decline to be interviewed – the data you collect will not be representative of both genders. In addition, people who have an extreme viewpoint, either positive or negative, about a specific issue are more likely to share their feelings than people who are uninterested. Sometimes non-response bias occurs because people decide not to answer a particular question in an interview or on a written questionnaire. For example, participants may not find an appropriate option for a closed question or they may not have the time to answer a range of open questions. In these situations, the researcher is not able to know the reasons for the missing data and so it can be difficult to draw accurate conclusions for the investigation.

Both response and non-response bias can be reduced if you spend time thinking about the type of questions to be asked and how to express them clearly. You should try to avoid revealing your own opinions in questions because this may influence the answers given by interviewees and respondents. Ensure that participants fully understand what they are being asked so that you can be confident that their responses are meaningful.

HINTS AND TIPS

PLAN AHEAD

It is essential that you carefully plan an investigation before making decisions about data sources, sampling methods and data collection techniques. Think about the goals of your research and consider the benefits and problems associated with each decision: use of primary or secondary data, matching resources to an appropriate sampling method, and whether you will conduct interviews or distribute written questionnaires. Above all, aim to make your sample representative of the population of interest and to reduce bias as much as possible when you collect data.

PILOT STUDY

Always use a **pilot study** to test the quality of the questions in your questionnaire or interview. This involves asking a small group of people, often friends or family members, to answer the questions and give their opinion on the clarity of them. It should help you find any questions that are difficult for people to understand or ones that they are reluctant to answer. It is useful to keep a record of the pilot study results and the changes you make to your questions as a result of the feedback.

IMPROVING RESPONSE RATE

Response rate is calculated as the number of questionnaires returned by respondents divided by the number of questionnaires distributed. To improve the response rate in your investigation:

- make sure all questions are clearly worded and easy to answer;
- include information about why the investigation is important and explain any potential positive impact of the results;
- contact people who do not respond using a follow-up telephone call or email;
- consider offering a reward to respondents, such as free advice or discount vouchers.

Practice Exercises

1   The management team of a mail order company is trying to decide which type of music to play in staff canteens in their office buildings. They plan to find out about the music preferences of their employees. However, it is too time-consuming to ask every person who works for the company, so they decide that only the employees aged 20–25 will be asked.
(a) Which group of people is the population and which group is the sample?
(b) Do you think that the sample data collected will be a good representation of the music preferences for the entire population? Give a reason for your answer.

2   The manager of a furniture store believes that improving customer service will result in an increase in sales. He decides to send a paper questionnaire to each of his customers, asking them to describe their purchasing experience in his store.
(a) How would the response rate be calculated?
(b) List three ways in which the manager could maximise the response rate.

3   Explain the difference in method between simple random sampling and systematic sampling.

4   Describe what is meant by response bias and give an example of a situation in which it might occur.

5 Decide if collecting data in the following scenarios involves convenience, cluster, systematic or stratified sampling:
   (a) An investigation is carried out into the amount paid annually per household on electricity in Glasgow. A simple random sampling method is used to choose 30 streets in the town, and then every house in each chosen street is visited to ask the occupants about their electricity bill.
   (b) A researcher is interested in whether men spend more money than women at airport shops whilst waiting to board their flight. He divides the passengers on a flight into two groups, male and female, and then uses a simple random sampling method to select 15 men and 15 women from whom he gathers information about their spending at the airport.

6 An award-winning pizza delivery store is passionate about the quality of its pizza toppings. Having decided to carry out a customer opinion survey during one week in July, they question every customer who orders a ham and pineapple pizza during that week.
   (a) Explain why this sample of customers is not representative of the whole population.
   (b) Describe how you could use stratified sampling to obtain a more representative sample.

7 Give an example of a leading or biased question that could be asked when interviewing people about whether more companies should encourage their employees to work from home.

8 Explain why it is often better to collect data using a sample rather than by carrying out a census.

9 With the aid of examples, explain two guidelines that could be given as advice to a researcher who is designing a questionnaire to investigate people's attitudes towards the recent increase in food prices.

10 In a modern city-centre complex, there are 15 building blocks each containing four spacious apartments. The on-site warden would like to find out about the residents' attitude towards recycling, but he does not have time to visit each one of the 60 apartments.
   (a) Describe how you would use cluster sampling to collect data from the residents of 20 apartments as a representative sample of the population.
   (b) Describe one advantage and one disadvantage of cluster sampling.

11 A retail analyst would like to investigate the number of sales assistants employed by the stores in a shopping mall located just outside a major city. There are 280 stores in the mall, but the analyst has limited resources for their investigation. He decides to use a simple random sampling method to select 45 stores from which to gather the information he needs.
   Describe how he would obtain the sample of stores using this method.

12 Six steps to ensure good question design are:
   • Avoid giving biased or leading questions.
   • Questions should be unambiguous.
   • Do not use overlapping intervals.
   • Avoid compound questions.

- Allow for all possible answers.
- Make sure questions can be answered.

Using this list, describe which problem applies to each of the questions below. Explain your reasons.

(a) How much did you spend on books, music and films last month?
(b) Making products from recycled materials will preserve natural resources for future generations. Do you agree that recycling household waste is important?
(c) What is your favourite flavour of ice-cream: strawberry, chocolate or vanilla?
(d) How many train journeys did you make last month?

| less than 5 ☐ | 5–10 ☐ | 10–15 ☐ | more than 15 ☐ |

(e) Have you ever booked a holiday online and did you find it easy to search for the type of holiday you required?   ☐ Yes ☐ No
(f) Do you spend a long time reading?

13 A sampling method in which every member of the population has an equal chance of being chosen for the sample is known as:
(a) Simple random sampling
(b) Convenience sampling
(c) Quota sampling

14 A councillor wants to ask 250 people living in the local area whether they are satisfied with the frequency of the bus services. He has a limited budget and needs to act quickly because the next local election will take place shortly. Explain why it would be better to use online questionnaires for data collection rather than conducting interviews.

15 A printing firm produces 5000 promotional flyers for an annual charity event. Describe how systematic sampling would be used to select a sample of 50 flyers in which the quality of the images could be checked, assuming that the starting number generated is 24.

16 Which of the following statements describe collecting data by conducting an interview and which describe using a written questionnaire?
(a) More complex questions can be asked because you can explain the meaning if a participant does not understand.
(b) The researcher will not know if a question has been left blank because the meaning was unclear or the person chose not to answer.
(c) A large amount of data can be gathered using only a limited amount of time and money.
(d) It can be expensive to collect data from geographically dispersed sample members.

17 A sampling frame is:
(a) A list of people who have been chosen for a sample.
(b) The list of groups chosen in stratified sampling.
(c) A list that includes information about every member of the population.

18 Describe two advantages and two disadvantages of using written questionnaires to collect data for an investigation.

19 For each of the scenarios below, describe a possible sampling frame that could be used for simple random sampling:
(a) A survey to find out which political party people intend to vote for at the next county council elections.
(b) An investigation into the length of time each member of a management team spends in meetings during one week.
(c) A research study about the number of lecturers at a university who have published a textbook.

20 Describe two advantages and two disadvantages of conducting interviews to collect data for an investigation.

21 To conduct a customer satisfaction survey, a restaurant manager records the name and telephone number of every customer who eats in his restaurant during a one-month period. From a random starting point in the list, he telephones that customer and every 25th customer until he has collected data from 50 people about their experience of eating in his restaurant. State which sampling method was used in this investigation.

22 The following question appears in an online questionnaire.

Many people feel that the current government do not spend enough money on health, transport, policing and education. Do you agree?

What do you think is wrong with the question?

23 Explain the difference between cluster sampling and stratified sampling.

24 A pilot study involves:
(a) Offering discount vouchers to improve your response rate.
(b) Testing the quality of your questions on a small group of people.
(c) Checking that your sample members wish to be interviewed.

25 Explain the difference between a population and a sample.

26 A researcher is investigating the amount of homework given to pupils at a large comprehensive secondary school. Every Year 9 pupil is asked to give information about the amount of homework they receive each week. Would the researcher be able to use the sample data collected to draw conclusions about the amount of homework given to all of the pupils at the school?

27 Decide whether the following data collection scenarios could result in response or non-response bias. Explain your reasons.
(a) A customer satisfaction questionnaire distributed to people eating in a restaurant.
(b) In an investigation about healthy eating, a researcher asks a question about the number of chocolate bars eaten last week.
(c) An interviewer lists all of the reasons why buying locally produced food is good for the environment, and then asks participants whether they prefer to buy tomatoes grown in the UK or overseas.

28 Explain two benefits and two problems associated with the use of online questionnaires.

29 For the investigations listed below, define the population and decide if it would be practical to carry out a census.
(a) Finding out if adults in England aged 25–30 prefer to take their summer holiday in the UK or abroad.
(b) Finding out if the people in a library on a Tuesday morning prefer to read fiction or non-fiction books.
(c) Finding out if the pencils made by a manufacturer break easily when they are dropped.

30 The management team of an online bookstore decide to investigate whether there is a link between where a person lives and whether they prefer to read fiction or non-fiction books. They choose 100 sample members from each of 24 English counties. Explain why it would be better to conduct interviews by telephone rather than in person.

31 For an article about fuel economy, a popular car magazine wishes to carry out research into the fuel efficiency of cars that are suitable for families. They decide to use stratified sampling with proportional allocation to create a sample of 100 cars from a population of 1200 that have been classified as follows: 420 medium-sized, 240 estates, 480 people carriers, and 60 luxury. How many cars of each type should be included in the sample?

32 Describe one similarity and one difference between convenience sampling and quota sampling.

33 Suppose you were asked to investigate a possible connection between the age of an employee and their weekly expenditure in the company cafeteria. Write a closed and an open question that would be suitable for collecting data in a questionnaire for this investigation.

34 A sports centre owner wishes to find out whether customers are using the centre to attend an exercise class, to use the gym facilities or to play a racquet sport. Waiting by the entrance turnstile on a Wednesday at 9.45am, she questions the next 50 people who enter the building about their plans for the morning.
(a) Do you expect that the data collected by the sports centre owner will be representative of all of the customers using the centre? Give three possible reasons for your answer.
(b) State which sampling method was used by the sports centre owner.

35 Describe the difference between a structured and an informal interview. Fully explain one advantage and one disadvantage for each type of interview.

36 A UK-based company operating a worldwide parcel delivery service carries out an investigation into the average length of time taken for a parcel to be delivered. Suggest three characteristics which could be used to divide the population of parcels into strata so that the delivery times for a representative sample can be recorded.

37 A local education authority wants to assess if an additional primary school should be built to meet the needs of the growing number of families moving into the area. They decide to find out how long it takes families to walk from home to their nearest school.

(a) State three pieces of information about each family that could be useful for the assessment.

(b) Do you think primary data or secondary data should be used in this investigation? Give a reason for your answer.

38 Give two reasons why a respondent might not be able to answer a question in a written questionnaire, potentially causing non-response bias to occur.

39 Explain why it is important to select a sample that is representative of the entire population.

40 Explain the difference between primary data and secondary data. Give one advantage and one disadvantage for each type of data.

Solutions to Practice Exercises

[1] (a) The population is all of the employees of the mail order company. The sample is the employees of the mail order company who are aged 20–25.
  (b) No, the sample data collected will not be a good representation of the music preferences for the entire population because age can be a factor that influences choice of music and the sample only includes employees from a specific age group. The views of employees younger than 20 and older than 25 will be ignored.

[2] (a) The response rate would be calculated as the number of questionnaires returned by customers divided by the number of questionnaires distributed by the manager of the furniture store.
  (b) Here are three ways in which the manager could maximise the response rate:
   • Make sure all questions are clearly worded and easy to answer.
   • Contact customers who do not respond using a follow-up telephone call or email.
   • Offer discount vouchers for the store as a reward to respondents.

[3] In simple random sampling we:
   • give a unique number to each member of the population;
   • use a computer program to randomly generate a subset of the allocated numbers according to the size of sample required;
   • create the sample by choosing the members of the population whose numbers match the generated random numbers.

  In systematic sampling we:
   • use a computer program to randomly generate a number as a starting point in a list of all members of the population;
   • systematically select the person associated with the random number, and then each person that occurs in the list at a specific interval.

[4] Response bias occurs when the answers given in an interview or a questionnaire do not reflect the true facts and opinions of the participant. Examples of situations in which it might occur: when someone chooses to misrepresent or exaggerate facts so that they present themselves more favourably, or when someone feels pressurised into giving an answer which they know is expected rather than an answer which accurately reflects their own viewpoint.

[5] (a) Cluster sampling is used for the investigation into the amount paid annually per household on electricity in Glasgow.
  (b) Stratified sampling is used to determine whether men spend more money than women at airport shops whilst waiting to board their flight.

[6] (a) This sample of customers is not representative of the whole population because it only includes people who ordered one specific type of pizza – ham and pineapple. It is possible that the quality of the ham and pineapple topping was particularly good, whilst the topping on other types of pizza was not satisfactory. In this case,

the sample of customers would rate the toppings highly, but this would not accurately reflect the views of all of the customers.

(b) Stratified sampling could be used to obtain a more representative sample as follows:

- Divide the customers into strata according to the type of pizza they ordered.
- Produce a sampling frame for each stratum and give each member of each stratum a unique number.
- Choose a selection of customers from each stratum corresponding to the numbers generated randomly by a computer program.

7 An example of a leading or biased question that could be asked when interviewing people about whether more companies should encourage their employees to work from home is:

'Employees who work from home enjoy increased flexibility and save money on commuting. Do you agree that more companies should offer their employees this excellent opportunity?'

8 It is often better to collect data using a sample rather than by carrying out a census because the population may be too large or not sufficiently well defined. Also a census might be very time-consuming or expensive to carry out, particularly if the members of the population are geographically dispersed.

9 Two guidelines that could be given as advice to a researcher who is designing a questionnaire to investigate people's attitudes towards the recent increase in food prices are:

- Do not use overlapping intervals:
  How much money did you spend on food at the supermarket last week?

| less than £50 ☐ | £50–£100 ☐ | £100–£150 ☐ | more than £150 ☐ |

- Avoid compound questions:
  Do you think you spend the same amount on food now as you did a year ago or has your weekly expenditure stayed the same? yes/no

10 (a) Cluster sampling could be used to collect data as follows:
- Using the building blocks as clusters, give each block a number from 1 to 15.
- Use random numbers generated by a computer program to choose five of the blocks.
- Visit each of the four apartments within the five chosen blocks to collect sample data from the residents of 20 apartments.

(b) Advantage – cluster sampling can be a very convenient and practical way of producing a sample, and it can reduce the time and money involved if the members of the population are spread throughout a wide geographical area. Disadvantage – if the people in each cluster have very similar characteristics then the sample may not be fully representative of the population.

11 The retail analyst would obtain a sample of 45 stores using simple random sampling as follows:
- Give a unique number to each store in the mall.
- Use a computer program to randomly generate 45 numbers between 1 and 280.

- Create the sample by choosing the stores whose numbers match the generated random numbers, without replacement, so that if a store is chosen once, it cannot be chosen again.

12 (a) Make sure questions can be answered: it is unlikely that a participant will remember how much money they spent on these items last month.
(b) Avoid giving biased or leading questions: the researcher is strongly expressing their viewpoint and encouraging the participant to agree.
(c) Allow for all possible answers: there is no option available if the participant's favourite ice-cream is mint.
(d) Do not use overlapping intervals: there are two boxes that could be ticked if 10 train journeys were made.
(e) Avoid compound questions: 'Yes' could mean they have booked a holiday online or they found it easy to search for the type of holiday required or both.
(f) Questions should be unambiguous: people will give a different meaning to 'a long time'.

13 Option (a). A sampling method in which every member of the population has an equal chance of being chosen for the sample is known as simple random sampling.

14 It would be better to use online questionnaires for data collection rather than conducting interviews because the councillor needs to act quickly before the next local election takes place. It will be quicker to ask 250 people to complete online questionnaires compared to interviewing them individually.

15 Systematic sampling would be used to select a sample of a 50 flyers as follows:
- Select the 24th flyer in the box and check the quality of its images.
- 5000 divided by 50 is 100, so systematically select flyers numbered 124, 224, 324, . . . until the flyer numbered 4924 is reached, giving a sample of 50 flyers.

16 (a) Conducting an interview: more complex questions can be asked because you can explain the meaning if a participant does not understand.
(b) Using a written questionnaire: the researcher will not know if a question has been left blank because the meaning was unclear or the person chose not to answer.
(c) Using a written questionnaire: a large amount of data can be gathered using only a limited amount of time and money.
(d) Conducting an interview: it can be expensive to collect data from geographically dispersed sample members.

17 Option (c). A sampling frame is a list that includes information about every member of the population.

18 Advantages of using written questionnaires to collect data for an investigation:
- Questionnaires are a time-efficient method of collecting data from a large sample of people; any postage costs incurred are likely to be less than telephone charges or interviewer fees.
- Respondents are more likely to give truthful answers to sensitive questions because they will be completing the questionnaire anonymously.

- Questionnaires can easily be sent to sample members when they are located across a wide geographical area; this allows the researcher to gather data from a wider variety of places.

Disadvantages of using written questionnaires to collect data for an investigation:
- Only straightforward questions can be used in a questionnaire; the researcher must make sure that they can easily be understood because no further clarification can be given.
- Members of the sample who receive a written questionnaire are more likely to ignore it, particularly if they do not have a strong opinion on the topic under investigation.
- If the researcher does not understand an answer given by a respondent, there is no opportunity to ask for more details and the collected data might not be usable.
- When you receive completed questionnaires that have been distributed by post or email, it is not possible to know if the intended sample member has actually answered the questions.

19 A possible sampling frame that could be used for simple random sampling is:
(a) The list of all the adults eligible to vote at the next county council elections.
(b) The list of all the members of the management team.
(c) The list of all the lecturers at the university.

20 Advantages of conducting interviews to collect data for an investigation:
- It is possible to ask more complex questions in an interview because the researcher is available to explain them more fully if the interviewee does not understand the meaning.
- Interviews usually have a higher response rate because people will generally find it harder to refuse a request for information when they are approached directly.
- In an informal interview, the researcher has the opportunity to ask additional questions if they need more explanation about a response from the interviewee.
- When conducting your own interviews to collect primary data, you know that the interviewees are the people you have chosen to answer the questions.

Disadvantages of conducting interviews to collect data for an investigation:
- Interviews are time-consuming because the researcher can only talk to one person at a time; data collection will be expensive if the researcher employs several interviewers.
- If the members of the sample are dispersed geographically then the researcher will have to spend more time and it is more expensive travelling to each location.
- An interviewee is more likely to give an untruthful or exaggerated answer when the researcher asks a direct question which is sensitive.

21 Systematic sampling was used by the restaurant manager.

22 There are two problems with this question. It is a biased or leading question because the researcher is encouraging the participant to agree with the viewpoint of many people. Also, it is a compound question which means that it is difficult to answer 'yes'

or 'no' if you agree that the government does not spend enough money on health, but feel that there is sufficient spending on education.

23 Both cluster sampling and stratified sampling involve dividing the population into groups. In cluster sampling, a simple random sample of clusters is chosen and then every member of each chosen cluster is included in the sample. In stratified sampling, a simple random sample of stratum members is chosen for the sample from every stratum.

24 Option (b). A pilot study involves testing the quality of your questions on a small group of people.

25 A population is the collection of all the people or objects in whom we are interested, whereas a sample is the part of the population from which we gather information.

26 The researcher would not be able to use the sample data collected to draw conclusions about the amount of homework given to all of the pupils at the school because it only includes pupils from one year group, Year 9. It is likely that the amount of homework given to pupils is associated with their year of schooling. Pupils in the earlier years may receive less homework as they settle into the unfamiliar teaching system of the secondary school, whereas pupils in later years may receive more homework as they prepare for their public examinations.

27 (a) A customer satisfaction questionnaire distributed to people eating in a restaurant could result in non-response bias. People who have had a very good experience or a very bad experience are more likely to complete a questionnaire than people who had a satisfactory experience, and so the data collected might not be representative of the entire population.

   (b) In an investigation about healthy eating, a researcher asks a question about the number of chocolate bars eaten last week; this question could result in response bias. People may choose to under-report the number of chocolate bars eaten so that they present themselves as being more healthy.

   (c) An interviewer lists all of the reasons why buying locally produced food is good for the environment, and then asks participants whether they prefer to buy tomatoes grown in the UK or overseas; this question could result in response bias. People may feel pressurised into agreeing with the interviewer rather than giving an answer which accurately reflects their own viewpoint.

28 Benefits associated with the use of online questionnaires:
   • It will reduce the resources required, in terms of money and time, for distribution and collection because there is no printing or posting involved.
   • You can design a questionnaire that looks attractive and interesting, using features such as pop-up images and drop-down menus to encourage people to participate.
   • Results can be input directly into a spreadsheet or other type of computer program for analysis, which reduces mistakes and saves time.

Problems associated with the use of online questionnaires:
- As the use of online distribution increases, people may become overloaded with electronic requests for information and so become more likely to delete or ignore the request.
- You are restricting your sample members to those who have regular access to the Internet; this may result in under-representation of part of the population such as older people.
- Even though a request for information via email or social media may be successfully received by a person, software incompatibility or other technical problems may mean that they are unable to access the questionnaire or return it to the researcher.

29 (a) The population is all of the adults in England aged 25–30; it would not be practical to carry out a census because the population is large and geographically dispersed so the census would be time-consuming and expensive.
(b) The population is all of the people in the library on a Tuesday morning; it would be practical to carry out a census because the population is quite small and all located in the same place during the same time period.
(c) The population is all of the pencils made by the manufacturer; it would not be practical to carry out a census because this would mean that all of the pencils would have to be dropped to see if they break easily.

30 It would be better to conduct interviews by telephone rather than in person because the 100 sample members are located in 24 counties throughout England. It will be less expensive to make telephone calls for interviewing than travelling to each county.

31 Using proportional allocation, the number of each type of car to be included in the sample would be as follows:
420 is 35% of 1200, and 35% of 100 = 35 medium-sized cars;
240 is 20% of 1200, and 20% of 100 = 20 estate cars;
480 is 40% of 1200, and 40% of 100 = 40 people carriers;
60 is 5% of 1200, and 5% of 100 = 5 luxury cars.

32 Both convenience sampling and quota sampling involve choosing the most convenient members of the population to form a sample. In convenience sampling, the characteristics of the people are not considered, whereas in quota sampling a specific number of people are chosen according to their characteristics, for example, 35 males and 35 females.

33 Closed question:
What is your age?

under 25 ☐	25–34 ☐	35–44 ☐	45–54 ☐	over 54 ☐

Open question:
Give your opinion on whether you think that eating lunch in the company cafeteria is more or less cost-effective than bringing in a home-made packed lunch.

34 (a) We would not expect the data collected by the sports centre owner to be representative of all of the customers using the centre because the sample of customers was taken only on a Wednesday morning at 9.45am. It is likely that that there were timetabled exercise classes starting at 10am on a Wednesday and so a high proportion of people questioned may have been intending to take part in these classes. The swimming pool may have been closed for maintenance and so no one would be arriving for a swim at this time. The courts for racquet sports may be bookable on the half hour, for example 10.30am to 11.30am, and so people intending to play a racquet sport are less likely to arrive 45 minutes before the start of their booked session.

   (b) Convenience sampling was used by the sports centre owner.

35 For a structured interview, the researcher prepares a set of questions in advance and asks only those questions during the interview. During an informal interview, the researcher is allowed to ask any questions that they feel would be relevant, based on the interviewee's responses.

Structured
Advantage: the data collected from different interviewees can be compared and analysed easily because each interview consists of the same questions.
Disadvantage: they limit the amount of rich data that can be gathered because the researcher is not able to pursue an unexpected direction in the interview leading from an interesting response from an interviewee.

Informal
Advantage: this method may result in the collection of very rich data.
Disadvantage: making comparisons and analysing responses from different interviewees will be difficult for the researcher; drawing conclusions from the sample data will be a complex process.

36 Characteristics which could be used to divide the population of parcels into strata so that the delivery times for a representative sample can be recorded are:
- size of parcel (for example, small, medium and large);
- arrival destination (for example, within the UK, or overseas);
- type of service purchased (for example, same-day delivery, next-day delivery).

37 (a) Three pieces of information that should be collected by the local education authority are: how long it takes to walk to school, their home address, and the name of their school attended.

   (b) It would be sensible to use primary data because it is unlikely that secondary data would be available for this type of information.

38 Reasons why a respondent might not be able to answer a question in a written questionnaire are:
- Participants may not find an appropriate option for a closed question.
- They may not have the time to answer a range of open questions.
- The respondent might not understand the meaning of the question.

39 It is important to select a sample that is representative of the entire population so that any observations made about the sample can be generalised to draw conclusions about the population.

40 Differences between primary data and secondary data are as follows:
- Primary data are collected by the researcher, whereas secondary data have been collected by someone else and are used by the researcher.
- Primary data are usually raw data, whereas secondary data have often been processed before being made available.

Primary
Advantage: when collecting your own data, they can be processed and presented in ways which best suit your research and results.
Disadvantage: it is difficult and time-consuming to use data collection methods to gather information from large samples of the population.

Secondary
Advantage: you could have easy and quick access to a large database of information that has been collected over a long period of time.
Disadvantage: it is likely that secondary data have already been processed and so may not be presented in the way you would prefer.

Data Distributions

This chapter explains how to:

- construct frequency distributions for both qualitative and quantitative data
- distinguish between
  - cumulative frequency
  - relative frequency
  - cumulative relative frequency
- understand the meaning of
  - class limits and class boundaries
  - class width and class mid-point
- choose appropriate classes for a grouped frequency distribution

class	cumulative relative frequency	lower class limit
class boundary	frequency distribution	relative frequency
class limit	grouped frequency distribution	raw data
class mid-point		upper class boundary
class width	lower class boundary	upper class limit
cumulative frequency		

Introduction

Use of the data collection methods described in Chapter 2 may result the accumulation of a very large data set, particularly if we are collecting data about every member of a population, or if a sample of considerable size has been chosen. Understanding and processing such a data set can be challenging, but we can use a frequency distribution or a grouped frequency distribution as a starting point to present our information in a concise form. Once our data set has been successfully tabulated, then we can apply some of the graphical and numerical techniques covered in Chapters 4 and 5.

In this chapter you will learn how to construct frequency distributions for summarising both qualitative and quantitative data. For grouped frequency distributions, we will discuss the importance of choosing sensible groups, or classes, and we will also introduce some new terminology and methods for identifying numerical characteristics of the classes.

Frequency Distributions

When qualitative or quantitative data values are recorded in the order in which they are collected, this is known as raw data. We can display raw data in an ordinary table with rows and columns, but sometimes the quantity of data collected makes it difficult to actually interpret their meaning or produce any summary statistics.

If the raw data are processed and simplified using a frequency distribution, then it may be possible to:

- determine characteristics of the data set such as the data value that occurs most often;
- highlight important features or underlying patterns which are hidden by the quantity of raw data;
- make a comparison more easily between two sets of data.

The construction of a frequency distribution involves producing a list of all the *distinct* pieces of data that could have been collected, between (and including) the smallest value and the largest value in the data set. We then count and record how many times each one of those distinct values occurs in our collected data.

The frequency distribution is presented as a table, usually with three columns. We use the first column to identify each distinct data value; the column heading should describe the data that have been collected. The second column, entitled 'tally', contains a tally mark (|) representing each occurrence of the distinct value listed on that row. Tally marks are grouped together in sets of five for clarity. The total of the tally marks for each distinct value is recorded in the third column. This is known as the frequency with which the distinct value occurs, shortened to *frequency*, which is used as the column heading; it is usually denoted *f*.

The number of rows in the table will depend on the number of distinct values that can occur between the smallest and largest values in the data set, inclusively. We often use the last row in the table to record the sum of the frequencies in the third column; this total is equal to the total number of data values contained in the set.

A template for a frequency distribution containing some tally marks is shown below; the data set represented by this template would contain three distinct values and 25 pieces of data in total.

Description of data	Tally	Frequency
value	⌊⌋⌋⌋ ⌊⌋⌋⌋ ||	12
value	||||	4
value	⌊⌋⌋⌋ ||||	9
Total		25

A frequency distribution is sometimes created without the tally marks; in this case, the table might be presented in column form like this:

Description of data	Frequency
value	12
value	4
value	9
Total	25

or in row form like this:

Description of data	value	value	value	Total
Frequency	12	4	9	25

For quantitative data, we should not have any missing distinct values in the first column of the frequency distribution table. However, for an individual row, it is possible to have no tally marks and zero in the frequency column when there are no data values in our collected data that match the distinct value.

We can use a frequency distribution to produce some basic summary statistics about our data set; for example, we can identify the value which occurs most often and least often in the data set. Whilst it is also possible to find these values using raw data, the procedure is simplified and less error-prone if a frequency distribution is used instead, particularly if we have collected data from a large sample or a population.

EXAMPLE – QUALITATIVE DATA

During the check-in procedure at an airport information desk, 50 adult passengers were asked for their preference of free drink to be served during the flight. The drinks available were tea, coffee, juice, wine and water.

The choices made by the passengers were recorded as raw data in the table below. The first passenger chose tea, the second preferred water and the last passenger requested juice as their free drink.

tea	water	water	tea	wine	coffee	water	water	coffee	water
wine	wine	juice	coffee	water	water	tea	coffee	water	coffee
wine	tea	coffee	coffee	wine	juice	wine	wine	juice	water
coffee	coffee	coffee	coffee	coffee	wine	juice	tea	coffee	tea
coffee	wine	juice	tea	water	juice	wine	water	tea	juice

Using a frequency distribution to summarise the choices of the first 10 passengers gives:

Drink preference	Tally	Frequency
tea	||	2
coffee	||	2
juice		
water	⊔⊦⊦⊤	5
wine	|	1
Total		10

The completed frequency distribution is shown below.

Drink preference	Tally	Frequency
tea	⊔⊦⊦⊤ |||	8
coffee	⊔⊦⊦⊤ ⊔⊦⊦⊤ ||||	14
juice	⊔⊦⊦⊤ ||	7
water	⊔⊦⊦⊤ ⊔⊦⊦⊤ |	11
wine	⊔⊦⊦⊤ ⊔⊦⊦⊤	10
Total		50

Total frequency represents one drink choice for each passenger

By examining the third column of the frequency distribution, we can see that the most popular free drink was coffee which was chosen by 14 passengers; only seven passengers stated that their preference was juice, so this drink was the least popular.

Adding up the frequencies for tea and coffee, we find that 22 of the passengers chose a hot drink, and similarly the frequency distribution shows that 40 out of 50 passengers requested a non- alcoholic drink.

EXAMPLE – QUANTITATIVE DATA

At a coffee shop located in the departure lounge of an airport, the manager recorded the number of items purchased by each customer.

The following table shows the data in the order in which it was collected from 50 customers.

2	3	1	1	2	5	6	2	5	3
2	2	2	1	1	1	3	3	6	1
1	1	2	2	5	5	6	2	6	2
6	6	3	2	5	3	1	1	2	3
5	2	6	3	3	2	2	1	1	1

Constructing the frequency distribution gives:

Number of items purchased	Tally	Frequency
1	𝍸 𝍸 III	13
2	𝍸 𝍸 𝍸	15
3	𝍸 IIII	9
4		0
5	𝍸 I	6
6	𝍸 II	7
Total		50

Total frequency equals number of values in the data set

The frequency distribution is shown without tally marks below in column form:

Number of items purchased	Frequency
1	13
2	15
3	9
4	0
5	6
6	7
Total	50

and in row form:

Number of items purchased	1	2	3	4	5	6	Total
Frequency	13	15	9	0	6	7	50

The frequency distribution shows us that there were no customers who purchased exactly four items. By multiplying each distinct value by its frequency, we can calculate how many items were purchased in total at the coffee shop as follows: $(1 \times 13) + (2 \times 15) + (3 \times 9) + (5 \times 6) + (6 \times 7) = 142$ items were purchased in total by the 50 customers.

Relative Frequency

Sometimes we would like to consider the frequency of each distinct value in terms of its proportion of all the values in the data set. **Relative frequency** is calculated as:

$$\text{relative frequency} = \frac{\text{frequency of distinct value}}{\text{sum of all frequencies}}$$

Whereas the frequency indicates how many times the distinct value occurs within the data set, the relative frequency shows what proportion of the data values in that set are the same as the distinct value.

Relative frequency generally provides a useful way of comparing two data sets. To help with interpretation, we often multiply relative frequency by 100 so that the decimal form is converted into a percentage.

EXAMPLE – RELATIVE FREQUENCY

Returning to our raw data consisting of the preferred free drinks for 50 passengers, the table below shows the relative frequency for each distinct value in the data set, in its decimal form and also as a percentage.

Drink preference	Frequency	Relative frequency	Relative frequency (as a percentage)
tea	8	$8/50 = 0.16$	$0.16 \times 100 = 16\%$
coffee	14	0.28	28%
juice	7	0.14	14%
water	11	0.22	22%
wine	10	0.20	20%
Total	50	1.00	100%

The relative frequencies provide the proportions of each drink preference in terms of the choices made by all of the 50 passengers. They show that 16% of the passengers chose tea, 28% chose coffee, 14% preferred juice, 22% preferred water, and wine was requested by 20% of the passengers.

Cumulative Frequency

For quantitative data, the concept of a frequency distribution can be extended to include the cumulative frequencies. The **cumulative frequency** for a distinct value represents the number of data values we have collected that are less than or equal to that distinct value; it is actually a running total of the frequencies in the table.

We calculate the cumulative frequency for an individual row by adding up all of the frequencies of the rows up to and including the current one. For the first row in a frequency distribution, the cumulative frequency is just equal to the frequency of the distinct value.

To display the cumulative frequencies, we would add an additional column to our frequency distribution, entitled 'cumulative frequency'.

EXAMPLE – CUMULATIVE FREQUENCY

Using our earlier example involving the number of items purchased at the coffee shop in the airport departure lounge, we can include the cumulative frequencies in the frequency distribution as follows:

Number of items purchased	Frequency	Cumulative frequency	
1	13	13	
2	15	28	→ 13+15 = 28
3	9	37	→ 13+15+9 = 37
4	0	37	→ 13+15+9+0 = 37
5	6	43	→ 13+15+9+0+6 = 43
6	7	50	→ 13+15+9+0+6+7 = 50
Total	50		

The frequency distribution now provides us with additional information. For example, the cumulative frequency column shows that 28 customers purchased two or fewer items at the coffee shop.

Cumulative Relative Frequency

The cumulative relative frequency allows us to express cumulative frequencies as a cumulative percentage. They are calculated using the formula:

$$\text{cumulative relative frequency} = \frac{\text{cumultive frequency of distinct value}}{\text{sum of all frequencies}}$$

As with relative frequencies, we often multiply the cumulative relative frequency by 100 to obtain a percentage; this is generally easier to interpret.

EXAMPLE – CUMULATIVE RELATIVE FREQUENCY

As well as the number of customers, now we can observe the percentage of customers at the coffee shop who purchased two or fewer items: 56%. This is shown by the cumulative relative frequency for two items purchased.

Number of items purchased	Cumulative frequency	Cumulative relative frequency	Cumulative relative frequency (as a percentage)
1	13	13/50 = 0.26	0.26 × 100 = 26%
2	28	0.56	56%
3	37	0.74	74%

(Continued)

Number of items purchased	Cumulative frequency	Cumulative relative frequency	Cumulative relative frequency (as a percentage)
4	37	0.74	74%
5	43	0.86	86%
6	50	1.00	100%

Grouped Frequency Distributions

In the previous sections, we have used frequency distributions to present two different types of data: firstly, qualitative data; and secondly, quantitative data where the data set contains relatively few distinct values. Recall our example about the number of items purchased at the airport coffee shop – there were only six distinct values listed in the frequency distribution.

When our quantitative data set consists of discrete data with a large number of distinct values, a frequency distribution would not be suitable because a list identifying each distinct value (for the first column) would be too long. There would as many rows as there are distinct values between the smallest and largest values in the data set, inclusively; many of the rows would have no tally marks where the distinct value does not appear in the data set, or a frequency of 1 because the distinct value appears only once.

In this case, and for continuous data, the frequency distribution would not provide us with a useful summary of the data set, and therefore a **grouped frequency distribution** is preferred. For a grouped frequency distribution, we condense the data set by forming a series of groups and then counting how many values from the data set are included in each group. Generally, we use the term **class** in preference to 'group'. The classes with their corresponding tally marks and frequencies are presented in a table similar to the type used for a frequency distribution. Once again, the tally marks may be omitted, and a column or row form can be used in presentation.

As discussed before, we can extend the concept of a grouped frequency distribution to include relative frequency, cumulative frequency and cumulative relative frequency. For this distribution, we are working with class frequencies rather than the frequency with which a distinct value appears, and therefore the following definitions apply:

- Relative frequency shows the proportion of the data values in the set that belong to each group or class.
- Cumulative frequency represents the number of data values we have collected that belong to that class or the classes that come before it in the table; it is a running total of the class frequencies.
- Cumulative relative frequencies allow us to express cumulative frequencies as a cumulative percentage of the total number of data values.

Although a grouped frequency distribution is a useful way of summarising a data set, it does have one disadvantage: the individual values from the data set can no longer be identified by looking at the table. The grouped frequency distribution only shows the number of data values that belong to each class. We can still determine characteristics of the data set and highlight important features or underlying patterns, but we are not able to comment on individual pieces of data that have been collected.

EXAMPLE – DISCRETE DATA

Suppose we recorded the number of boarding gates for passengers at 75 international airports. Our raw data might be presented as follows:

114	46	43	61	38	21	75	40	94	51
96	10	92	19	17	39	70	27	46	114
35	68	81	114	74	95	38	17	14	74
20	108	76	28	108	45	56	38	36	17
46	17	103	109	41	88	125	14	121	44
106	55	44	38	17	16	40	85	34	103
101	66	64	50	86	61	60	42	99	59
19	33	50	38	110					

The smallest data value is 10 and the largest is 125, so a frequency distribution would give the table below. It can be seen that this is not a suitable way to summarise our information.

Number of passenger boarding gates	Tally	Frequency
10	|	1
11		
12		
13		
14	||	2
15		
. . .		
. . .		
. . .		
. . .		
120		
121	|	1
122		
123		

(Continued)

Number of passenger boarding gates	Tally	Frequency
124		
125	|	1
Total		75

Choosing appropriate classes, the grouped frequency distribution is shown below; this is a more appropriate distribution for our data.

Number of passenger boarding gates	Tally	Frequency
10–29	ⅬⅢ ⅬⅢ ⅬⅢ	15
30–49	ⅬⅢ ⅬⅢ ⅬⅢ ⅬⅢ |	21
50–69	ⅬⅢ ⅬⅢ ||	12
70–89	ⅬⅢ ||||	9
90–109	ⅬⅢ ⅬⅢ ||	12
110–129	ⅬⅢ |	6
Total		75

Total frequency equals number of values in the data set

Examining the grouped frequency distribution, we can easily see that the number of boarding gates at nine of the airports was 70–89 inclusive. Without the detailed raw data, it is not possible to identify individual pieces of data so we cannot say, for example, how many airports had 73 boarding gates.

Including relative frequencies, in decimal and percentage form, provides the following grouped frequency distribution:

Number of passenger boarding gates	Frequency	Relative frequency	Relative frequency (as a percentage)
10–29	15	15/75 = 0.20	0.20 × 100 = 20%
30–49	21	0.28	28%
50–69	12	0.16	16%
70–89	9	0.12	12%
90–109	12	0.16	16%
110–129	6	0.08	8%
Total	75	1.00	100%

The relative frequencies show that the highest proportion of airports, 28%, had 30–49 boarding gates, whilst there were 110–129 boarding gates at only 8% of the airports.

EXAMPLE – CONTINUOUS DATA

The management team of a UK-based airline were considering making changes to their checked-in baggage allowance policy. As an information gathering exercise, they decided to record the weight (in kilograms) for a sample of 75 luggage items checked in on their flights during the same week.
The data collected are listed below.

20.5	23.5	28.2	16	18.1	28	23.8	22.7	23.7	20.1
25.1	31.2	20.5	21.5	21.4	20.1	30.9	22.1	27.4	20.8
23.3	21.3	21	22.4	26.1	22.3	22.9	25.3	21.2	17.5
22.1	22.8	15.8	25.9	20.7	28.4	18.3	21.9	21.4	27.2
17.4	22.5	21.8	23.6	31	27.7	21.6	15.6	21.8	22.4
16.9	22.3	23.6	26.7	28.9	21.7	27.1	23.6	18.4	18.7
20.9	23.4	22.6	22.2	20.9	23.9	21.3	26.9	21.9	28.6
22.4	18.6	23.9	15.7	21.8					

Using a grouped frequency distribution to summarise the data gives:

Weight of luggage item (kg)	Frequency
15.0–17.4	6
17.5–19.9	6
20.0–22.4	30
22.5–24.9	15
25.0–27.4	9
27.5–29.9	6
30.0–32.4	3
Total	75

The grouped frequency distribution shows that the largest number of the luggage items (30 out of 75) weighed between 20.0 kg and 22.4 kg, inclusive. The smallest number of luggage items belonged to the class with the largest weights, 30.0–32.4 kg.

Omitting the tally marks and using the row form for the grouped frequency distribution gives:

Weight of luggage item (kg)	15.0– 17.4	17.5– 19.9	20.0– 22.4	22.5– 24.9	25.0– 27.4	27.5– 29.9	30.0– 32.4	Total
Frequency	6	6	30	15	9	6	3	75

Using cumulative and cumulative relative frequencies, we can extend our distribution as follows:

Weight of luggage item (kg)	Cumulative frequency	Cumulative relative frequency	Cumulative relative frequency (as a percentage)
15.0–17.4	6	6/75 = 0.08	$0.08 \times 100 = 8\%$
17.5–19.9	12	0.16	16%
20.0–22.4	42	0.56	56%
22.5–24.9	57	0.76	76%
25.0–27.4	66	0.88	88%
27.5–29.9	72	0.96	96%
30.0–32.4	75	1.00	100%

The figures for the third class in the table tell us that 42 luggage items, or 56% of the total number of luggage items, weighed between 15.0 kg and 22.4 kg, inclusive.

Numerical Class Characteristics

For any given class, we can find the class limits, boundaries, width and mid-point. The definitions of these numerical characteristics are given below. The first three classes in each of our earlier grouped frequency distribution examples are used again here.

CLASS LIMITS

The **lower class limit** and **upper class limit** are simply the end-points of the class interval when it is included in the table for the grouped frequency distribution.

Number of passenger boarding gates	Lower class limit	Upper class limit
10–29	10	29
30–49	30	49
50–69	50	69

Weight of luggage item (kg)	Lower class limit	Upper class limit
15.0–17.4	15.0	17.4
17.5–19.9	17.5	19.9
20.0–22.4	20.0	22.4

CLASS BOUNDARIES

The **lower class boundary** is the half-way point between the upper class limit of the previous class and the lower class limit of this class; similarly, the **upper class boundary** is the half-way point between the upper class limit of this class and the lower class limit of the next class. The half-way points are found by adding the appropriate class limits and then dividing by 2.

Number of passenger boarding gates	Lower class boundary	Upper class boundary
10–29	9.5	$(29 + 30)/2 = 29.5$
30–49	$(29 + 30)/2 = 29.5$	$(49 + 50)/2 = 49.5$
50–69	$(49 + 50)/2 = 49.5$	69.5

The table above shows that the upper class boundary of one class is equal to the lower class boundary of the next class in the distribution. So the upper class boundary of 10–29 is the same as the lower class boundary of 30–49.

Weight of luggage item (kg)	Lower class boundary	Upper class boundary
15.0–17.4	14.95	$(17.4 + 17.5)/2 = 17.45$
17.5–19.9	$(17.4 + 17.5)/2 = 17.45$	$(19.9 + 20.0)/2 = 19.95$
20.0–22.4	$(19.9 + 20.0)/2 = 19.95$	22.45

CLASS WIDTH

We calculate the **class width** by subtracting the lower class boundary from the upper class boundary.

Number of passenger boarding gates	Lower class boundary	Upper class boundary	Class width
10–29	9.5	29.5	$29.5 - 9.5 = 20$
30–49	29.5	49.5	$49.5 - 29.5 = 20$
50–69	49.5	69.5	20

Weight of luggage item (kg)	Lower class boundary	Upper class boundary	Class width
15.0–17.4	14.95	17.45	$17.45 - 14.95 = 2.5$
17.5–19.9	17.45	19.95	$19.95 - 17.45 = 2.5$
20.0–22.4	19.95	22.45	2.5

CLASS MID-POINT

To find the **class mid-point**, simply divide the sum of the class limits by 2; alternatively, you can divide the sum of the class boundaries by 2 as the result is the same.

Number of passenger boarding gates	Lower class limit	Upper class limit	Class mid-point
10–29	10	29	(10 + 29)/2 = 19.5
30–49	30	49	(30 + 49)/2 = 39.5
50–69	50	69	59.5

Weight of luggage item (kg)	Lower class boundary	Upper class boundary	Class mid-point
15.0–17.4	14.95	17.45	(14.95 + 17.45)/2 = 16.2
17.5–19.9	17.45	19.95	(17.45 + 19.95)/2 = 18.7
20.0–22.4	19.95	22.45	21.2

CHOOSING CLASSES

The choices we make about the classes for a grouped frequency distribution are a matter of judgement based on the values in the data set; there is no 'right' way to devise the classes, but some classes are less suitable than others.

Our aim should be to make sensible decisions so that any underlying patterns and interesting features in the data set are revealed by appropriate grouping of the data values. If our choices do not summarise the data effectively, we can always start the process again with a different number of classes or an alternative class width. We can use the following guidelines to help inform our decisions.

1. **Starting point**
   To decide on a starting point for the grouped frequency distribution, examine the data and identify the smallest value. The lower class limit of the first class should then be fixed at a convenient value slightly lower than the smallest value, or the smallest value itself.
2. **Number of classes**
   We should generally use between 5 and 15 classes in the distribution, depending on the size of the data set. If we use too few classes, then there will probably be a large proportion of data values in a single class and so patterns in the data might be hidden. On the other hand, too many classes will result in distribution with many empty classes. For larger data sets, a larger number of classes might be required.
3. **Non-overlapping intervals**
   When we created a frequency distribution, we listed every distinct value just once in the first column. Applying the same approach to a grouped frequency distribution, there should be no overlap in our list of classes: it should be possible to place each value from the data set into one, and only one, class in the grouped frequency distribution.

4. **Class width**

Although not essential, using equal widths for the classes is preferred. When all the classes will be of equal width, the width can be calculated using the formula below, rounding the result up to a convenient value:

$$\text{class width} = \frac{\text{largest data value} - \text{smallest data value}}{\text{number of classes}}$$

However, this method does not work effectively in all circumstances and should therefore be used only as a guideline. It is equally acceptable to decide upon a class width of 5 or 10, for example, to create a smooth structure to the distribution.

As an alternative method, we might choose to devise classes for continuous data using 'less than' in the description of the class interval. Returning to our example about the weight of luggage items checked in on flights, we could rewrite the classes as:

15 kg to less than 17.5 kg,
17.5 kg to less than 20 kg,
20 kg to less than 22.5 kg,

and so on. Any luggage item that weighs 15 kg or more, but less than 17.5 kg, would be placed in the first class.

Which Distribution?

Figure 3.1 shows a flowchart summarising when it is appropriate to use a frequency distribution or a grouped frequency distribution, assuming that the decision is based only on the values in the data set.

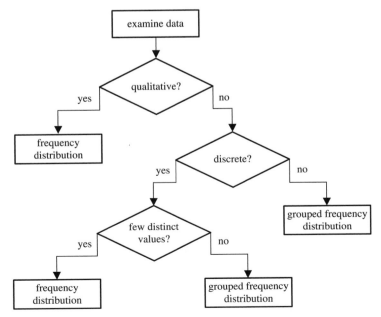

FIGURE 3.1   Flowchart for deciding when to use a frequency or grouped frequency distribution

HINTS AND TIPS

SUM OF RELATIVE FREQUENCIES

Where we have calculated the relative frequency in some of the examples described in this chapter, the sum of the column has been equal to 1.00 or 100% depending on whether decimals or percentages are used.

Depending on the level of accuracy used, sometimes the column total will differ slightly from 1.00 or 100% due to rounding that may be necessary in the calculation of the relative frequency values.

In the table below, the relative frequencies sum to 1.001 when three decimal places are used, and to 100.1% when we have converted each relative frequency value to a percentage.

x	Frequency	Relative frequency	Relative frequency (as a percentage)
15	8	0.077	$0.077 \times 100 = 7.7\%$
16	16	0.154	15.4%
17	22	0.212	21.2%
18	35	0.337	33.7%
19	19	0.183	18.3%
20	4	0.038	3.8%
Total	104	1.001	100.1%

CROSSING OFF DATA VALUES

When you are constructing a frequency or a grouped frequency distribution, it may be useful to cross off each data value as you make a tally mark in the distribution table. This technique should ensure that no data value is missed out from the table, and no value is added to the table more than once. It can be particularly helpful if your data set is very large, or contains many values that are the same or very similar.

Practice Exercises

1   For the following classes, find the class limits and the class mid-point:
(a) 25–34
(b) 4.1–5.5

2   The creators of an online price comparison website wanted to assess the effectiveness of advertising using a variety of media. Customers who purchased car insurance were asked how they had found out about the website, and their responses are shown below.

Response	Frequency
search engine	247
television advertisement	534
recommended by a friend	109
magazine/newspaper article	75
radio advertisement	139
other	261

(a) How many customers responded?
(b) Calculate the relative frequencies for each response.
(c) What percentage of customers said that they found out about the comparison website by watching a television advertisement?
(d) What proportion of respondents answered 'recommended by a friend'?

3   For the data collected in each scenario listed below, decide whether a frequency distribution or a grouped frequency distribution would be more appropriate. Give a reason for each answer.
(a) In a survey, 100 employees were asked what they did in their lunchtime earlier in the day. The possible responses to the question were: meet a friend, read a book, browse the Internet, continue to work, go shopping, eat lunch, and other activity.
(b) At a car manufacturing facility, the time taken to produce a specific engine component was recorded for a sample of 2500 components. The times were measured in seconds, accurate to three decimal places.
(c) At the entrance to a busy supermarket, a market researcher asked 85 shoppers to state how many times they had visited the supermarket in the past seven days. None of the shoppers had visited the supermarket more than four times during the specified period.
(d) The manager of a multi-screen cinema complex noted the number of empty seats at every scheduled film screening on a Saturday in April. For 67 screenings in total, the screening with the least empty seats had only six, and the largest number of empty seats was 42.

4　For a grouped frequency distribution with ten classes of equal width and a first class of 501–600, decide whether the following statements are TRUE or FALSE. Explain your response for any FALSE statements.

(a) The lower class boundary of the second class is 600.5.

(b) The mid-point of the first class is 550.5.

(c) The class width is 101.

(d) The upper class limit of the fourth class is 801.

5　The number of cars produced (in thousands) by 45 different countries during a single year was recorded as follows:

507	965	1360	110	90	1123	474	1016	541
185	1128	220	411	265	634	326	368	660
148	626	540	10	161	46	78	107	278
450	3	475	975	291	138	104	266	97
221	41	57	264	865	751	145	685	412

(a) Construct a grouped frequency distribution for these data using classes 1–200, 201–400, 401–600, 601–800, 801–1000 and 1001–1200.

(b) Calculate the relative frequency for each class. Write your answers in percentages, using one decimal place.

6　The frequency distribution below shows the number of days taken for council services to respond to complaints received from local residents about schools, leisure facilities and environmental health.

Number of days	Frequency
7	35
8	44
9	12
10	32
11	47
12	33
13	29
14	68

(a) How many complaints were received from local residents?

(b) Work out the relative frequencies for this distribution.

(c) For what percentage of complaints did council services take exactly nine days to respond?

7 Two friends decide to write down the number of text messages that they send to each other during every week for a year. The data are summarised in a grouped frequency distribution using classes 1–20, 21–40, 41–60, 61–80, 81–100. Decide if it is possible to use the grouped frequency distribution to state the number of weeks in which the following occur:

(a) Exactly 27 text messages
(b) Fewer than 81 text messages
(c) Fewer than 40 text messages
(d) Between 1 and 20 text messages inclusive
(e) 21 or more text messages
(f) Between 21 and 61 messages inclusive

8 The frequency distribution below shows the number of people in each car that arrived in a shopping centre car park.

Number of people in the car	Frequency
1	52
2	231
3	74
4	39

For these data, decide whether the following statements are TRUE or FALSE. For FALSE statements, give the correct numerical value.

(a) In total, 396 people travelled by car to the shopping centre.
(b) 18.69% of the cars arriving at the car park contained exactly four people.
(c) 283 cars contained less than three people.
(d) Approximately 90% of cars arriving at the shopping centre contained three people or fewer.

9 The time spent in a coffee shop was recorded for customers who had three people in their group. The shortest time was 12 minutes and the longest time was 148 minutes. We want to summarise these data into classes of equal width, starting with a lower limit of 10 for the first class and using 25 as the class width. Write down the class limits and mid-point for every class.

10 Describe three reasons for processing and simplifying raw data using a frequency distribution.

11 Using a property sales website, the following data were collected about the number of bedrooms in 3733 houses for sale in the same county.

Number of bedrooms	Frequency
1	454
2	943

(Continued)

Number of bedrooms	Frequency
3	985
4	830
5	362
6	108
7	25
8	10
9	8
10	5
11	3

Calculate and explain the meaning of the cumulative relative frequencies for this distribution.

12 In the context of a grouped frequency distribution, explain the difference between frequency, relative frequency and cumulative frequency.

13 At a manufacturing plant, the quality control process involves counting the items in a sample of stationery products. A box of paper clips should contain 100 items; the table below shows the actual contents of 500 boxes.

Number of paper clips in a box	Frequency
97	10
98	23
99	74
100	286
101	69
102	30
103	8

(a) Are the data collected discrete or continuous?
(b) Work out the relative frequencies, cumulative frequencies and cumulative relative frequencies for the distribution.
(c) Did more than half or less than half of the sampled boxes contain the correct number of paper clips?
(d) How many boxes in the sample contained 99 or fewer paper clips?
(e) What percentage of sampled boxes did not contain the correct number of paper clips?

14 Over a two-month period, a city-centre café kept a record of how many traditional cooked breakfasts were served to its customers.

134	110	116	135	129	130	111	116
118	113	133	128	113	110	132	131
140	125	127	125	118	138	111	132
143	126	144	124	139	144	129	141
111	123	127	119	142	147	121	148

Construct a grouped frequency distribution for these data using equal class widths, the first class having a lower limit of 110 and a class width of 5. Include a column for cumulative frequency.

15 For the following grouped frequency distribution:
(a) State the number of classes and the class limits of the third class.
(b) Find the upper class boundary of the third class and the mid-point of the fifth class.
(c) Calculate the class width.

Number of words in a sentence	Frequency
1–4	8
5–9	15
10–14	68
15–19	27
20–24	18
25–29	4

16 In an assessment of the attractions offered to tourists at a coastal town in the UK, the number of tickets sold for each sailing of a harbour tour is recorded during the summer period. At full capacity, the tour boat can accommodate 230 passengers. To summarise these data in a report, fully explain why a grouped frequency distribution would be chosen rather than a frequency distribution.

17 Quantitative data are summarised in a grouped frequency distribution with six classes of equal width and using 15–29 as the first class. Find the following numerical class characteristics:
(a) The upper class limit of the third class.
(b) The class width of all six classes.
(c) The lower class boundary of the second class.

18   The total number of points scored in 55 games of snooker played in a professional tournament was noted down. The lowest total scored was 69 and the highest total was 141 points. Write down the limits of each class in a grouped frequency distribution if we choose to create eight classes of equal width with the third class 85–94. Determine the mid-point for each class.

19   In an online questionnaire, primary school pupils were asked to give their favourite flavour of a well-known brand of crisps. Their responses are shown below:

cheese & onion	salt & vinegar	ready salted	salt & vinegar	ready salted
steak & onion	salt & vinegar	ready salted	ready salted	other
other	roast chicken	smoky bacon	cheese & onion	prawn cocktail
cheese & onion	salt & vinegar	other	steak & onion	steak & onion
ready salted	smoky bacon	smoky bacon	cheese & onion	prawn cocktail
steak & onion	salt & vinegar	steak & onion	steak & onion	ready salted
salt & vinegar	ready salted	prawn cocktail	cheese & onion	salt & vinegar
cheese & onion	ready salted	cheese & onion	other	cheese & onion
roast chicken	roast chicken	ready salted	ready salted	roast chicken
other	other	ready salted	roast chicken	steak & onion
prawn cocktail	prawn cocktail	ready salted	salt & vinegar	other
roast chicken	salt & vinegar	steak & onion	salt & vinegar	other

(a) Create a frequency distribution for the responses.
(b) Which flavour of crisps was chosen as favourite by the largest number of children? How many children preferred this flavour?

20   Explain why it would not be appropriate to construct a grouped frequency distribution for each of these types of collected data.
(a) Qualitative data
(b) Discrete data with few distinct values

21   In a frequency distribution, what should the sum of the relative frequencies be equal to?
(a) Approximately 1.00 or 100%, depending on whether decimals or percentages were used.
(b) Exactly 1.00 or 100%, depending on whether decimals or percentages were used.
(c) The number of data values in the set.

22   Explain what is meant by the term 'raw data'.

23   An independent researcher conducted a survey to find out the ticket prices of journeys made by rail passengers arriving at a central London station on a Saturday afternoon. The results of the survey are shown below.

Ticket price (£)	Frequency
10–29	11
30–49	64
50–69	0
70–89	31
90–109	12
110–129	25
130–149	19
150–169	0
170–189	6

Based on this grouped frequency distribution, decide whether the following statements are TRUE or FALSE. For FALSE statements, give the correct numerical value.
(a) The independent researcher found out the price of 168 tickets.
(b) The upper class limit of the third class is 69.5.
(c) The mid-point of the second class is 39.5.
(d) The class width for every class is 20.
(e) The lower class boundary of the fifth class is 89.

24 Fruit and vegetables form part of a balanced diet and contribute towards good health. Healthcare organisations recommend that we eat five portions of fruit and vegetables each day. The following tables show the number of portions of fruit and vegetables eaten on a specific day by 40 males and 40 females.

males

3	5	3	0	5	2	1	1	3	5
3	4	4	5	4	1	4	1	3	4
0	5	2	0	2	5	1	4	0	5
1	4	3	0	2	3	3	1	1	4

females

1	2	1	0	1	0	0	3	1	2
3	4	3	3	1	4	2	2	3	4
5	3	4	1	1	4	5	1	5	3
0	3	0	2	3	2	1	2	0	3

(a) Create a frequency distribution for each gender, including cumulative frequencies.
(b) Did more males or females eat five portions of fruit and vegetables?

25 The customer services department of a major clothing retailer recorded the reason why customers returned the items that had been ordered online. The collected data are shown in the following table.

Reason for return	Frequency
faulty	11
do not like colour	24
too large	6
too small	17
poor quality material/fabric	46
arrived too late	9
incorrect item received	16

(a) Calculate the relative frequencies for each response.
(b) What percentage of items was returned because they were too large or too small?
(c) How many faulty items were returned?
(d) If you were asked to advise the management team about how improvements could be made to products, which aspect of the clothing would you suggest they focus on? Explain your response.

26 Discrete data are summarised in a grouped frequency distribution with eight classes of equal width. The lower limit of the first class is 100 and the class width is 25. Which class would include the data value 175?
(a) we cannot know which class contains the data value 175
(b) the class 175–179
(c) the third class in the grouped frequency distribution

27 The table below shows the time taken (in seconds) to accelerate from 0 to 60 miles per hour for a sample of 42 convertible cars.

11.2	8.1	13.0	11.1	12.4	8.4	10.0
6.6	6.2	6.5	12.6	10.6	7.4	8.3
9.8	10.9	10.3	4.5	9.8	12.8	7.8
13.0	11.9	7.6	5.9	13.2	11.2	10.1
9.3	8.6	8.7	10.1	9.6	10.6	10.6
10.5	7.7	9.1	12.3	12.0	7.3	5.8

Using 4.5 as the lower limit of the first class and 1.0 as the class width, construct a grouped frequency distribution using nine classes of equal width. Calculate the cumulative relative frequency for each class, leaving your answers in decimal form.

28 Life expectancy is the average number of years a person can expect to live, if in the future they experience the current age-specific mortality rates in the population. The table below shows the grouped frequency distribution constructed from data collected for 50 countries.

Life expectancy (in years)	Frequency
40–49	1
50–59	9
60–69	11
70–79	13
80–89	16

(a) Find the lower and upper class boundaries for each class.
(b) Do all the classes have the same width?
(c) How many countries have a life expectancy of less than 70 years?

29 Calculate the class boundaries and the class width for the following classes:
(a) 140–149
(b) 16.9–27.8

30 The manager of an Italian restaurant records the number of children in each family who order the set menu for children that includes baked dough balls, pizza or pasta and an ice-cream sundae for £6.99. His data are shown below.

3	0	1	2	0	0	1	3	0	2
2	2	4	2	1	3	0	1	2	2
3	5	2	1	1	2	1	2	0	0
4	4	1	1	3	3	1	2	2	0
0	5	3	2	0	2	5	2	1	3
2	1	3	0	0	2	5	0	1	1

(a) Create a frequency distribution for these data.
(b) In total, how many children ordered the £6.99 set menu?

31 Find the following numerical class characteristics if a set of continuous data is summarised in a grouped frequency distribution with eight classes of equal width and using 2.1–3.5 as the first class.
(a) The upper class boundary of the first class.
(b) The mid-point of the fourth class.
(c) Upper and lower limits for the last class.

32 For 80 hospitals in the UK, the frequency distribution below shows the number of patients who were waiting to start treatment after a referral from their doctor.

Number of patients	Frequency
0–9999	18
10,000–19,999	36
20,000–29,999	15
30,000–39,999	6
40,000–49,999	3
50,000–59,999	1
60,000–69,999	0
70,000–79,999	1

(a) Work out the relative frequencies for each class.
(b) What percentage of hospitals had between 20,000 and 29,999 patients waiting for their treatment?
(c) Can we say how many hospitals had between 45,000 and 47,000 patients on waiting lists? Explain your answer.

33 Fill in the blank spaces in the following statements about frequency distributions. Use these words:

tally	sum	distinct	first	last	values	largest	frequency

(a) The construction of a frequency distribution involves producing a list of all the _____ pieces of data that could have been collected, between (and including) the smallest value and the _____ value in the data set.
(b) The _____ column in a frequency distribution is used to identify each distinct data value.
(c) The total of the _____ marks is the _____ with which each distinct value occurs.
(d) We often use the _____ row in the table to record the _____ of the frequencies; this total is equal to the total number of data _____ contained in the set.

34 Explain what is wrong with each of the following statements:
(a) For qualitative data, class width is calculated by subtracting the lower class boundary from the upper class boundary.
(b) To find the mid-point of a class, simply multiply the sum of the class limits by 2.

35 The frequency distribution below summarises the data collected at a local fitness centre when customers were asked to state the day and time segment in which they would prefer to attend an exercise class.

Preferred day and time segment	Frequency
weekday morning	16
weekday afternoon	9

(Continued)

Preferred day and time segment	Frequency
weekday evening	37
weekend morning	44
weekend afternoon	12
weekend evening	25

(a) Are the collected data qualitative or quantitative?
(b) Work out the relative frequencies for the frequency distribution.
(c) If you were responsible for organising exercise classes at the fitness centre, when would you choose to schedule the widest variety of classes to maximise the number of potential participants? During which session might you decide to arrange a weekly staff training session instead of running classes? Explain how you reached the decisions.

36 The height of 35 professional basketball players was measured in centimetres. The data are shown below.

177	202	178	180	186	216	225
217	214	200	190	212	214	218
205	207	219	224	187	217	177
217	181	184	225	187	201	219
179	185	195	192	195	181	199

(a) Using equal class widths of 10 and a lower class limit of 175 for the first class, identify all of the classes that would be created in a grouped frequency distribution for this data.
(b) Based on the classes you have identified in part (a), construct the distribution and include a column for cumulative frequencies.
(c) Using the grouped frequency distribution, can you say how many basketball players have a height of exactly 182 centimetres? Explain your response.

37 For a grouped frequency distribution, decide whether the following statements are TRUE or FALSE. Explain your response for any FALSE statements.
(a) The groups used to categorise the data values are also known as classes.
(b) The relative frequency for a group shows the proportion of the data values in the set that belong to that group.
(c) When a grouped frequency distribution has been constructed, it is still possible to identify each individual data value that belongs to the original data set.

38 In a healthcare survey, participants were asked to describe the most effective way of ensuring that they fell asleep quickly at bedtime. The suggestions made were as follows:

count sheep	listen to music	have a bath	listen to music
listen to music	read a book	read a book	read a book
have a warm drink	have a bath	read a book	listen to music

(*Continued*)

have a warm drink	count sheep	relaxation exercises	have a bath
have a warm drink	read a book	relaxation exercises	have a bath
read a book	listen to music	have a bath	other
other	read a book	listen to music	count sheep
have a bath	listen to music	count sheep	other

Present these data in a frequency distribution, including a column for relative frequencies.

39 At a company providing bespoke logistic solutions to the retail industry, every employee earning more than £40,000 per year was asked how many meetings they attended on the previous working day. The data collected are shown in the table below.

Number of meetings	Frequency
1	87
2	62
3	21
4	15
5	9
6	1

(a) How many employees in the company earn more than £40,000?
(b) Calculate the cumulative frequencies.
(c) How many employees attended fewer than three meetings on the previous working day?

40 For a sample of 80 football matches, the table below shows the number of minutes that elapsed before the first goal was scored.

12	89	65	78	29	34	66	15	21	87
8	84	63	76	31	24	72	73	5	46
18	68	78	32	10	80	80	38	15	36
25	35	57	1	59	46	22	30	25	23
1	83	21	55	21	43	20	71	50	78
23	81	46	11	67	17	78	80	88	69
54	56	45	31	29	11	6	39	15	90
29	27	57	50	69	43	23	2	90	73

(a) Construct a grouped frequency distribution for these data using 0–9 as the first class.
(b) Work out the cumulative frequencies.

Solutions to Practice Exercises

1. (a) lower class limit is 25
       upper class limit is 34
       class mid-point is $(25 + 34)/2 = 29.5$
   (b) lower class limit is 4.1
       upper class limit is 5.5
       class mid-point is $(4.1 + 5.5)/2 = 4.8$

2. (a) 1365 customers responded; this is calculated as the sum of the frequencies.
   (b)

Response	Frequency	Relative frequency	Relative frequency (as a percentage)
search engine	247	0.181	18.1%
television advertisement	534	0.391	39.1%
recommended by a friend	109	0.080	8.0%
magazine/newspaper article	75	0.055	5.5%
radio advertisement	139	0.102	10.2%
other	261	0.191	19.1%

   (c) 39.1% of customers said that they found out about the comparison website by watching a television advertisement.
   (d) A proportion 0.080 of respondents answered 'recommended by a friend'.

3. (a) frequency distribution because the data are qualitative
   (b) grouped frequency distribution because the data are continuous
   (c) frequency distribution because the data are discrete with few distinct values
   (d) grouped frequency distribution because the data are discrete with many distinct values

4. (a) TRUE
   (b) TRUE
   (c) FALSE
       The class width is 100; this can be calculated for the first class as $600.5 - 500.5$.
   (d) FALSE
       801 is the lower class limit of the fourth class, 801–900; the upper class limit is 900.

5. (a)

Number of cars produced (in 000s)	Tally	Frequency
1–200	⦀⦀⦀⦀ ⦀⦀⦀⦀ ⦀⦀⦀⦀ ⎪	16
201–400	⦀⦀⦀⦀ ⎪⎪⎪	9
401–600	⦀⦀⦀⦀ ⎪⎪⎪	8

(Continued)

Number of cars produced (in 000s)	Tally	Frequency
601–800	ЖГ	5
801–1000	|||	3
1001–1200	|||	3
1201–1400			1
Total		45

(b)

Number of cars produced (in 000s)	Frequency	Relative frequency (as a percentage)
1–200	16	16/45 × 100 = 35.6%
201–400	9	20.0%
401–600	8	17.8%
601–800	5	11.1%
801–1000	3	6.7%
1001–1200	3	6.7%
1201–1400	1	2.2%
Total	45	

6   (a) 300 complaints were received from local residents; this is calculated as the sum of the frequencies.

(b)

Number of days	Frequency	Relative frequency	Relative frequency (as a percentage)
7	35	0.117	11.7%
8	44	0.147	14.7%
9	12	0.040	4.0%
10	32	0.107	10.7%
11	47	0.157	15.7%
12	33	0.110	11.0%
13	29	0.097	9.7%
14	68	0.227	22.7%

(c) Council services responded to 4% of complaints in exactly nine days.

7   (a) not possible
    (b) possible
    (c) not possible
    (d) possible
    (e) possible
    (f) not possible

8   (a) TRUE
    (b) FALSE
        9.85% of the cars arriving at the car park contained exactly four people; this is
        calculated using $39/396 \times 100 = 9.85\%$.
    (c) TRUE
    (d) TRUE

9   The classes for the grouped frequency distribution would be:

Lower class limit	Upper class limit	Class mid-point
10	34	$(10 + 34)/2 = 22$
35	59	47
60	84	72
85	109	97
110	134	122
135	159	147

10 Three reasons for processing and simplifying raw data using a frequency distribution are:
    • To determine characteristics of the data set such as the data value that occurs most
      often.
    • To highlight important features or underlying patterns which are hidden by the
      quantity of raw data.
    • To make a comparison between two sets of data more easily.

11

Number of bedrooms	Frequency	Cumulative frequency	Cumulative relative frequency (as a percentage)
1	454	454	12.2%
2	943	1397	37.4%
3	985	2382	63.8%
4	830	3212	86.0%
5	362	3574	95.7%

(Continued)

Number of bedrooms	Frequency	Cumulative frequency	Cumulative relative frequency (as a percentage)
6	108	3682	98.6%
7	25	3707	99.3%
8	10	3717	99.6%
9	8	3725	99.8%
10	5	3730	99.9%
11	3	3733	100.0%

The cumulative relative frequency for a data value represents the percentage of properties that have that quantity or fewer bedrooms. For example, 86.0% of the properties on the website have four bedrooms or fewer.

12 The frequency of a class is the number of data values that belong to that class. Relative frequency shows the proportion of the data values in the set that belong to each class. Cumulative frequency represents the number of data values we have collected that belong to that class or the classes that come before it in the table.

13 (a) The data are discrete.
(b)

Number of paper clips in a box	Frequency	Relative frequency	Cumulative frequency	Cumulative relative frequency (as a percentage)
97	10	2.0%	10	2.0%
98	23	4.6%	33	6.6%
99	74	14.8%	107	21.4%
100	286	57.2%	393	78.6%
101	69	13.8%	462	92.4%
102	30	6.0%	492	98.4%
103	8	1.6%	500	100%

(c) 57.2%, so more than half of the sampled boxes contain the correct number of paper clips.
(d) 107 boxes in the sample contained 99 or fewer paper clips.
(e) 42.8% of sampled boxes did not contain the correct number of paper clips.

14

Number of cooked breakfasts served	Tally	Frequency	Cumulative frequency
110–114	LHT II	7	7
115–119	LHT	5	12
120–124	III	3	15
125–139	LHT LHT LHT II	17	32
140–144	LHT I	6	38
145–149	II	2	40
Total		40	

15 (a) number of classes is six
class limits of the third class 10–14 are 10 and 14
(b) upper class boundary of the third class 10–14 is $(14 + 15)/2 = 14.5$
mid-point of the fifth class 20–24 is $(24 + 20)/2 = 22$
(c) class width is $9.5 - 4.5 = 5$

16 We would choose to construct a grouped frequency distribution rather than a frequency distribution for these data because, although they are discrete, many distinct values could occur. A frequency distribution would not be suitable because a list identifying each distinct value would be too long and many of the rows would have no tally marks where the distinct value does not appear in the data set, or a frequency of 1 because the distinct value appears only once.

17 (a) The third class is 45–59, so the upper class limit of the third class is 59.
(b) The class width can be calculated from the first class, $15-29 : 29.5 - 14.5 = 15$.
(c) The second class is 30–44, so the lower class boundary of the second class is $(29 + 30)/2 = 29.5$.

18 The eight classes for the grouped frequency distribution are: 65–74, 75–84, 85–94, 95–104, 105–114, 115–124, 125–134, 135–144.
The mid-points for the classes are: 69.5, 79.5, 89.5, 99.5, 109.5, 119.5, 129.5 and 139.5.

19 (a)

Flavour of crisps	Tally	Frequency
cheese & onion	LHT III	8
prawn cocktail	LHT	5

(Continued)

Flavour of crisps	Tally	Frequency
ready salted	ЖЖ ЖЖ II	12
roast chicken	ЖЖ I	6
salt&vinegar	ЖЖ ЖЖ	10
smoky bacon	III	3
steak&onion	ЖЖ III	8
other	ЖЖ III	8
Total		60

(b) Ready salted was chosen as favourite by the largest number of children; 12 out of 60 children preferred this flavour.

20 (a) A grouped frequency distribution cannot be used for qualitative data because there are no numerical values on which the classes can be based.

(b) For discrete data with only a few distinct values, a grouped frequency distribution would not be appropriate because there is not a large enough range of different values to support the construction of 5 to 15 classes.

21 Option (a). Approximately 1.00 or 100%, because sometimes the total will differ slightly from 1.00 or 100% due to rounding that may have been necessary in the calculation of the relative frequency values.

22 When qualitative or quantitative data values are recorded in the order in which they are collected, this is known as raw data. We can display raw data in an ordinary table with rows and columns.

23 (a) TRUE
(b) FALSE
    The upper class limit of the third class 50–69 is 69.
(c) TRUE
(d) TRUE
(e) FALSE
    The lower class boundary of the fifth class 90–109 is $(89 + 90)/2 = 89.5$.

24 (a) males

Portions of fruit and vegetables	Frequency	Cumulative frequency
0	5	5
1	8	13
2	4	17

(*Continued*)

Portions of fruit and vegetables	Frequency	Cumulative frequency
3	8	25
4	8	33
5	7	40
Total	40	

females

Portions of fruit and vegetables	Frequency	Cumulative frequency
0	6	6
1	9	15
2	7	22
3	10	32
4	5	37
5	3	40
Total	40	

(b) More males than females ate five portions of fruit and vegetables.

25 (a)

Response	Frequency	Relative frequency	Relative frequency (as a percentage)
faulty	11	0.085	8.5%
do not like colour	24	0.186	18.6%
too large	6	0.047	4.7%
too small	17	0.132	13.2%
poor quality material/ fabric	46	0.357	35.7%
arrived too late	9	0.070	7.0%
incorrect item received	16	0.124	12.4%

(b) 17.9% of items were returned because they were too large or too small.
(c) 11 faulty items were returned.
(d) I would advise the management team to focus on the quality of the material/fabric because the highest percentage of items (35.7%) was returned for this reason.

26 Option (b). The fourth class, 175–179, would include the data value 175.

27

Time taken for 0–60 mph (in seconds)	Frequency	Cumulative frequency	Cumulative relative frequency (as a percentage)
4.5–5.4	1	1	0.02%
5.5–6.4	3	4	0.10%
6.5–7.4	4	8	0.19%
7.5–8.4	6	14	0.33%
8.5–9.4	4	18	0.43%
9.5–10.4	7	25	0.60%
10.5–11.4	8	33	0.79%
11.5–12.4	4	37	0.88%
12.5–13.4	5	42	1.00%

28 (a)

Life expectancy (in years)	Frequency	Lower class boundary	Upper class boundary
40–49	1	$(39 + 40)/2 = 39.5$	$(49 + 50)/2 = 49.5$
50–59	9	49.5	59.5
60–69	11	59.5	69.5
70–79	13	69.5	79.5
80–89	16	79.5	89.5

(b) Yes, all of the classes have the same width; this is calculated as $49.5 - 39.5 = 10$.
(c)

Life expectancy (in years)	Frequency	Cumulative frequency
40–49	1	1
50–59	9	10
60–69	11	21
70–79	13	34
80–89	16	50

21 countries have a life expectancy of less than 70 years.

29 (a) lower class boundary is $(139 + 140)/2 = 139.5$
upper class boundary is $(149 + 150)/2 = 149.5$
class width is $149.5 - 139.5 = 10$

(b) lower class boundary is $(16.8 + 16.9)/2 = 16.85$
upper class boundary is $(27.8 + 27.9)/2 = 27.85$
class width is $27.85 - 16.85 = 11$

30 (a)

Number of children in each family who ordered the set menu	Tally	Frequency
0	$\cancel{||||}\ \cancel{||||}\ |||$	13
1	$\cancel{||||}\ \cancel{||||}\ ||||$	14
2	$\cancel{||||}\ \cancel{||||}\ \cancel{||||}\ ||$	17
3	$\cancel{||||}\ ||||$	9
4	$|||$	3
5	$||||$	4
Total		60

(b) The total number of children who ordered the set menu is calculated as:
$(1 \times 14) + (2 \times 17) + (3 \times 9) + (4 \times 3) + (5 \times 4) = 107$.

31 (a) The first class is 2.1–3.5, so the upper class boundary of the first class is $(3.5 + 3.6)/2 = 3.55$.

(b) The fourth class is 6.6–8.0, so the mid-point of the fourth class is $(6.6 + 8.0)/2 = 7.3$.

(c) The last class is 12.6–14.0, so the limits of the last class are 12.6 and 14.0.

32 (a)

Number of patients	Frequency	Relative frequency	Relative frequency (as a percentage)
0–9999	18	0.225	22.5%
10000–19999	36	0.450	45.0%
20000–29999	15	0.188	18.8%
30000–39999	6	0.075	7.5%
40000–49999	3	0.038	3.8%
50000–59999	1	0.013	1.3%

(Continued)

Number of patients	Frequency	Relative frequency	Relative frequency (as a percentage)
60000–69999	0	0.000	0.0%
70000–79999	1	0.013	1.3%

(b) 18.8% of hospitals had between 20000 and 29999 patients waiting for their treatment.

(c) No, we cannot say how many hospitals had between 45000 and 47000 patients on waiting lists because we do not have a class representing exactly these values in the grouped frequency distribution.

33 (a) distinct, largest
   (b) first
   (c) tally, frequency
   (d) last, sum, values

34 (a) Qualitative data cannot be described using classes, and so it is not possible to calculate class widths. The correct statement would be:

   For *quantitative* data, class width is calculated by subtracting the lower class boundary from the upper class boundary.

   (b) In this statement, the calculation is incorrect for the mid-point of a class. It should say:

   To find the mid-point of a class, simply *divide* the sum of the class limits by 2.

35 (a) The collected data are qualitative.
   (b)

Preferred day and time segment	Frequency	Relative frequency	Relative frequency (as a percentage)
weekday morning	16	0.112	11.2%
weekday afternoon	9	0.063	6.3%
weekday evening	37	0.259	25.9%
weekend morning	44	0.308	30.8%
weekend afternoon	12	0.084	8.4%
weekend evening	25	0.175	17.5%

(c) I would schedule the widest variety of classes on a weekend morning because the highest percentage of customers (30.8%) stated that they would prefer to attend an exercise class at this time. I might decide to arrange a weekly staff training session on a weekday afternoon instead of running classes because this was the least popular day and time segment chosen by the customers.

36 (a) The classes for the grouped frequency distribution are: 175–184, 185–194, 195–204, 205–214, 215–224 and 225–234.

(b)

Height in centimetres	Tally	Frequency	Cumulative frequency
175–184	⦀⦀ ⦀⦀⦀	8	8
185–194	⦀⦀ ⦀	6	14
195–204	⦀⦀ ⦀	6	20
205–214	⦀⦀	5	25
215–224	⦀⦀ ⦀⦀⦀	8	33
225–234	⦀⦀	2	35
Total		35	

(c) No, we cannot say how many basketball players have a height of exactly 182 cm because we can no longer identify individual data values.

37 (a) TRUE
(b) TRUE
(c) FALSE

Although a grouped frequency distribution is a useful way of summarising a data set, it does have one disadvantage: the individual values from the data set can no longer be identified by looking at the table. The grouped frequency distribution only shows the number of data values that belong to each class.

38

Suggestion	Frequency	Relative frequency	Relative frequency (as a percentage)
count sheep	4	0.125	12.5%
listen to music	7	0.219	21.9%
have a warm drink	3	0.094	9.4%
read a book	7	0.219	21.9%
have a bath	6	0.188	18.8%
relaxation exercises	2	0.063	6.3%
other	3	0.094	9.4%

39 (a) 195 employees in the company earn more than £40,000.

(b)

Number of meetings	Frequency	Cumulative frequency
1	87	87
2	62	149
3	21	170
4	15	185
5	9	194
6	1	195

(c) 149 employees attended fewer than three meetings on the previous working day.

40 (a)

Number of minutes before first goal	Tally	Frequency
0–9	⊬⊤ I	6
10–19	⊬⊤ ⊬⊤ I	11
20–29	⊬⊤ IIII	9
30–39	⊬⊤ IIII	9
40–49	⊬⊤ III	8
50–59	III	3
60–69	⊬⊤ ⊬⊤ ⊬⊤ II	17
70–79	⊬⊤ IIII	9
80–89	⊬⊤ II	7
90–99	I	1
Total		80

(b)

Number of minutes before first goal	Frequency	Cumulative frequency
0–9	6	6
10–19	11	17

(Continued)

Number of minutes before first goal	Frequency	Cumulative frequency
20–29	9	26
30–39	9	35
40–49	8	43
50–59	3	46
60–69	17	63
70–79	9	72
80–89	7	79
90–99	1	80
Total	80	

Graphical Representation

This chapter explains how to:

- construct charts to display qualitative data
  - bar chart
  - pie chart
- draw graphs to display quantitative data
  - scatter diagram
  - histogram
  - time series plot
  - stem and leaf diagram
- visually compare multiple data sets using a single graph or chart
- understand some of the ways that diagrams can be misinterpreted
- choose the appropriate diagram for your data

bar chart	**pie chart**	**stem and leaf diagram**
histogram	**scatter diagram**	**time series plot**

Introduction

Graphs and charts provide a useful method for showing what your data mean in a visual way. When you are working with a small amount of data, a simple table may be sufficient for presenting the data and results. However, if you have collected large sets of data using a questionnaire or through interviewing then a diagram will help you to summarise your results in a concise way, highlight important facts and patterns in the data and describe comparisons between different data sets. When information is presented in a visual form, it is more likely that people will be able to understand and remember the results you are trying to show about the data you have collected.

Whether you need to describe your results by writing a report, displaying details on a website or giving a verbal presentation to an audience, the use of graphs and charts is not always straightforward. You should aim to choose a diagram that is appropriate for the data you have collected, the audience you are writing for, and the type of results to be shown. It is also important that diagrams are drawn carefully and accurately so that the audience does not misinterpret their meaning because of the way in which the data are presented.

Bar Charts

Qualitative data are often displayed using a **bar chart**. This is a diagram drawn with rectangular bars where each bar represents a different category in the data set. Categories are labelled on one axis and the frequency of the category on the other. The bars in the chart should be the same width and separated an equal distance from each other. Bars can be drawn horizontally or vertically, and the frequency of the category is represented by the length or height of the corresponding bar. Horizontal bar charts are particularly useful if category names are lengthy.

The following bar charts show the number of small, medium and large portions of chips sold in a single hour at a fast food restaurant. Each chart shows the same data – one using vertical bars, the other using horizontal bars.

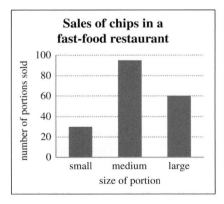
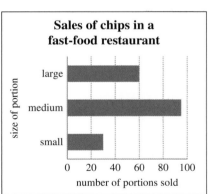

From these bar charts, we can see that:

- the most popular portion size was medium;
- half as many small portions of chips were sold compared to large;
- 60 large portions of chips were sold.

The scale on a bar chart must always be carefully drawn, starting at zero, so that the diagram provides an accurate picture of the data it is representing. The example below shows how changing the scale can give a false impression of the data set.

In a trial of new milkshake flavours, 300 customers were asked to taste a sample of each flavour and record their favourite. Looking only at the relative height of the bars, the chart on the left suggests that twice as many people preferred the popcorn-flavoured sample compared to the maple syrup milkshake. The vertical axis scale on this chart does not start at zero and so the difference between the heights of the bars is exaggerated. The bar chart on the right provides a more accurate visual representation of the data collected.

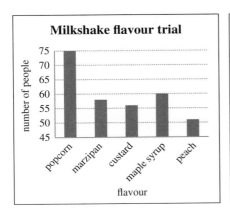 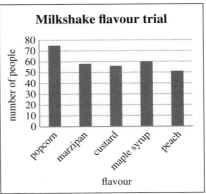

Bar charts are particularly useful if we want to make a comparison between different data sets on the same diagram. Either a grouped bar chart or a stacked bar chart can be used for this purpose.

In an online questionnaire about food shopping preferences, respondents were asked whether they preferred to buy frozen, tinned or fresh vegetables. Using a grouped bar chart, a separate bar represents each subcategory of data and these are usually shaded differently so that the audience can distinguish between them. Subcategory bars are then grouped together for each category.

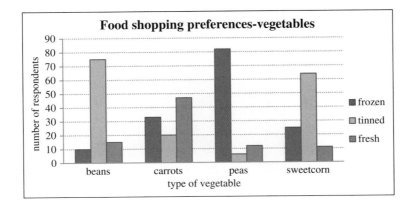

In a stacked bar chart, we place the bars representing the subcategories on top of each other to make a single bar for each category. Once again, shading is used to help with interpreting the data.

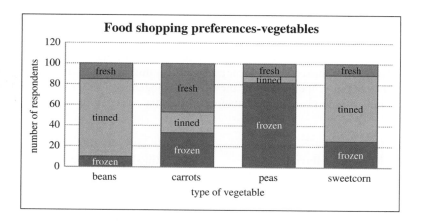

Pie Charts

A **pie chart** is a circular diagram that can also be used to display qualitative data. The circle is divided into segments, each one representing a category as a proportion of the whole data set. The area of a segment is proportional to the frequency of its corresponding category.

As there are 360 degrees in a circle representing the whole data set, each segment angle in the pie chart is calculated using

$$\text{relative frequency} \times 360$$

where

$$\text{relative frequency} = \frac{\text{category frequency}}{\text{total frequency}}$$

The pie chart below shows the responses of 60 people who were asked the question 'How often do you eat in a restaurant?' during an interview about eating habits.

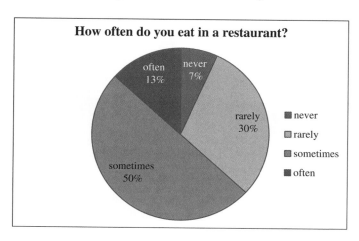

From this pie chart, we can see that:

- exactly half of the interviewees said that they sometimes eat in a restaurant;
- more than twice as many people responded with 'rarely' compared to 'often';
- 7% of people questioned said they never eat in a restaurant.

The segment angles were calculated as follows:

Response	Frequency	Relative frequency	Segment angle
never	4	$4/60 = 7\%$	$4/60 \times 360 = 24°$
rarely	18	$18/60 = 30\%$	$18/60 \times 360 = 108°$
sometimes	30	$30/60 = 50\%$	$30/60 \times 360 = 180°$
often	8	$8/60 = 13\%$	$8/60 \times 360 = 48°$

The main advantage of pie charts is that they are easy to construct and simple to understand. They are visually appealing and therefore attract the attention of the audience. However, there are several problems associated with presenting and analysing data using this method.

They cannot easily be used to compare proportions of the same category in different data sets. Consider the charts below which show the percentage of fruit and vegetables grown in allotments in 2009 and 2010. Comparing the size of the corresponding segments, such as the proportion of potatoes grown in each year, is difficult because it relies on visual inspection.

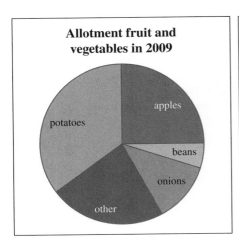

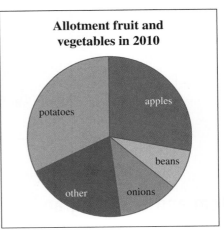

Making a visual comparison of the relative size of segments within a pie chart can also be difficult if percentage values are not shown. The diagram below describes the responses from 260 shoppers when asked about the factor that most influences their product choice when buying a loaf of bread. Deciding whether more shoppers choose their bread based on familiarity compared to brand is problematic because the segments representing these two factors appear to be very similar in size.

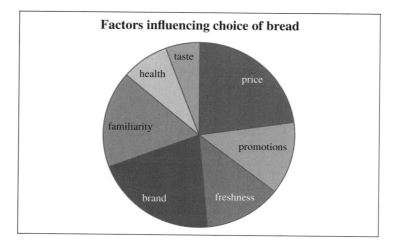

This type of diagram is less useful when a data set includes many different categories because the circle becomes cluttered with too many very small segments. The following pie chart shows the worldwide production of bananas by country. With so many countries to be displayed, the chart becomes confusing and difficult to interpret.

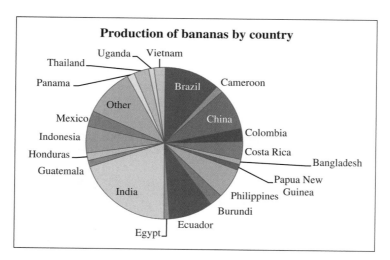

Stem and Leaf Diagrams

A technique for organising quantitative data is to draw a **stem and leaf diagram**. We can use this type of diagram to observe patterns in our data set and highlight interesting features. Each individual data value is retained when we draw the stem and leaf diagram, but for large data sets it can be a time-consuming process.

To draw the diagram, we need to separate the digits in each data value into a stem and a leaf. The stem consists of all but the rightmost digits and the leaf is the rightmost digit only. For single digits, use 0 as the stem.

Data value	Stem	Leaf
36	3	6
417	41	7
9	0	9

each leaf should consist of the single rightmost digit only

There are three steps involved in drawing the diagram for a data set.

1. Write the stem digits in ascending order in a vertical column, drawing a vertical line to the right of the column.
2. For each stem, write all of the corresponding leaves in the data set along the same horizontal line.
3. Rearrange each line of leaves in ascending order.

Within the range of the data values, all stems should be shown on the diagram even if the data set does not contain any corresponding leaves. Every stem and leaf diagram should have a key to provide information about how the data in the diagram should be interpreted.

The data set in the following example consists of the scores achieved in an aptitude test taken by applicants for a graduate marketing role in a leading food and drink manufacturing company.

22	36	8	56	14	54	25	49	19	16
45	31	11	55	72	72	49	56	46	22
85	47	42	85	41	39	13	33	78	93
92	75	24	83	38	91	84	85	28	7

The stem and leaf diagram for these data is constructed as follows:

```
0 |              0 | 8  7                      0 | 7  8
1 |              1 | 4  9  6  1  3             1 | 1  3  4  6  9
2 |              2 | 2  5  2  4  8             2 | 2  2  4  5  8
3 |              3 | 6  1  9  3  8             3 | 1  3  6  8  9
4 |              4 | 9  5  9  6  7  2  1       4 | 1  2  5  6  7  9  9
5 |              5 | 6  4  5  6                5 | 4  5  6  6
6 |              6 |                           6 |
7 |              7 | 2  2  8  5                7 | 2  2  5  8
8 |              8 | 5  5  3  4  5             8 | 3  4  5  5  5
9 |              9 | 3  2  1                   9 | 1  2  3

  Step 1          Step 2                         Step 3
```

Adding a title and an information key gives the final diagram:

Aptitude test scores

9 | 3 = 93%

```
0 | 7 8
1 | 1 3 4 6 9
2 | 2 2 4 5 8
3 | 1 3 6 8 9
4 | 1 2 5 6 7 9 9
5 | 4 5 6 6
6 |
7 | 2 2 5 8
8 | 3 4 5 5 5
9 | 1 2 3
```

Two data sets can be displayed at the same time for comparison in a back-to-back stem and leaf diagram. Here, one data set is shown to the left of the stem and the other set is shown to the right. Leaves are written in ascending order on each side, with the smallest values closest to the stems.

The following back-to-back stem and leaf diagram shows the age of male and female customers who use an online pizza ordering service.

Customer age by gender

8 | 1 = age 18   2 | 3 = age 23

male   female

```
            9 9 9 9 8 8 | 1 |
6 6 5 5 2 1 1 0 0 | 2 | 3 4 4 4 8 8 9 9 9
                4 | 3 | 0 0 1 4 5 5 8
                5 | 4 | 2 5 6
              5 4 | 5 |
              6 3 | 6 |
```

In the diagram above, we may feel that there are too many leaves on each side of the stem '2'. In this case, we could split the stem into two lines instead of one, writing leaves 0–4 on the first lines and leaves 5–9 on the second line, as follows:

Customer age by gender

8 | 1 = age 18   2 | 3 = age 23

male   female

```
9 9 9 9 8 8 | 1 |
    2 1 1 0 0 | 2 | 3 4 4 4
    6 6 5 5 | 2 | 8 8 9 9 9
        4 | 3 | 0 0 1 4 5 5 8
        5 | 4 | 2 5 6
      5 4 | 5 |
      6 3 | 6 |
```

A stem and leaf diagram can also be used to display data when the individual values are not whole numbers, but you may need to round the values before constructing the diagram. You will also need to change the information key to reflect the way in which the data should be interpreted by the audience.

The data below shows the price in £s per kilogram of 30 types of cheese.

5.92	9.35	8.70	6.00	8.78	7.32	9.13	8.27	7.50	7.08
7.69	9.35	6.67	5.71	6.17	8.56	6.67	9.09	5.66	5.66
8.78	8.33	5.71	7.12	7.38	5.54	8.49	6.67	9.12	8.20

To ensure that the leaves in the diagram have only a single digit, we would need to round the data as follows:

5.9	9.4	8.7	6.0	8.8	7.3	9.1	8.3	7.5	7.1
7.7	9.4	6.7	5.7	6.2	8.6	6.7	9.1	5.7	5.7
8.8	8.3	5.7	7.1	7.4	5.5	8.5	6.7	9.1	8.2

Our stem and leaf diagram would then be constructed as follows:

Price in £s of cheese per kg

5|5 = £5.50 per kg

```
5 | 5  5  7  7  7  9
6 | 0  2  7  7  7
7 | 1  1  3  4  5  7
8 | 2  3  3  5  6  7  8  8
9 | 1  1  1  4  4
```

Histograms

A **histogram** can be used to display quantitative data that have been organised into groups or classes. It is visually similar in style to a bar chart, but the bars are drawn next to each other without gaps and the width of the bars has a specific meaning.

To draw a histogram, we use the vertical axis to represent the frequency of the classes. The horizontal axis is used to record the class intervals and is labelled with each class limit. If we have used classes of the same width for our data set, then the bars will all have equal width and the height of each bar will represent the frequency of the corresponding class.

The data set below shows the weight (in grams) of each packet of savoury crackers in a sample of 60 packets.

200	125	125	200	500	150	125	150	150	200
125	120	150	150	300	125	200	192	200	185
150	80	125	300	250	140	130	150	300	200
140	150	200	125	125	100	175	175	125	150
240	150	250	123	200	150	150	150	150	150
300	200	190	200	150	125	200	150	150	80

Organising the data into classes of equal size, with inclusive lower class limits, gives:

Class	0–100	100–200	200–300	300–400	400–500
Frequency	2	39	14	4	1

The histogram for these data would be drawn as follows:

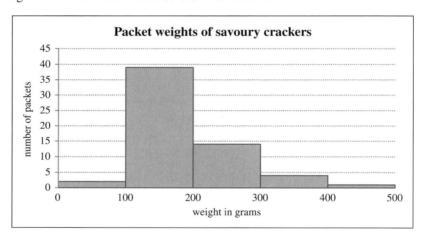

We need to be careful when using unequal class sizes for our data set. In this case, the frequency of each class will be represented by the *area* of the corresponding bar instead of the height.

In this example, the height (in cm) of 40 employees was measured at a sugar production company.

172	179	166	181	173	164	175	172	178	163
184	176	169	175	173	179	163	174	165	177
177	168	179	174	176	182	177	170	180	176
173	184	172	169	184	180	171	170	177	172

We could organise the data into classes as follows:

Class	160–170	170–175	175–180	180–185
Frequency	8	12	13	7

The width of the first class is twice as large as the width of the other classes, and therefore the height of the corresponding bar in the histogram must be reduced to half of the frequency value.

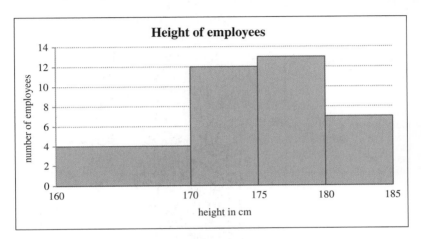

Time Series Plots

If you have data values which change over time, a **time series plot** can be used to display this information. It is a graph on which you plot each observation against its corresponding time period. Time periods could include minutes, hours, days, weeks, months and years, depending on the data set. Time is always plotted on the horizontal axis and the points on the graph are usually connected with straight lines.

In the following time series plot, we can observe how the average price of a pint of milk has varied each year between 2000 and 2009.

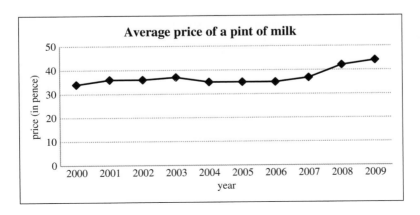

From this time series plot, we can see that:

- the price increase over the decade was approximately 10 pence;
- prices did not change during 2004, 2005 and 2006;
- between 2003 and 2004 there was a decrease in the average price of a pint of milk.

Time series plots provide a very effective way of showing patterns or trends in a data set over time. However, the vertical axis scale for a plot must be chosen with caution because using an inappropriate scale can exaggerate the trends over time and therefore lead to misinterpretation of the data.

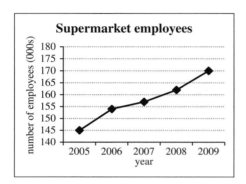 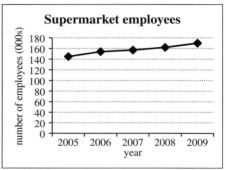

Consider the example above in which the number of employees at a leading supermarket is displayed for a five-year period. The time series plot on the left uses a *y*-axis scale from 140,000 to 180,000 and gives the impression that the number of employees has risen quite sharply over the five years. Using a vertical axis scale that begins at zero, the right-hand plot gives a more appropriate representation of the data set whilst still showing the increase in employees at the supermarket.

It is easy to compare two or more data sets over the same time period using a single time series plot. In this situation, it is important to include an information key, or legend, so that the audience knows which set of connected points belongs to each data set.

The following example shows how the market share of three leading supermarkets changed during the 1990s. The diagram provides information about the relationship between the different supermarkets and allows us to make comparisons between their percentage market shares.

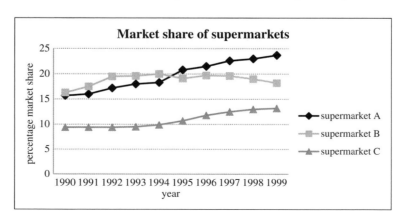

Scatter Diagrams

A scatter diagram is a graph that can be used to display the values of two quantitative variables so that we can observe any potential relationship between them. Each point on a scatter diagram represents a pair of data values for an individual entity, such as a person, a product or a company. The plotted points are not joined with lines.

The diagram provides visual information about the pattern of data values, showing whether an increase in one variable is associated with an increase or decrease in the other variable. Sometimes, the scatter diagram indicates that there is no obvious relationship between the variables.

The scatter diagram below shows the temperature (in degrees Celsius) recorded at 12 noon and the number of ice-creams sold at a seaside café on the first day of each month in a year.

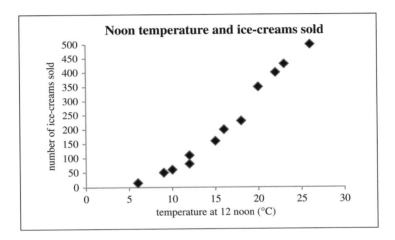

From this scatter diagram, we can see that:

- the highest temperature recorded was less than 30°C;
- when the recorded temperature was 20°C, the seaside café sold 350 ice-creams;
- as the temperature increases, the number of ice-creams sold also increases.

A scatter diagram is particularly useful for showing whether the data sets contain any extreme values. In the example below, the amount of sugar and salt was measured for ten different types of breakfast cereal.

The graph clearly shows that one of the cereals contained a low amount of sugar but a high salt content and so it does not follow the same data pattern as the other varieties.

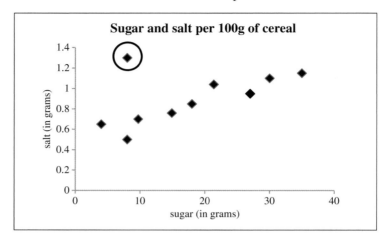

A multiple scatter diagram can be used to compare two different data sets on the same graph, although sometimes these diagrams can become very cluttered and difficult to interpret.

Consider the example below, which shows the annual salary and the average weekly expenditure in the company cafeteria for 30 men and 30 women who work at the same company.

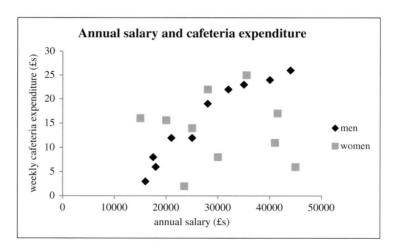

HINTS AND TIPS

BACKGROUND IMAGES

When you are presenting results using one of the graphical methods discussed in this chapter, do not use unnecessary background images in an attempt to make your report look more attractive. As shown in the example below, the image is likely to distract your audience from understanding the real meaning of the data displayed in the graph or chart.

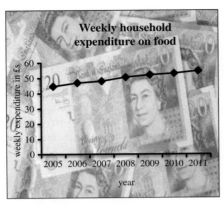

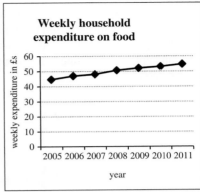

GENERAL GUIDELINES

Follow these straightforward guidelines to ensure that graphs and charts are always well presented:

1. Choose the graphical method that is most suitable to represent your results, depending on the type of data collected and the information you are trying to convey.
2. Keep your diagram simple and uncluttered, avoiding three-dimensional effects, background images and unnecessary gridlines.
3. Ensure that both axes are clearly labelled with a consistent scale and a useful title including units of measurement, if appropriate.
4. Use a short but meaningful title that describes the data displayed in the diagram.
5. When you have finished constructing your chart or drawing your graph, check that the meaning of the data and the results cannot be misinterpreted by the audience.

VISUAL PERSPECTIVE

Many people use three-dimensional effects in their pie chart or bar chart because they feel that it draws the attention of the audience and makes the diagram look more attractive. Unfortunately, this technique can make it difficult for the data values to be read accurately from the diagram. It can also make some segments of the chart look bigger than they actually are, in proportion to the other segments, so that comparing relative sizes of bars or pie segments is problematic.

The charts shown below have been drawn using exactly the same data that was collected by asking 160 people about the fruit they preferred to eat at lunchtime.

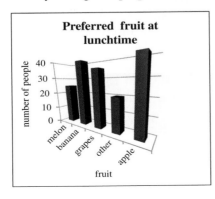

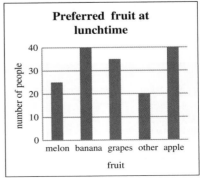

Using the bar chart on the left, it is difficult to accurately read the number of people associated with each fruit because the bars are not lined up horizontally with the values on the axis scale; the chart seems to indicate that more than 40 people preferred to eat an apple at lunchtime, but using the diagram on the right, you can see that the correct data value is exactly 40.

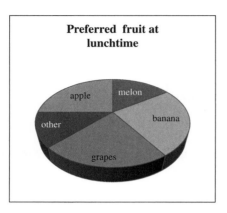

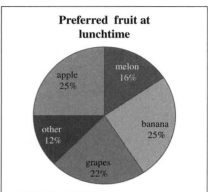

In the bar chart and pie chart on the left, the rotated three-dimensional perspective distorts the way in which we compare the relative size of each segment. In the bar chart, it looks as though more people prefer to eat an apple than a banana, but the diagram on the right clearly shows that the same number of people like these fruits. Similarly, the pie chart on the left seems to imply that grapes are the most popular fruit for eating at lunchtime, but the diagram on the right shows that this is a false interpretation.

Using Excel

CREATING CHARTS AND GRAPHS

Excel can be used to create charts and graphs to display your data in a visual form. Data should be entered into spreadsheet cells using a row and column format with column headings above the data and row headings to the left.

For qualitative data, Excel provides bar charts and pie charts. Scatter diagrams and time series plots can be created if your data are quantitative.

All of the charts and graphs can be accessed using the **Insert** tab on the ribbon. To create a diagram, highlight the cells that contain your data and click the chart type required.

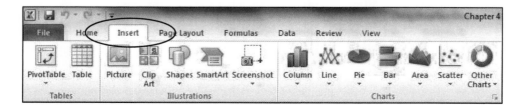

When you select a chart type, you will see that there are a range of different styles available for that chart. Always choose the style that is appropriate for your data set, taking into consideration what you are trying to show with your statistics in a particular situation.

As an example, the screenshot below shows the style choices for time series plots.

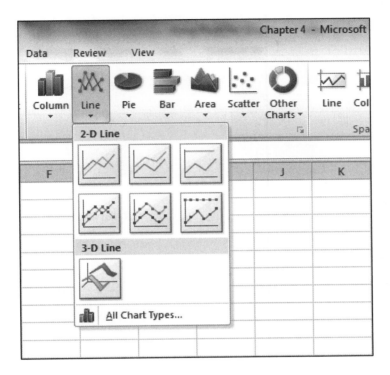

When you have chosen the style, Excel will create a chart based on your highlighted data. The chart will be displayed in a white rectangle which you can reposition as an object, using your mouse.

The software package automatically determines the best way to plot the data in the selected chart, but you may wish to make changes to its content or appearance. Once a chart has been created, you can use the **Chart Tools** tabs on the ribbon: **Design**, **Layout** and **Format**. These tabs display options that are specific to the each chart type and they are only visible when a chart has been selected in the spreadsheet.

The **Design** options for a pie chart are shown below.

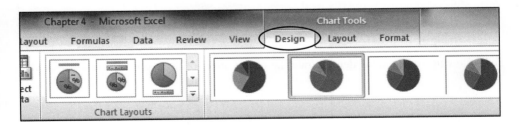

Using the **Design** tab, you can choose alternative predefined chart layouts; for example, you could include a chart title, legend and data labels. You can also change the background and foreground colours of your chart.

The following screenshots show some example layouts that are available for pie charts.

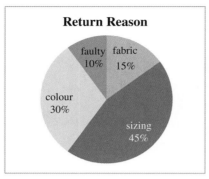
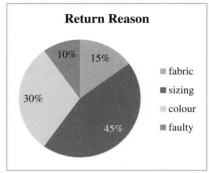
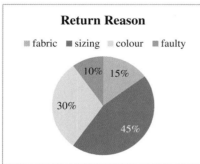
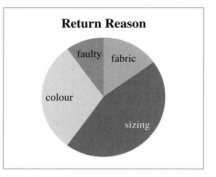

The **Layout** tab provides options for making changes to many aspects of your chart such as the positioning and style of the chart title, axis titles, legend, data labels, axis scales and gridlines. The **Layout** options for a bar chart are shown below.

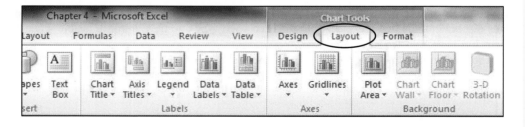

The following screen shots demonstrate the use of some of these options for a bar chart.

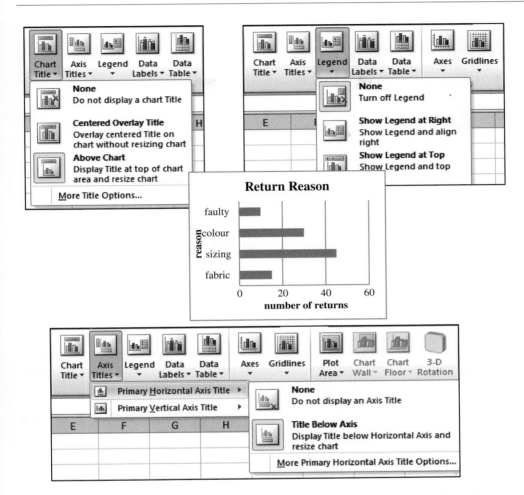

Any text and borders on the chart can be modified using the **Format** tab. Here you can apply different colours, text effects and shape effects to make your chart visually appealing.

Practice Exercises

1   Describe three ways in which graphs and charts can be useful for displaying data and results.

2   The time series plot below shows the number of male and female patients who visit a doctor at a walk-in health centre during one week.

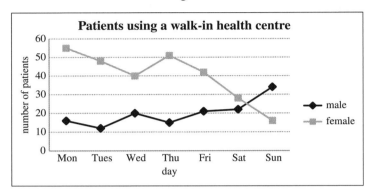

Use the graph to decide whether the following statements are TRUE or FALSE:
(a) There were twice as many male patients compared to female patients on Wednesday.
(b) On every day of the week, most of the patients using the walk-in health centre are female.
(c) The most popular day for men to visit a doctor was Sunday.

3   The payment method of 640 supermarket shoppers spending less than £30 on groceries was recorded. The results are shown below.

Payment method	debit card	cash	credit card
Frequency	352	192	96

Calculate the segment angle that would be used for each payment method in the construction of a pie chart for these data.

4   The histogram below shows the number of hotel rooms occupied each night during June, July and August.

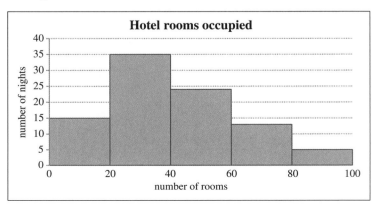

(a) Which class has the lowest frequency?

(b) On how many nights were 20–40 rooms occupied during the three months?

5 Explain how the use of three-dimensional effects can give a false interpretation of data being presented in a bar chart or pie chart.

6 Use this stem and leaf diagram to write down the original data set: the highest level recorded (in metres) for 25 rivers in the North of England.

Highest river levels recorded

1 | 3 = 1.3 metres

1	3	7					
2	0	0	0	2	2	4	4
2	5	5	6	6	6		
3	1	3	3	5	8	9	
4	0	3	7				
5	0	0					

7 The prize money for winning a sporting competition for men and women between 1990 and 1999 is given in the table below.

Year	Men	Women
1990	£45,100	£27,000
1991	£47,900	£28,400
1992	£48,200	£29,300
1993	£49,800	£31,800
1994	£51,300	£32,100
1995	£56,200	£34,900
1996	£56,200	£44,400
1997	£56,200	£45,400
1998	£60,400	£46,900
1999	£61,100	£46,900

Draw a time series plot to graphically display the prize money for both men and women on the same diagram.

8 Decide which type of graph or chart would be most suitable for presenting each of the following data sets. Give a reason for your choice.

(a) UK interest rates recorded each year between 1960 and 1980

(b) The number of male and female customers who made purchases at three different stores in a shopping mall

(c) Estimated annual earnings and height of the ten highest-paid actors in 2007

9 In a survey conducted by an environmental consultancy, house owners were asked: 'Would you have solar panels fitted to your house if the total up-front cost was less than £3000?' Of the 450 respondents, 60% answered 'yes', 25% answered 'no' and the remainder answered 'don't know'.

Construct a pie chart to visually illustrate the responses of the house owners.

10 One of Europe's leading airlines specifies a weight allowance of 20 kg of luggage per person on its flights. Fees are charged for excess baggage at £7 per kilogram. The weight (in kilograms) of each bag checked in for a flight from Gatwick Airport was recorded.

Comparing the histogram below with the table of data, explain how the diagram has been drawn incorrectly.

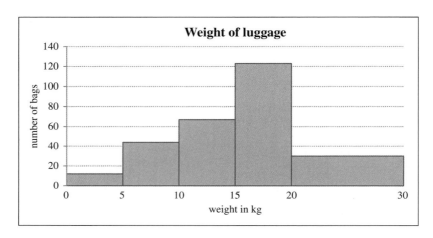

Class	0–5	5–10	10–15	15–20	20–30
Frequency	12	44	67	123	30

11 The following table shows the current energy efficiency rating and advertised price for 30 houses for sale in the same postcode area.

Energy efficiency rating	73	45	56	32	62	63	70	47	50	54
Price (£000s)	155	185	295	180	725	225	135	390	300	190

Energy efficiency rating	58	55	36	72	77	73	58	70	54	50
Price (£000s)	490	480	175	475	565	175	390	575	180	340

Energy efficiency rating	65	65	53	61	65	49	59	71	68	55
price (£000s)	285	220	420	350	150	280	750	350	250	160

Draw a scatter diagram for these data.

12 Describe the purpose of a time series plot and give two examples of data that a marketing company might present using this type of diagram.

13 The back-to-back stem and leaf diagram shown below has been created so that a comparison can be made between the ages of men and women who have been nominated in the 2013 Oscars for leading and supporting acting roles.

Age of Oscar nominees 2013

8 | 3 = 38 years old   0 | 9 = 9 years old

         male   female

	0	9
	1	
	2	2
8 8	3	0 6 8
5 4	4	4
8 6 6	5	0
9 6	6	6 6
9	7	
	8	6

(a) What was the age of the youngest nominee? Were they male or female?
(b) Which gender had the most nominees in their fifties?

14 In each of the four car parks on a university campus, a researcher recorded the number of hatchbacks, saloon cars and estates parked on a Monday morning. The results are shown below.

	Hatchback	Saloon	Estate
Car park 1	25	14	8
Car park 2	12	24	16
Car park 3	9	11	24
Car park 4	27	29	25

Use a stacked bar chart to display these data, with each car park labelled on the horizontal axis.

15 Although pie charts are easy to construct and are visually appealing, there are disadvantages associated with using them to display qualitative data. Describe two possible disadvantages.

16 This time series plot displays the number of people who visit a science museum each week in the autumn.

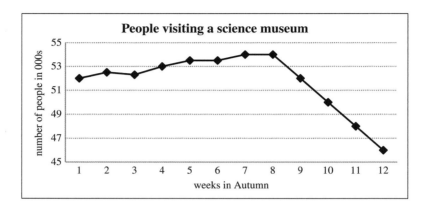

Describe how this diagram is misleading. What change should be made if the diagram were to be redrawn to give a more appropriate representation of the data?

17 The following table shows the length of telephone calls (in minutes) made by a household during one month.

Class	0–10	10–20	20–30	30–60
Frequency	37	22	8	12

Use an appropriate graphical method to display this information.

18 Draw a stem and leaf diagram to show the price of 60 pairs of men's trainers displayed on the website for a large sports retailer. Split any stems that contain more than ten leaves.

20	20	20	80	25	25	15	65	50	15	20	21
31	15	55	22	22	22	27	27	42	25	65	23
68	80	57	68	55	14	76	30	102	45	89	49
47	38	57	41	29	27	39	76	65	62	19	66
36	38	17	54	59	78	86	36	49	27	44	36

19 On returning from a Caribbean cruise trip, 900 customers completed a questionnaire about the on-board entertainment shows provided by the operating company. The diagram below shows their responses.

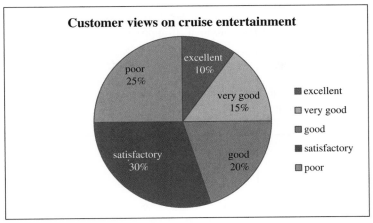

Customer views on cruise entertainment

(a) How many customers reported that the on-board entertainment was very good?
(b) Did more or less than half of the customers indicate that the entertainment shows were satisfactory or poor?

20 The following data show the number of gold, silver and bronze Olympic medals won in 2012 by Great Britain, China and the United States. Display these data in an appropriate diagram, using the *x*-axis for the type of medal: gold, silver and bronze.

	Gold	Silver	Bronze
Great Britain	29	17	19
China	38	27	23
United States	46	29	29

21 The following table shows the quarterly electricity bills for a household over a two-year period.

	Year 1				Year 2			
Quarter	1	2	3	4	1	2	3	4
Cost of electricity in £s	127	163	92	167	187	208	131	176

Use an appropriate graphical method to display this information.

22 Use the words provided to fill in the blank spaces in the following guidelines for ensuring that graphs and charts are always well presented.

images	meaningful	units	uncluttered	short	axes	effects

(a) Keep your diagram simple and _____, avoiding three-dimensional _____, background _____, and unnecessary gridlines.

    (b) Ensure that both _____ are clearly labelled with a consistent scale and a useful title including _____ of measurement, if appropriate.

    (c) Use a _____ but _____ title that describes the data displayed in the diagram.

23 For 25 employees working in the accounts department of a distribution company, the scatter diagram below shows the number of years employed by the company and the level of job satisfaction on a scale of 1–10.

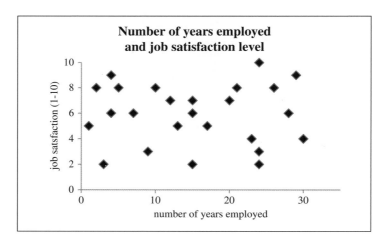

What does the pattern of data values show?

(a) An increase in one variable is associated with an increase in the other.

(b) As the number of years employed increases, the job satisfaction level decreases.

(c) There is no obvious relationship between number of years employed and job satisfaction.

24 Describe one advantage and one disadvantage of using a stem and leaf diagram to display data.

25 The following table shows the number of domestic passengers who used Heathrow Airport from 2008 to 2012.

Year	2008	2009	2010	2011	2012
Number of domestic passengers (millions)	4.7	4.7	4.8	5.3	5.6

Construct a time series plot for these data.

26 In a local primary school, 60 boys and 60 girls were asked what they would like to do for a job when they were older. The diagram below shows their responses.

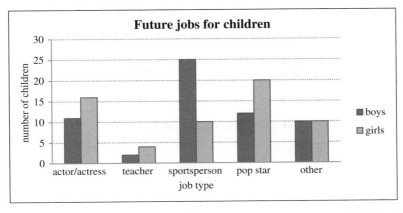

Use the bar chart to decide whether the following statements are TRUE or FALSE:
(a) Twice as many boys wanted to be a sportsperson compared to girls.
(b) For both genders, the least popular job was becoming a teacher.
(c) 50% of the girls wanted to be either a pop star or a sportsperson.

27 A mail order company is planning to build a new distribution centre on a business park in a rural location. The management team decide to ask some existing employees about the distance (in miles) they commute each day to work. The data collected are shown below.

45	10	16	38	29	27	14	31	48	19	17	11	24
20	23	37	14	29	22	27	18	13	26	26	15	10

Draw a suitable diagram that retains the individual commuting distances for each employee.

28 The average temperature and average wind speed in July for 10 cities in the northern hemisphere and 10 cities in the southern hemisphere are given in the table below.

Northern hemisphere		Southern hemisphere	
Average temperature (°C)	Average wind speed (km/h)	Average temperature (°C)	Average wind speed (km/h)
28	12	11	10
25	10	22	8
23	16	21	9
16	14	27	12
11	19	23	8
18	7	17	12
28	15	8	6
26	16	11	9
16	14	8	25
25	17	11	12

Draw a scatter diagram to graphically display this information for the northern and southern hemispheres on the same diagram.

29 This bar chart shows the preferred European destination for a summer holiday chosen by a sample of 130 adults who visited a travel agent.

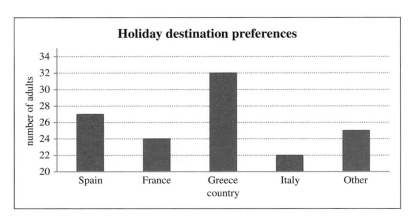

By comparing the height of the bars and the frequency values for two specific countries, explain why the information displayed this diagram could be misinterpreted by the audience.

30 The following table shows the overall length (in centimetres) of 500 caravans advertised at the Caravan and Motorhome Show.

Class	550–600	600–650	650–700	700–750	750–800
Frequency	20	150	71	223	36

Construct a histogram for these data.

31 Decide which statement below applies to the construction of a scatter diagram.
(a) Both variables must be quantitative.
(b) Only one variable must be quantitative.
(c) The data type is not important.

32 The management team of a leading UK-based fashion retailer decided to compare the time spent browsing by customers in two of its city-centre stores. They recorded the time spent in each store (in minutes) by 20 customers who made a purchase on the same Saturday afternoon.

store A

| 67 | 38 | 42 | 51 | 57 | 43 | 41 | 28 | 36 | 68 |
| 41 | 36 | 34 | 29 | 64 | 59 | 52 | 53 | 44 | 41 |

store B

| 12 | 31 | 26 | 19 | 22 | 30 | 23 | 30 | 16 | 23 |
| 27 | 19 | 22 | 30 | 21 | 14 | 47 | 31 | 17 | 25 |

Draw a back-to-back stem and leaf diagram for these data.

33 Explain how a grouped bar chart is drawn differently from a stacked bar chart.

34 In a series of interviews about overseas travel, a random sample of 100 women aged 45–55 were asked how many times they had flown to an overseas destination in the past 5 years. Their responses are given in the table below.

Class	0–5	5–10	10–20
Frequency	63	27	10

Draw a histogram to graphically display the information obtained during the interviews.

35 The pie chart below shows the favourite flavour of ice-cream chosen by 400 tourists who were staying at a luxury villa complex in Spain.

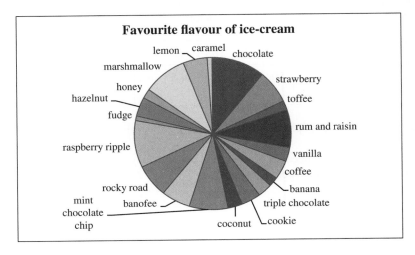

Favourite flavour of ice-cream

Explain why a pie chart is not the most useful diagram for displaying this data set.

36 Customers who purchased a satellite navigation system for their car were given a questionnaire in which they were asked:

Which type of voice do you prefer for spoken navigation instructions?

| male ☐ | female ☐ | no preference ☐ |

Of the 300 respondents, 180 answered 'male', 40 answered 'female' and the remainder did not have a preference.

Construct a bar chart for these data.

37 In a recent series of interviews about financial issues, undergraduate students who work part-time to supplement their income were asked about their job type. The responses are shown below.

bar work	22%
clothing store	34%
supermarket	18%
coffee shop	16%
other	10%

Display these data in an appropriate diagram so that each type of part-time work is represented visually as a proportion of the whole data set.

38 The following table shows the height (in centimetres) and estimated earnings (in millions of pounds (£)) of the ten highest-paid actors in 2012–2013.

Height (cm)	174	185	188	173	196	183	178	170	185	193
Estimated earnings (£ millions)	50	40	36.5	34.5	30	25.8	24.5	23.1	21.8	21.1

Use an appropriate graphical method to display this information.

39 Students at a sixth-form college were asked whether they would vote in a general election if the voting age was lowered to 16.

Comparing the pie chart below with the students' responses given in the table, explain why the information in this diagram might be misleading.

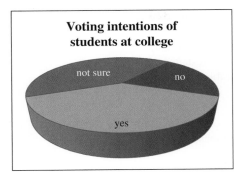

Response	Percentage
no	20
yes	38
not sure	42

40 Decide which statement below applies to the construction of a histogram.
(a) The height of a bar always represents the frequency of the corresponding class.
(b) A histogram can be used to display both quantitative and qualitative data.
(c) The bars in a histogram never have spaces between them.

Solutions to Practice Exercises

1. Graphs and charts can be useful for displaying data and results because they:
   - summarise results in a concise way;
   - highlight important facts and patterns in the data;
   - describe comparisons between different data sets;
   - are easy to understand and memorable.

2. (a) FALSE
   The time series plot shows that there were twice as many female patients compared to male patients on Wednesday.
   (b) FALSE
   From Monday to Saturday, more women used the walk-in health centre compared to men, but on Sunday the majority of the patients were male.
   (c) TRUE
   The graph shows that the number of male patients who visited a doctor on Sunday was more than 30, whereas on every other day there were less than 30 male patients at the health centre.

3. The segment angles would be calculated as follows:

Payment method	Frequency	Relative frequency	Segment angle
debit card	352	$352/640 = 55\%$	$352/640 \times 360 = 198°$
cash	192	$192/640 = 30\%$	$192/640 \times 360 = 108°$
credit card	96	$96/640 = 15\%$	$96/640 \times 360 = 54°$

4. (a) 80–100 rooms is the class that has the lowest frequency.
   (b) 20–40 rooms were occupied on 35 nights during the three months.

5. Using three-dimensional effects in a pie chart or bar chart can make some sections of the chart look bigger than they actually are, in proportion to the other sections, so that comparing relative sizes of bars or pie segments is problematic.

6. The original data set for the highest level recorded (in metres) for 25 rivers in the North of England is as follows:

1.3	1.7	2.0	2.0	2.0
2.2	2.2	2.4	2.4	2.5
2.5	2.6	2.6	2.6	3.1
3.3	3.3	3.5	3.8	3.9
4.0	4.3	4.7	5.0	5.0

7

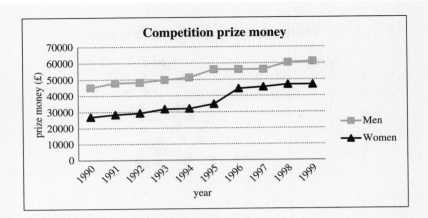

8 (a) A time series plot would be the most suitable graph for presenting UK interest rates recorded each year between 1960 and 1980 because the data are quantitative and it is important to show how the data values change over time.

(b) A bar chart would be the most suitable chart for presenting the number of male and female customers who made purchases at three different stores in a shopping mall. The data are qualitative and it is important to show a comparison of each gender and each store on the same diagram.

(c) A scatter diagram would be the most suitable graph for presenting estimated annual earnings and height of the ten highest-paid actors in 2007 because the data are quantitative and it is important to show any potential relationship between the two variables.

9

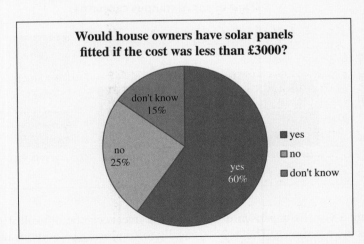

10 This histogram has unequal class sizes and so the frequency of each class will be represented by the *area* of the corresponding bar instead of the height. The width of the last class is twice as large as the width of the other classes, and therefore the height of the corresponding bar in the histogram must be reduced to half of the frequency value.

11

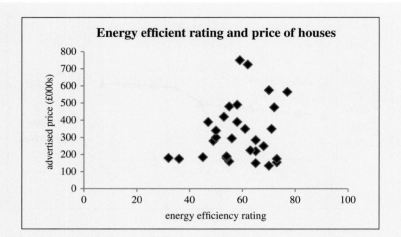

Energy efficient rating and price of houses

12 A time series plot is used to display data collected during a specific time period so that we can show patterns or trends in the data set over time. A marketing company might use a time series plot to present:
- the weekly amount of money spent on advertising by a client;
- the number of times that a television advertisement is shown each month.

13 (a) The youngest nominee was a 9-year-old girl.
(b) There were more male nominees in their fifties than female.

14

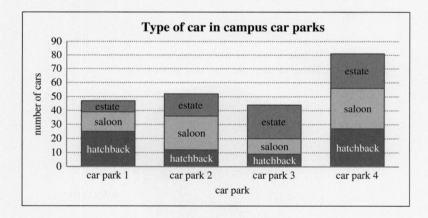

Type of car in campus car parks

15 Making a visual comparison of the size of segments can be difficult if percentage values are not shown. This applies equally to comparing proportions of the same category in different data sets and also to comparing the relative size of segments in the same pie chart. This type of diagram is less useful when a data set includes many different categories because the circle becomes cluttered with too many very small segments.

16 The time series plot uses a y-axis scale from 45,000 to 55,000 and gives the false impression that the number of people visiting the science museum has fallen sharply over the last four weeks in the autumn. If the diagram were to be redrawn, a vertical axis scale that begins at zero should be used to give a more appropriate representation of the data set whilst still showing the decline in visitors to the science museum.

17 A histogram should be used to display the length of telephone calls made by a household during one month.

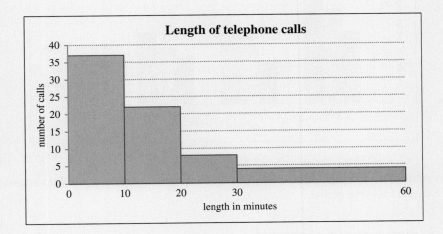

18

Price of men's trainers in £s

1 | 5 = £15

1	4	5	5	5	7	9			
2	0	0	0	0	1	2	2	2	3
2	5	5	5	7	7	7	7	9	
3	0	1	6	6	6	8	8	9	
4	1	2	4	5	7	9	9		
5	0	4	5	5	7	7	9		
6	2	5	5	5	6	8	8		
7	6	6	8						
8	0	0	6	9					
9									
10	2								

19 (a) 15% of the 900 customers = 135 reported that the on-board entertainment was very good.
    (b) 30% of the customers indicated satisfactory and 25% indicated poor, so in total 55% (more than half) said that the entertainment shows were satisfactory or poor.

20   The Olympic medal data should be displayed using a grouped bar chart so that the number of medals can be easily compared.

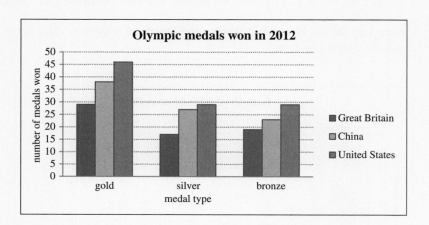

21   A time series plot should be used to display the quarterly electricity bills for a household over a two-year period.

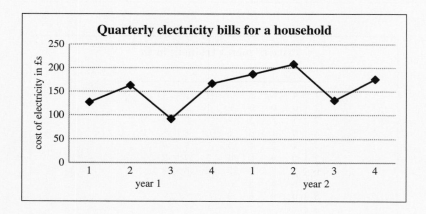

22   (a) uncluttered, effects, images
    (b) axes, units
    (c) short, meaningful

23   Option (c). The scatter diagram shows that there is no obvious relationship between number of years employed and job satisfaction.

24   Advantage – each individual data value is retained when a stem and leaf diagram is used to display data.
    Disadvantage – for large data sets, constructing the diagram can be a time-consuming process.

25

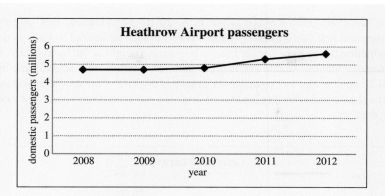

26 a) FALSE

The bar chart shows that 25 boys wanted to be a sportsperson, whereas the corresponding figure for girls was 10.

b) TRUE

The shortest bar for both genders represents being a teacher, so this is the least popular choice.

c) TRUE

The diagram shows that 20 girls wanted to be a pop star and a further 10 girls wanted to be a sportsperson. A total of 60 girls were asked about their future job and so 50% of them wanted to be either a pop star or a sportsperson.

27 A stem and leaf diagram would retain the individual commuting distances for each employee.

Commuting distances of employees

$1 \mid 0 = 10$ miles

1	0	0	1	3	4	4	5	6	7	8	9
2	0	2	3	4	6	6	7	7	9	9	
3	1	7	8								
4	5	8									

28

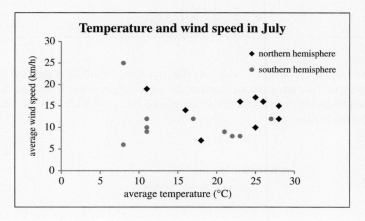

29 The bar chart uses a *y*-axis scale from 20 to 34. Visually, this gives the false impression that twice as many people chose France compared to Italy as a favourite destination because the bar for France is twice the height of the bar for Italy. Using the frequency values, we can see that the number of adults who actually preferred Italy was 22 and the equivalent figure for France is 24. This chart should be redrawn with a vertical axis scale that begins at zero to give a more accurate visual representation of the data set.

30

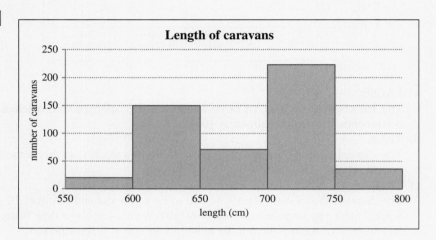

31 Option (a). Both variables must be quantitative for the construction of a scatter diagram.

32

Time spent in store browsing

8 | 2 = 28 minutes   1 | 2 = 12 minutes

						store A		store B						
						1	2	4	6	7	9	9		
				9	8	2	1	2	2	3	3	5	6	7
		8	6	6	4	3	0	0	0	1	1			
4	3	2	1	1	1	4	7							
	9	7	3	2	1	5								
		8	7	4	6									

33 In a grouped bar chart, a separate bar represents each subcategory of data and subcategory bars are grouped together for each category. For a stacked bar chart, the bars representing the subcategories are placed on top of each other to make a single bar for each category.

34

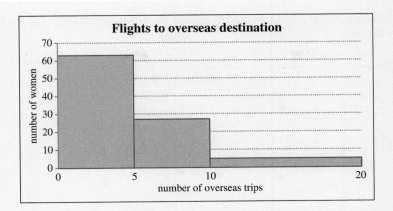

35 A pie chart is less useful when a data set includes many different categories because the circle becomes cluttered with too many very small segments. This pie chart shows 20 flavours of ice-cream, making the relative proportions difficult to interpret.

36

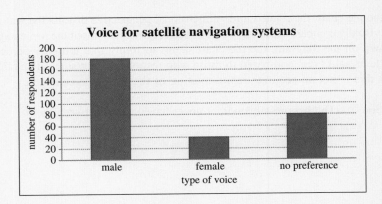

37 The responses from the student interviews should be displayed using a pie chart so that each type of part-time work can be represented visually as a proportion of the whole data set.

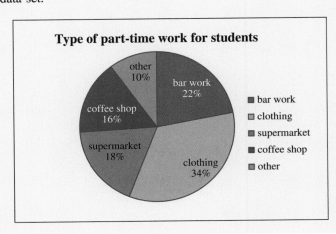

38 A scatter diagram should be used to display the estimated earnings and the height of the actors.

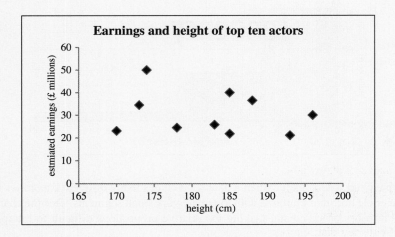

39 In the pie chart, the rotated three-dimensional perspective distorts the way in which we visually compare the relative size of each segment. Without the percentage figures shown on the diagram, the pie chart seems to imply that a higher percentage of students said 'yes' compared to those who responded 'not sure'. The table shows that this is not an accurate representation of the actual percentages.

40 Option (c). The bars in a histogram never have spaces between them.

5 Measures of Central Tendency

Introduction

In Chapter 3, we explored a variety of techniques that allowed us to represent data in a pictorial form. These graphical methods are important for showing structure and presenting data clearly, but it can sometimes be helpful to use a numerical value to summarise a data set.

A **measure of central tendency** describes a set of data by identifying a 'typical value' that is representative of the set. Such a value could be typical because it occurs most frequently in the data set (mode), because it is the average for the data set (mean), or because it is the middle point when the data set is ordered (median). Each measure requires a different type of calculation and has advantages and disadvantages associated with its use.

The Mode

The mode of a set of data is the value which occurs most frequently. If no data value appears more frequently than any other values in the set, then there will be no mode. A data set with two modes is known as **bimodal**, while a data set with more than two modes is described as **multimodal**.

When finding the mode of a set of raw data, it can be useful to put the data in order so that values which are the same will appear together in the list. In a frequency distribution, we look for the data value which has the highest associated frequency. For grouped frequency distributions, we aim to identify the modal *class* rather than a specific value for the mode because the individual data values are not available in this type of distribution. The modal class is the class which has the highest frequency.

The mode is easy to calculate and is usually used as a suitable measure of central tendency when the data are qualitative. It can also be used for quantitative data, but it is not very informative when a data set is multimodal or has no mode at all.

EXAMPLES: MODE

MODE – RAW DATA

The table below shows the average price in pence for a litre of unleaded petrol in the UK in 2010.

| 111.8 | 112.1 | 116.1 | 120.5 | 121.5 | 118.1 | 117.5 | 116.1 | 115.2 | 111.7 | 119.1 | 122.1 |

Putting the data in numerical order, we have:

| 111.7 | 111.8 | 112.1 | 115.2 | 116.1 | 116.1 | 117.5 | 118.1 | 119.1 | 120.5 | 121.5 | 122.1 |

The mode is 116.1, which occurs twice.

MODE – FREQUENCY DISTRIBUTION

The quality control department in a factory records the number of defective items produced by a particular machine each day for two months. The data collected are shown below.

Number of defective items	Frequency (f)
0	5
1	16
2	10
3	10

(Continued)

Number of defective items	Frequency (f)
4	12
5	4
6	4

The mode is 1 because this is the number of defective items that occurs most often; a single defective item occurs on 16 days in the two-month period in which data were collected.

MODE – GROUPED FREQUENCY DISTRIBUTION

The frequency table below shows the time, in minutes, that a sample of users spent browsing a website during a single visit.

Time spent	Frequency (f)
1–15	10
16–30	26
31–45	42
46–60	36
61–75	15
76–90	9

The modal class is 31–45 because it is the class with the highest frequency.

The Mean

The **mean** is more precisely known as the **arithmetic mean**, but also commonly referred to as the **average**. It is calculated as the sum of the data values divided by the number of values in the set. To simplify the way in which the formula is written down, we use:

- $\bar{x}$ as the symbol for the mean of a sample;
- $\sum$ (the Greek letter sigma) instead of 'the sum of';
- n to represent 'the number of values in the set';
- f to denote the frequency with which a data value occurs.

For a raw data set, the formula then becomes

$$\bar{x} = \frac{\sum x}{n}$$

If our data are summarised in a frequency distribution, the mean of a sample is calculated using

$$\bar{x} = \frac{\sum fx}{\sum f}$$

where $\sum fx$ means that we multiply each value of x by its corresponding f and find the sum. The same formula can be applied to a grouped frequency distribution but in this case, each class mid-point must be used to represent the value of x because the individual data values are not available to us.

The Greek symbol μ (pronounced 'mu') is used to represent the mean of a population; however, we use the same formulae as above to calculate its value.

The mean is suitable for discrete or continuous quantitative data; it is not suitable for a qualitative data set which does not contain numerical values. It is the most popular measure of central tendency because the calculation uses all of the data values and therefore it is truly representative of the whole set. Unfortunately, the mean can be highly influenced by extreme values which, if excluded from the calculations, would have a noticeable effect on the result.

COMBINED MEAN

If we know the number of data values and the mean for each of two sets of data, the formula below can be used to calculate the **combined mean** of the two data sets:

$$\bar{x} = \frac{n_1 \bar{x}_1 + n_2 \bar{x}_2}{n_1 + n_2}$$

where:

- $\bar{x}_1$ is the mean of the first data set and $\bar{x}_2$ is the mean of the second data set;
- n_1 and n_2 represent the number of data values in sets 1 and 2 respectively.

This formula can be extended for use with more than two data sets.

WEIGHTED MEAN

In calculating the arithmetic mean, each data value in the set contributes equally to the final result. However, we can have a situation where some data values in the set have a higher importance, or weighting, than others. In this case, it is useful to calculate the **weighted mean** for the data set, using

$$\bar{x} = \frac{w_1 x_1 + w_2 x_2 + \ldots + w_n x_n}{w_1 + w_2 + \ldots + w_n}$$

where:

- $w_1, w_2, \ldots, w_n$ represents the level of importance, or weighting, placed on an individual data value;
- $x_1, x_2, \ldots x_n$ represents each individual data value in the set.

EXAMPLES: MEAN

MEAN – RAW DATA

The table below shows the average price in pence for a litre of unleaded petrol in the UK in 2010.

| 111.8 | 112.1 | 116.1 | 120.5 | 121.5 | 118.1 | 117.5 | 116.1 | 115.2 | 111.7 | 119.1 | 122.1 |

The mean is

$$\bar{x} = \frac{\sum x}{n} = \frac{111.8 + 112.1 + \ldots + 119.1 + 122.1}{12} = \frac{1401.8}{12} = 116.817$$

MEAN – FREQUENCY DISTRIBUTION

The quality control department in a factory records the number of defective items produced by a particular machine each day for two months. The data collected are shown below:

Number of defective items (x)	Frequency (f)	fx
0	5	0
1	16	16
2	10	20
3	10	30
4	12	48
5	4	20
6	4	24
	$\sum f = 61$	$\sum fx = 158$

The mean is

$$\bar{x} = \frac{\sum fx}{\sum f} = \frac{158}{61} = 2.590$$

MEAN – GROUPED FREQUENCY DISTRIBUTION

The frequency table shows the time, in minutes, that a sample of users spent browsing a website during a single visit.

Time spent	Mid-point (x)	Frequency (f)	fx
1–15	8	10	80
16–30	23	26	598
31–45	38	42	1596

(*Continued*)

Time spent	Mid-point (x)	Frequency (f)	fx
46–60	53	36	1908
61–75	68	15	1020
76–90	83	9	747
		$\sum f = 138$	$\sum fx = 5949$

The mean is

$$\bar{x} = \frac{\sum fx}{\sum f} = \frac{5949}{138} = 43.109$$

MEAN – COMBINED

A broadband provider has three UK-based call centres for dealing with customer enquiries and complaints. The number of employees at each call centre and their mean age is shown in the table below.

	Manchester	Glasgow	Cardiff
Number of employees	1560	1240	985
Mean employee age	32	28	25

The combined mean age for all call centres is

$$\bar{x} = \frac{n_1\bar{x}_1 + n_2\bar{x}_2 + n_3\bar{x}_3}{n_1 + n_2 + n_3} = \frac{(1560 \times 32) + (1240 \times 28) + (985 \times 25)}{1560 + 1240 + 985} = \frac{109265}{3785} = 28.868$$

MEAN – WEIGHTED

The business school at a university in Yorkshire teaches a compulsory undergraduate first-year module in business statistics. The following table gives details of the module assessment.

Component	Weighting
Weekly homework	20%
Term test	30%
Project report	50%

If an individual student scores 74% in the weekly homework, 88% in the term test and 52% in the project report, their weighted average for the module is

$$\bar{x} = \frac{w_1 x_1 + w_2 x_2 + w_3 x_3}{w_1 + w_2 + w_3} = \frac{(0.2 \times 0.74) + (0.3 \times 0.88) + (0.5 \times 0.52)}{0.2 + 0.3 + 0.5} = 67.2\%$$

The Median

The **median** for a set of ordered data is the middle value which divides the set into two halves; one half contains all of the data that are less than the median, and the other half includes all values greater than the median.

For an odd number of data values, the median is actually one of the values in the set: the middle one. However, when there is an even number of values in a set, there is no actual middle value and therefore the median is calculated as the average of the two values closest to the middle.

Consider the following sets of data, which represent the amount of money spent by the customers queuing at till 10 and till 14 in a supermarket.

	Customer 1	Customer 2	Customer 3	Customer 4	Customer 5
Till 10	£6.04	£12.99	£30.22	£56.70	£58.94

In the queue at till 10, there are an odd number of customers, and so you can clearly identify the amount of money that is in the middle position – it is an actual value in the data set, £30.22 spent by customer 3.

	Customer 1	Customer 2	Customer 3	Customer 4	Customer 5	Customer 6
Till 14	£4.68	£19.01	£45.66	£47.12	£61.25	£61.27

However, in the data set for till 14 there is an even number of customers, so there is no middle position. In this case, we should identify the two values closest to the middle and then find the average of these amounts; these two values would be £45.66 and £47.12 for customers 3 and 4 queuing at till 14.

If we have a small set of raw data, it is easy to identify the middle value (or the two values closest to the middle) by simply writing down an ordered list and choosing the appropriate data value. However, when there are many data values or the data are described by a frequency distribution we need a more generalised way of finding the position of the middle data value(s). Representing 'the number of values in the set' as n, we can proceed as follows.

- When n is an odd number, and a single middle value exists, the **position** of the median in the ordered set of data is found using

$$\tfrac{1}{2}(n+1)$$

Using the same example of money spent at a supermarket, there are 5 customers queuing at till 10, so the position of the median is found using $\tfrac{1}{2}(5+1)$ which identifies the 3rd customer's expenditure.

- When n is an even number, we need to identify the two values closest to the middle. Their **positions** in an ordered set of data are found using

$$\tfrac{1}{2}n \quad \text{and} \quad \tfrac{1}{2}n+1$$

For example, there are 6 customers in the queue for till 14, so the position of the two values closest to the middle are found using $\tfrac{1}{2}(6)$ and $\tfrac{1}{2}(6)+1$, which identifies the amount of money spent by the 3rd and 4th customers.

For a frequency distribution, it is helpful to use the cumulative frequency to identify the middle values in the data set. Use these four steps to find the median:

1. Work out whether the distribution contains an odd or an even number of data values by looking at the total of the frequencies.
2. Establish the *position* of the middle data value(s) using either $\frac{1}{2}(n+1)$ or $\frac{1}{2}n$ and $\frac{1}{2}n+1$.
3. Use cumulative frequencies to identify the actual middle data value(s).
4. If you are working with an odd number of data values, you have now found the median. For a data set that contains an even number of values, the median is equal to the average of the two values closest to the middle.

Finding the median for a grouped frequency distribution requires a more complex method because we are not able to determine the individual data values from the distribution. In this case, we work out an estimate for the median by applying the formula given below to the class which contains the middle value(s) of the data set:

$$b + \left(\frac{\frac{1}{2}n - f}{f_m} \right) w$$

where:

- b represents the lower class boundary for the median class;
- f is the sum of all the frequencies that occur before the median class;
- f_m represents the frequency of the median class;
- w is the class width for the median class.

So, for a grouped frequency distribution, the four steps to find the median are as follows:

1. Work out whether the distribution contains an odd or an even number of data values by looking at the total of the frequencies.
2. Establish the *position* of the middle data value(s) using either $\frac{1}{2}(n+1)$ or $\frac{1}{2}n$ and $\frac{1}{2}n+1$.
3. Use cumulative frequencies to identify the class which contains the middle value(s) – this is called the 'median class'.
4. Apply the formula to the median class.

The median is suitable for discrete or continuous quantitative data; it is not suitable for a qualitative data set which does not contain numerical values. It can be described as a **resistant** measure because it is not particularly influenced by extreme data values that are unusual in numerical size compared to the rest of the data set.

EXAMPLES: MEDIAN

MEDIAN – RAW DATA

The table below shows the average price in pence for a litre of unleaded petrol in the UK in 2010.

| 111.8 | 112.1 | 116.1 | 120.5 | 121.5 | 118.1 | 117.5 | 116.1 | 115.2 | 111.7 | 119.1 | 122.1 |

Putting the data in numerical order, we have:

111.7	111.8	112.1	115.2	116.1	116.1	117.5	118.1	119.1	120.5	121.5	122.1

There is an even number of values in the data set, 12, so the median is calculated as the average of the two values closest to the middle. Using $\frac{1}{2}(12)$ and $\frac{1}{2}(12) + 1$ identifies the 6th and 7th data values; the 6th value is 116.1 and the 7th value is 117.5, so the median is calculated as

$$\frac{116.1 + 117.5}{2} = 116.8$$

MEDIAN – FREQUENCY DISTRIBUTION

The quality control department in a factory records the number of defective items produced by a particular machine each day for two months. The data collected are shown below:

Number of defective items (x)	Frequency (f)	Cumulative frequency
0	5	5
1	16	21
2	10	31
3	10	41
4	12	53
5	4	57
6	4	61
	$\sum f = 61$	

There is an odd number of values in the data set, 61, so the median is the middle data value. Using $\frac{1}{2}(61 + 1)$ identifies the 31st data value as the middle one. The cumulative frequency column shows that the first five data values are 0, the 6th to 21st data values are 1, and the 22nd to 31st data values are 2. The 31st value, and hence the median, is 2 for this distribution.

MEDIAN – GROUPED FREQUENCY DISTRIBUTION

The frequency table shows the time, in minutes, that a sample of users spent browsing a website during a single visit.

Time spent	Frequency (f)	Cumulative frequency
1−15	10	10
16−30	26	36
31−45	42	78

(Continued)

Time spent	Frequency (f)	Cumulative frequency
46–60	36	114
61–75	15	129
76–90	9	138
	$\sum f = 138$	

There is an even number of values in the data set, 138, so the median is calculated as the average of the two values closest to the middle. Using $\frac{1}{2}(138)$ and $\frac{1}{2}(138) + 1$ identifies the 69th and 70th values.

The cumulative frequency column shows that the first 10 data values are in class 1–15, the 11th to 36th data values are in class 16–30, and class 31–45 contains the 37th to 78th data values (including the 69th and 70th). Therefore, the median class is 31–45, to which we apply the formula to calculate an estimate of the median:

$$b + \left(\frac{\frac{1}{2}n - f}{f_m}\right)w = 30.5 + \left(\frac{\frac{1}{2} \times 138 - 36}{42}\right) \times 15 = 42.286$$

where:

- b represents the lower class boundary for the median class = 30.5;
- f is the sum of all the frequencies that occur before the median class = $10 + 26 = 36$;
- f_m represents the frequency of the median class = 42;
- w is the class width for the median class = $45.5 - 30.5 = 15$.

Advantages and Disadvantages

We can summarise the advantages and disadvantages of the three measuers of central tendency as follows.

	Mean	Mode	Median
Easy to understand and calculate	mostly	always	sometimes
Uses all of the data values in the set	yes	no	no
Can be used for qualitative data	no	yes	no
Can be used for quantitative data	yes	yes	yes
Is influenced by extreme values	affected	unaffected	mostly unaffected
Is one of the data values in the set	rarely	always	sometimes
Provides only a single result	yes	sometimes	yes

Which Measure?

Choosing whether to use the mode, mean or median as a measure of central tendency will often depend on the type of values included in your data set.

When the data values in the set are qualitative, then the mode should be used because there are no numerical values available on which to calculate the mean or the median. The mode can be used for quantitative data, but it is less useful when the data are multimodal or have no mode. The mean and the median are generally the preferred measures when the data set contains numerical values.

If your data set contains extreme values which are unlike the rest of the data, it is important to consider using the median rather than the mean which can be influenced by such values. The mean is usually the preferred measure when you have a set of numerical data which does not contain any extreme values, because the calculation makes use of all of the data values in the set and therefore it is a truly representative measure.

Consider this set of data which represents the annual salary paid to workers at a factory:

| £16,000 | £14,000 | £18,000 | £65,000 | £16,000 | £60,000 | £17,000 | £15,000 |

Calculating the mean annual salary for these workers gives us a result of £27,625, which is clearly not representative of the whole data set because six out of eight of the workers are paid a salary that is £9000 or more below this amount. For this data set, the value of the mean is highly influenced by the two large salaries and so it may not be the most useful measure of central tendency in this situation.

If we now put our annual salaries into numerical order, the data set becomes:

| £14,000 | £15,000 | £16,000 | £16,000 | £17,000 | £18,000 | £60,000 | £65,000 |

The median value would be £16,500, which is much more representative of the majority of values in the data set and therefore the most appropriate measure to use. In this case, the median has not been affected by the two large salaries.

Sometimes, it is equally appropriate to calculate the mode, mean and median to find a single value that is representative of a data set. In this case, we may decide to report only one result, choosing the measure of central tendency which best supports what we are trying to achieve.

Consider the example used earlier in this chapter describing a frequency distribution for the number of defective items produced by a particular machine each day in a factory. The following results were calculated:

Mode	Mean	Median
1	2.590	2

If a sales manager from the factory wished to highlight a measure of central tendency during a sales pitch to a potential customer, he would be likely to choose the mode because this shows the lowest average defective items per day. However, if the supervisor at the factory wished to persuade the management that they should purchase a new machine, then the mean would show the machine in the least positive way and therefore would probably be quoted in a report about the machine's performance.

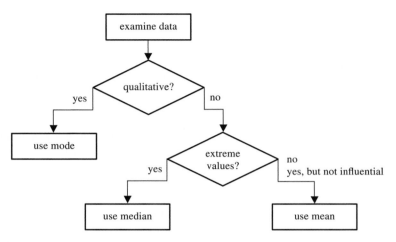

FIGURE 5.1   Flowchart for deciding when to use the mean, median or mode

Figure 5.1 shows a flowchart summarising when it is appropriate to use each measure, assuming that the decision is based only on the type of values in the data set. It is important to choose the most appropriate measure, firstly based on the type of values in your data set, and secondly taking into consideration what you are trying to show with your statistics in a particular situation.

HINTS AND TIPS

MODE – FREQUENCY DISTRIBUTION

When trying to find the mode for a frequency distribution, ensure that you write down the actual data value rather than quoting the associated frequency. In the following distribution, the mode is 4, not 47.

x	Frequency (f)
1	5
2	14
3	36
4	47
5	22

MEAN – FREQUENCY DISTRIBUTION

For a frequency distribution, remember that the denominator of the mean formula is the sum of the frequencies, not the number of rows in your distribution.

In the table below, the denominator for the mean calculation is 79, not 6.

x	Frequency (f)	fx
52	8	416
53	10	530
54	16	864
55	17	935
56	16	896
57	12	684
	$\Sigma f = 79$	$\Sigma fx = 4325$

6 rows

MEDIAN – RAW DATA

Make sure that you put raw data in ascending numerical order before identifying the median value.

For the data set

42	37	96	12	71	43	22

the median is 42, not 12, as you can see by putting the data in numerical order:

12	22	37	42	43	71	96

MEDIAN – GROUPED FREQUENCY DISTRIBUTION

For a grouped frequency distribution, it is essential that individual components are calculated in the appropriate order to gain a correct result when you are using the median formula.

1. Find $\frac{1}{2}n$.
2. Subtract f from the result.
3. Divide the result by f_m.
4. Multiply the result by w.
5. Add b to the result.

Practise using the correct order with this example:

$$b + \left(\frac{\frac{1}{2}n - f}{f_m}\right) w = 24.5 + \left(\frac{\frac{1}{2} \times 42 - 12}{17}\right) \times 10 = 29.794$$

Using Excel

It is possible to use the statistical built-in functions in Excel for calculating the mode, mean and median for a set of raw data. Enter each data value into a cell, using a single row or column and then use the **Formulas** tab on the ribbon to select the appropriate function.

The following screen shots demonstrate the procedure for each measure of central tendency using the raw data from an earlier example in this chapter which represented the average price in pence for a litre of unleaded petrol in the UK in 2010.

| 111.8 | 112.1 | 116.1 | 120.5 | 121.5 | 118.1 | 117.5 | 116.1 | 115.2 | 111.7 | 119.1 | 122.1 |

MODE

Function	Description	Syntax
MODE.SNGL	displays the most frequently occurring value in a set of data	MODE.SNGL(number1, number2, . . .)

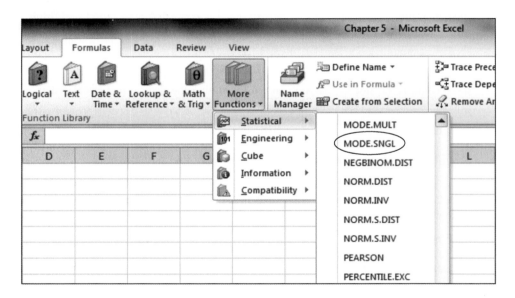

In terms of functionality, the **MODE.SNGL** function will return a 'value not available' error if the data set does not have a value that occurs more frequently than any other value; in this case an error **#N/A** will be returned in the cell. If the data set has more than one mode, then the function will return the mode with the smallest numerical value.

MEAN

Function	Description	Syntax
AVERAGE	calculates the mean of a set of data	AVERAGE(number1, number2, . . .)

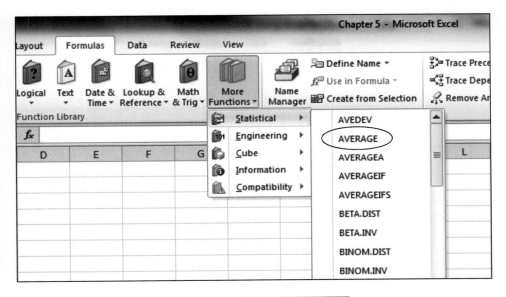

	A	B	C	D	E	F	G	H	I	J	K	L	M	N
1														
2		111.8	112.1	116.1	120.5	121.5	118.1	117.5	116.1	115.2	111.7	119.1	122.1	
3														
4		mean:	116.817											
5														

C4   =AVERAGE(B2:M2)

MEDIAN

Function	Description	Syntax
MEDIAN	displays the median of a set of data	MEDIAN(number1, number2, . . .)

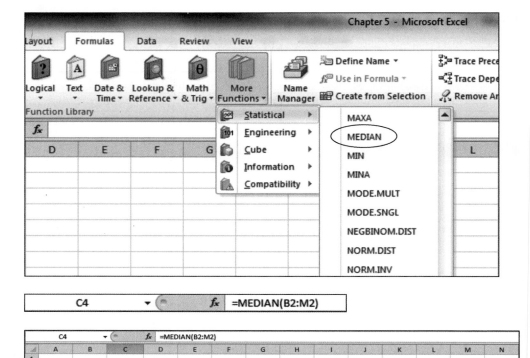

FREQUENCY AND GROUPED FREQUENCY DISTRIBUTIONS

If your data set is represented by a frequency distribution or a grouped frequency distribution, it is necessary to use a combination of formulae and built-in functions to find the mode, mean and median using Excel.

The built-in function **SUMPRODUCT** is particularly useful in these situations.

Function	Description	Syntax
SUMPRODUCT	multiplies corresponding components in the given sets of data (also known as arrays) and calculates the sum of those products	SUMPRODUCT(array1, array2, . . .)

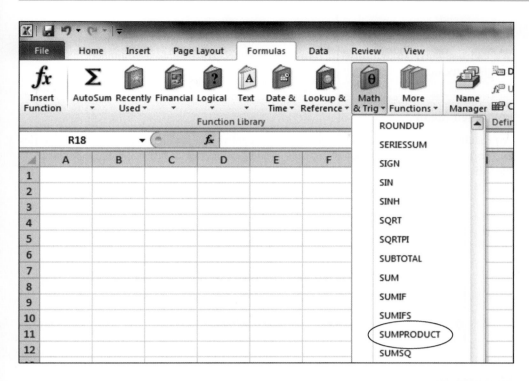

Returning to our example where the quality control department in a factory records the number of defective items produced by a particular machine each day for two months, we can use Excel to calculate the mean of this frequency distribution as follows:

C12		f_x =SUMPRODUCT(B4:B10,C4:C10)/SUM(C4:C10)

	A	B	C	D
1				
2		number of defective items	frequency	
3		x	f	
4		0	5	
5		1	16	
6		2	10	
7		3	10	
8		4	12	
9		5	4	
10		6	4	
11				
12		mean:	2.590	
13				

COMBINED AND WEIGHTED MEANS

We can use fairly straightforward formulae in Excel to calculate a combined mean and a weighted mean.

Combined Mean

A broadband provider has three UK-based call centres for dealing with customer enquiries and complaints. The number of employees at each call centre and their mean age is shown in the table.

C6	▼	f_x	=((C3*C4)+(D3*D4)+(E3*E4))/(C3+D3+E3)

	A	B	C	D	E	F
1						
2			Manchester	Glasgow	Cardiff	
3		number of employees	1560	1240	985	
4		mean employee age	32	28	25	
5						
6		combined mean:	28.868			
7						

Weighted Mean

The business school at a university in Yorkshire teaches a compulsory undergraduate first-year module in business statistics. The table below gives details of the module assessment. If an individual student scores 74% in the weekly homework, 88% in the term test and 52% in the project report, their weighted average for the module is calculated as shown below.

C7	▼	f_x	=((C3*0.74)+(C4*0.88)+(C5*0.52))/(C3+C4+C5)

	A	B	C	D
1				
2		component	weighting	
3		weekly homework	20%	
4		term test	30%	
5		project report	50%	
6				
7		weighted mean:	67.2%	
8				

Practice Exercises

1 The pre-tax profits of a leading supermarket were recorded for the past six years; the figures are shown below in billions of pounds (£):

| 48.35 | 40.28 | 39.11 | 44.76 | 42.87 | 38.65 |

(a) Find the median for these data.
(b) Calculate the mean for these data.
(c) The supermarket wishes to give a press release to the media, announcing its average profit over this time period. Should the supermarket use the mean or median value in its press release? Give a reason for your answer.

2 A group of undergraduate students who work as Saturday sales assistants in high-street stores were asked to state their hourly rate of pay. The male students claimed that the female students are paid a higher hourly rate, but the female students disagreed. The frequency table for their rates of pay is shown below.

Hourly rate (to the nearest 50p)	Frequency for males	Frequency for females
£5.25	5	6
£5.75	8	3
£6.25	8	3
£6.75	3	15
£7.25	6	3

(a) Calculate the mean hourly rate for males and for females.
(b) Decide which students receive the higher rate of pay.

3 The number of students who enrolled on a teacher training course for secondary school level mathematics was recorded for the past five years. The mean number of enrolled students was calculated to be 981. As a result of a televised recruitment campaign, 1002 students have enrolled in the current year.
(a) State the effect this will have on the mean number of students enrolled.
(b) Calculate the mean value for the data collected over the six-year period.

4 The frequency table shows the number of rooms occupied each night at a city-centre hotel over a period of 12 weeks.

Number of rooms occupied	Frequency (f)
50–59	6
60–69	17

(Continued)

Number of rooms occupied	Frequency (f)
70–79	32
80–89	21
90–99	5
100–109	3

(a) Write down the modal class.

(b) Calculate an estimate of the mean and median number of rooms occupied.

(c) The hotel manager knows that a profit will be made if at least 70 rooms are occupied per night. Using your answers from (b), write down whether or not you think that the hotel manager should be worried about profitability. Give an explanation for your judgement.

5   A population survey counted the number of people in each household in a street. The data collected are shown below.

5	2	2	1	3	4	2	5	6	3
2	4	4	4	1	3	1	3	5	4
6	2	3	3	1	2	5	4	5	4
2	1	2	4	3	5	3	4	4	6

(a) Construct a frequency distribution for these data.

(b) Calculate the mean number of people per household.

(c) Write down the number of households that have more occupants than the mean number of people.

(d) Is the mean for these data greater than the modal number of people?

(e) Work out the median for these data.

6   Which measures of central tendency are largely unaffected by extreme data values?

(a) median and mode

(b) mean and mode

(c) median and mean

7   A water company decides to record and compare the daily water usage of the households in two neighbouring streets. A frequency table was produced for the collected data as follows:

Daily water usage, in litres	Street A frequency	Street B frequency
135–139	6	4
140–144	14	12
145–149	16	11
150–154	24	28
155–159	27	26

(Continued)

Daily water usage, in litres	Street A frequency	Street B frequency
160–164	15	18
165–169	15	14

(a) What is the modal class for each street?

(b) By comparing the estimated means for each street, state which street has the highest average daily usage.

8 The total annual salary for a team of eight business analysts working for a multinational organisation is £639,480. What is the mean annual salary for a business analyst employed by this organisation?

9 An accountancy firm has many international customers. The firm decides to analyse the cost of telephone calls, per minute, to the destinations in which its clients live, and the data set collected is shown in the table.

Pence per minute	Number of destinations
5–14	10
15–24	7
25–34	3
35–44	18
45–54	4
55–64	1

(a) Calculate an estimated mean cost per minute of an international telephone call.

(b) Write down the modal class for this frequency distribution.

(c) Work out an estimate of the median for these data.

10 The table below shows the results of a survey where shoppers in a busy newsagent store were asked how many lottery tickets they had purchased.

Number of tickets	0	1	2	3	4	5	6	7	8	9	10
Frequency (f)	15	8	12	26	24	32	9	8	8	2	1

(a) How many shoppers gave information about the number of lottery tickets that they had purchased?

(b) Write down the modal number of tickets purchased.

(c) Calculate the mean and the median values for these data.

(d) If you asked one more shopper in the same store, how many tickets would you expect them to have bought?

11 A leading estate agent has 11 branches throughout the South East of England. During last year, the average number of days' sickness taken by each member of staff at each branch office was as follows:

Branch office	A	B	C	D	E	F	G	H	I	J	K
Average number of sickness days	4.3	6.1	3.2	55.9	8.2	3.9	2.6	1.7	3.7	6.4	1.6

(a) Calculate the mean and median of these data.
(b) Explain why the mean is not good measure of the average number of days of sickness taken for this data set.

The Human Resources Department realises that the figure 55.9 has been recorded incorrectly and that the staff working at branch office D actually took 5.9 sickness days during last year.
(c) Recalculate the mean and median using the correct value for branch office D.
(d) What effect does this correction have on the median and mean?

12 For any set of data, which measures of central tendency can only have one value?
(a) median and mode
(b) mean and mode
(c) median and mean

13 A company decides to launch a free mobile application for sports enthusiasts and one for music enthusiasts, for a three-month period, and compare the number of daily downloads (to the nearest thousand) for each application. The data were recorded as follows:

Number of daily downloads (000s)	Science application	Music application
1–5	2	78
6–10	10	6
11–15	28	3
16–20	45	2
21–25	6	2
26–30	1	1

(a) What is the modal class for each application?
(b) By comparing the estimated means for each application, state which one has the highest average daily download rate.

14 The table below shows the monthly sales of new cars for a leading car manufacturer, in thousands.

92	137	84	70	95	102	110	146	84	68	97	86

(a) Write down the mode.
(b) Work out the median for these data.
(c) Calculate the mean monthly sales.

15 The table below shows the frequency distribution for the price charged for each different type of 800 g loaf of bread available at a large supermarket.

Price (to nearest 10p)	Frequency (f)	Cumulative frequency
90	4	4
100	8	12
110	11	23
120	23	46
130	19	65
140	5	70

(a) How many types of 800 g loaf are available at the supermarket?
(b) Write down the modal price.
(c) Calculate the median for these data.
(d) Work out the mean price for a loaf of bread.

16 Over an eight-year period, the punctuality of charter flights at the UK airports was analysed by recording the average flight delay in minutes.

22.9	19.6	23.4	27.7	26.9	26.8	30.5	19.1

(a) Find the mean for these data.
(b) Calculate the median for these data.

In the following year, the average flight delay was 28.5 minutes.
(c) Write down the effect this will have on the mean and the median.

17 The length of telephone calls, to the nearest minute, made between two sisters during a two-month period was recorded as follows:

126	90	83	68	85	114	88	80	103	90	93	92	72	79	117

(a) Write down the mode.
(b) Calculate the mean call length.
(c) Calculate the median call length.

18 A class of 90 undergraduate students achieved the following grades in the summer examination for their module on advanced macroeconomics.

B	D	D	C	C	A	D	C	F	C	C	D	B	D	C	B	C	A	B	B
E	D	A	E	A	C	A	A	E	C	E	D	E	A	D	B	F	C	C	C
C	D	B	A	D	A	D	C	C	C	B	E	E	D	B	D	A	D	C	C
A	C	C	C	B	B	F	E	E	B	B	B	B	F	C	D	C	C	C	C
A	C	C	E	B	D	D	C	B	D										

(a) Construct a frequency distribution table.

(b) Identify the mode for these data.

19 The table below shows the scores achieved by job applicants in a multiple-choice psychometric test focused on numeric ability.

Score out of 10	Frequency (f)
0	2
1	3
2	0
3	2
4	12
5	26
6	23
7	19
8	16
9	8
10	5

(a) Write down the number of applicants who scored 7 or more in the test.

(b) Calculate the median and mean values for these data.

(c) What is the modal test score?

20 700 lawyers working in the City of London were asked for their annual salary, in thousands of pounds (£). The data collected are shown below.

Salary	Frequency (f)
20–39	16
40–59	53
60–79	85
80–99	104
100–119	214
120–139	162
140–159	36
160–179	21
180–250	9

(a) Write down the modal class.
(b) Calculate an estimate of the mean and median annual salary.
(c) As part of a recruitment campaign, a law firm decides to quote the average annual salary for lawyers working in London. Write down, with reasons, whether the mean value or the median value should be used in the campaign.

21 The bar chart below shows the classification of employment type for males and females who live in a large city.

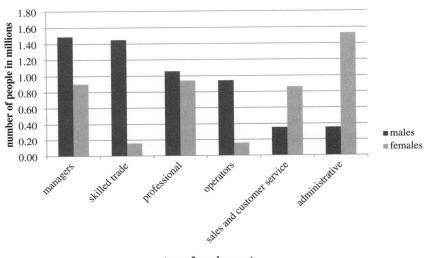

type of employment

(a) What is the modal type of employment for males?
(b) What is the modal type of employment for females?

22 The table shows the frequency distribution for the number of hours spent in a high-street car park by shoppers on the Saturday before Christmas.

Number of hours	Frequency (f)	Cumulative frequency
1	32	32
2	44	76
3	83	159
4	30	189
5	24	213

(a) How many shoppers used the high-street car park on that day?
(b) Write down the modal number of hours spent in the car park.
(c) Calculate the median for these data.
(d) Work out the mean number of hours spent in the car park by the shoppers.

23 The number of text messages sent by 90 teenagers in a single day is shown in the table.

Number of text messages	Frequency (f)
20–39	5
40–69	14
70–99	20
100–129	35
130–159	12
160–200	4

For these data:
(a) Write down the modal class.
(b) Work out an estimate of the mean.
(c) Estimate the median.

24 The table below shows the prices, in pounds (£) per person, of a one-week self-catering holiday at a popular continental resort during July and August.

July				August			
Week 1	Week 2	Week 3	Week 4	Week 1	Week 2	Week 3	Week 4
505	545	575	575	355	585	560	565

(a) Find the mean for these data.
(b) Calculate the median for these data.
(c) What is the modal price per person?

The travel company realises that the figure £355 has been incorrectly printed in the holiday brochure and that the price per person for the first week in August is actually £555.
(d) What effect does this correction have on the mean, the median and the mode?

25 Three IT companies based in the South East have recruited new graduates to work in their offices in a variety of roles. The number of graduates recruited and their mean starting salary are shown in the following table.

	Company 1	Company 2	Company 3
Number of graduates recruited	5	16	2
Mean starting salary	£21,712	£23,160	£18,933

Calculate the mean salary for the new graduates employed by all three companies.

26   The following table shows the number of employees in companies with offices located in two business parks.

Number of employees	1–10	11–50	51–150	151–250
Number of companies	4	17	21	18

(a) What percentage of companies employ more than 150 people?
(b) Write down the modal class.
(c) Calculate the difference between the estimated mean and the estimated median for these data.

27   The following table shows the monthly rent (in pounds (£)) for two-bedroom apartments in a town-centre location.

2000	1750	1500	1250	1750	2000	1500
2250	2250	1250	2500	2000	1750	1500
1750	2000	1250	1250	1250	2250	1250
1750	2500	2500	1750	1500	2500	1250

(a) Construct a frequency distribution for these data.
(b) Calculate the mean monthly rental amount.
(c) Write down the number of apartments that have a higher monthly rental than the mean amount.
(d) Is the mean for these data greater than the modal rent?
(e) Work out the median for these data.

28   A broadband provider has three UK-based call centres for dealing with customer enquiries and complaints. The number of employees at each call centre and their mean age is shown in the table.

	Manchester	Glasgow	Cardiff
Number of employees	1560	1240	985
Mean employee age	32	28	25

Calculate the mean age for all of the call centre employees.

29   An insurance company with offices in many different countries around the world wishes to conduct a survey to find out the nationality of its employees. Which measure of central tendency would provide the best way of summarising the data collected?
(a) mode
(b) median
(c) mean

30   The number of tourists that visit a popular town museum is 20.7 million over a five-year period. Calculate the mean number of visitors per year.

31 A car rental company in Edinburgh decides to record the age for a random sample of its customers. The data collected are shown in the table.

Age (in years)	Number of customers
20–29	15
30–39	22
40–49	57
50–59	33
60–69	21

(a) Calculate the estimated mean age of a customer.
(b) Write down the modal class for this frequency distribution.
(c) Work out an estimate of the median for these data.

32 The manager of a manufacturing company is interested in how many times his employees are late for work in a week. In particular, he would like to know if the male workers are better at arriving at work on time than the female workers. Taking a random sample of 55 male and 55 female workers, the results were recorded as follows:

Number of late arrivals in a week	Frequency for males	Frequency for females
0	9	23
1	10	14
2	8	9
3	12	6
4	9	2
5	7	1

Calculate the mean value for male workers and the mean value for female workers and decide which employees have the lower number of average late arrivals in a week.

33 The amount of gas and electricity units used over the winter months by a household was measured. The data are shown in the table below.

Month	September	October	November	December	January	February
Gas	39	47	49	56	64	66
Electricity	430	418	436	439	441	425

(a) Calculate the mean units of gas used per month.
(b) Calculate the mean electricity usage per month.
(c) Work out the median for each set of data.
(d) The owners decide that they would like to sell their house and need to provide prospective buyers with the average monthly gas and electricity usage for the property. Write down, with reasons, whether they should quote the mean or median value for each utility to prospective buyers.

34 The property prices for sale in a South Eastern town are shown in the table below.

Advertised sale price (£000s)	Number of properties
101–200	87
201–300	161
301–400	115
401–500	60
501–600	33
601–700	14
701–800	9
801–900	9

For these data:
(a) Write down the modal class.
(b) Work out an estimate of the mean.
(c) Estimate the median.

35 If there is an even number of observations, the median is:
(a) The average value of the two middle items of the data set.
(b) Impossible to calculate.
(c) The average value of the two middle items when the data are arranged in ascending numerical order.

36 A traffic monitoring system recorded the speed of vehicles travelling along a town-centre street with a 30 mph speed limit.

Speed in mph	28	29	30	31	32	33	34	35	36	37	38
Number of cars	2	5	12	20	26	23	19	16	9	4	1

(a) Write down the modal speed.
(b) Calculate the mean and the median values for these data.
(c) Based on the answers to parts (a) and (b), at what speed would you expect a car to be travelling along this street?

37 A well-known car insurance company decides to launch an expensive television advertising campaign to attract new customers. The manager of the company selects a random sample of 20 online quotation rates, to the nearest pound (£), as shown below:

371	256	239	472	412	365	227	416	509	367
262	198	343	375	299	659	701	325	361	218

(a) Find the median for these data.
(b) Calculate the mean for these data.
(c) Which measure of central tendency should the insurance company use in its advertising campaign? Give a reason for your answer.

38 A store specialising in cameras and video equipment wanted to know how much time its customers were spending with an experienced sales assistant before deciding to make a purchase. The following data were recorded:

Time spent with a sales assistant (in minutes)	Number of customers
0–4	11
5–9	16
10–14	23
15–19	39
20–24	15
25–29	14

(a) What percentage of customers spent less than 15 minutes with a sales assistant?
(b) Write down the modal class.
(c) Calculate the difference between the estimated mean and the estimated median for these data.

39 During an election day, the number of votes received per hour was recorded for the two most popular political parties. The data are shown in the table below.

Party A	Party B
56	35
64	98
66	133
79	142
116	168

(*Continued*)

Party A	Party B
134	151
106	103
124	98
112	64
79	32
62	29
50	14

(a) Calculate the mean number of votes per hour for each political party.
(b) Write down the modal amount of votes in each case.
(c) Work out the median for each set of data.
(d) Write down, with reasons, which of the median or mean would be quoted by the members of party B if they were demonstrating their popularity.

40 The table below shows the number of tickets booked in a single transaction for the Saturday night performance of *Romeo and Juliet* at a theatre in Cardiff.

Number of tickets booked	Frequency (f)
2	75
3	41
4	62
5	27
6	12
7	11
8	7

(a) Write down the number of transactions in which four or more seats were booked.
(b) Calculate the median and mean values for these data.
(c) What is the modal number of tickets booked?

Solutions to Practice Exercises

1 (a) $n = 6$, so the median is half the sum of 3rd and 4th observations. The 3rd observation is 40.28 and the 4th observation is 42.87, so the median is 41.575.
   (b) $\sum x = 254.02$, $n = 6$; mean is 42.337
   (c) The supermarket should use the mean value in its press release because it is the larger of the two values and therefore represents the profits of the supermarket most favourably.

2 (a) males: $\sum x = 186$, $n = 30$; mean is £6.20
      females: $\sum x = 190.50$, $n = 30$; mean is £6.35
   (b) On average, females receive the higher rate of pay.

3 (a) It will increase the mean value because $1002 > 981$.
   (b) The total number of students enrolled in six years is $(981 \times 5) + 1002 = 5907$, so the new mean is 984.5.

4 (a) The modal class is 70–79, with the largest frequency of 32.
   (b) $\sum fx = 6368$, $\sum f = 84$; mean is 75.810
      $n = 84$, so the median is half the sum of the 42nd and 43rd observations. The 42nd and 43rd observations are in the 70–79 class, so this is the median class.
      b is lower class boundary = 69.5
      f is sum of frequencies below median class = 23
      f_m is frequency of median class = 32
      w is width of median class = 10
      median is 75.438
   (c) The hotel manager should not be worried about profitability because the estimated mean and median values are both greater than 70.

5 (a) The frequency distribution is as follows:

Number of people in a household (x)	Frequency (f)	Cumulative frequency	fx
1	5	5	5
2	8	13	16
3	8	21	24
4	10	31	24
5	6	37	30
6	3	40	18
	$\sum f = 40$		$\sum fx = 133$

(b) $\sum fx = 133$, $\sum f = 40$; mean is 3.325

(c) 19 households have more than the mean number of people.

(d) The mode is 4, with the largest frequency of 10, so the mean is not greater than the mode.

(e) $n = 40$, so the median is half the sum of 20th and 21st observations.
The 20th observation is 3 and the 21st observation is 3, so the median is 3.

6 Option (a). The median and mode are largely unaffected by extreme data values.

7 (a) street A: modal class is 155–159 with the largest frequency of 27
street B: modal class is 150–154 with the largest frequency of 28

(b) street A: $\sum x = 17984$ $n = 117$; mean is 153.709
street B: $\sum x = 17461$ $n = 113$; mean is 154.522
On average, street B has a higher daily usage rate than street A.

8 $\sum x = 639480$ $n = 8$; mean is £79,935

9 (a) $\sum fx = 1288.5$ $\sum f = 43$; mean is 29.965p/min

(b) The modal class is 35–44, with the largest frequency of 18.

(c) $n = 43$, so the median is the 22nd observation in the 35–44 class, so this is the median class.
b is lower class boundary = 34.5
f is sum of frequencies below median class = 20
f_m is frequency of median class = 18
w is width of median class = 10
median is 35.333p/min

10 (a) 145 shoppers gave information about the number of lottery tickets that they had purchased.

(b) The mode is 5, with the largest frequency of 32.

(c) $\sum fx = 568$, $\sum f = 145$; mean is 3.917
$n = 145$, so the median is the 73rd observation, which is 4.

(d) The next shopper would be expected to buy 4 tickets because this is the value closest to the mean and the median.

11 (a) $\sum x = 97.6$, $n = 11$; mean is 8.873
$n = 11$, so the median is the 6th observation, which is 3.9.

(b) The mean is not a good measure because it is influenced by the extreme value 55.9.

(c) new $\sum x = 47.6$, $n = 11$; new mean is 4.327
$n = 11$, so the median is 6th observation, which is 3.9.

(d) The median is unaffected by the correction, and the mean is reduced.

12 Option (c). The median and mean can only have one value.

13 (a) For the science application, the modal class is 16–20, with the largest frequency of 45.
For the music application, the modal class is 1–5, with the largest frequency of 78.

(b) science application: $\sum fx = 1426$, $\sum f = 92$; mean is 15.5
music application: $\sum fx = 431$, $\sum f = 92$; mean is 4.685
The science application has the highest average daily download rate.

14 (a) The mode is 84, which occurs twice.
(b) $n = 12$, so the median is half the sum of the 6th and 7th observations.
The 6th observation is 92 and the 7th observation is 95, so the median is 93.5.
(c) $\sum x = 1171$, $n = 12$; mean is 97.583

15 (a) There are 70 types of 800 g loaf available at the supermarket.
(b) The mode is 120, with the largest frequency of 23.
(c) $n = 70$, so the median is half the sum of the 35th and 36th observations.
The 35th observation is 120 and the 36th observation is 120, so the median is 120.
(d) $\sum fx = 8300$, $\sum f = 70$; mean is 118.571

16 (a) $\sum x = 196.9$, $n = 8$; mean is 24.613
(b) $n = 8$, so the median is half the sum of the 4th and 5th observations.
The 4th observation is 23.4 and the 5th observation is 26.8, so the median is 25.1.
(c) It will increase the mean value because $28.5 > 24.613$.
new $\sum x = 225.4$, $n = 9$; new mean is 25.044
(d) $n = 9$, so the median is the 5th observation, which is 26.8.
The median is increased.

17 (a) The mode is 90, which occurs twice.
(b) $\sum x = 1380$, $n = 15$; mean is 92
(c) $n = 15$, so the median is the 8th observation, which is 90.

18 (a) The frequency distribution table is as follows:

Grade	Tally	Frequency (f)
A	ⅢⅢ ⅢⅢ ‖	12
B	ⅢⅢ ⅢⅢ ⅢⅢ ‖	17
C	ⅢⅢ ⅢⅢ ⅢⅢ ⅢⅢ ⅢⅢ ‖‖	29
D	ⅢⅢ ⅢⅢ ⅢⅢ ‖‖	18
E	ⅢⅢ ⅢⅢ	10
F	‖‖	4
		$\sum f = 90$

(b) The mode is C, with the largest frequency of 29.

19 (a) 48 applicants scored 7 or more in the test.

(b) $n = 116$, so the median is half the sum of the 58th and 59th observations.
The 58th observation is 6 and the 59th observation is 6, so the median is 6.
$\sum fx = 708$, $\sum f = 116$; mean is 6.103

(c) The mode is 5, with the largest frequency of 26.

20 (a) The modal class is 100–119, with the largest frequency of 214.

(b) $\sum fx = 73599.5$, $\sum f = 700$; mean is 105.142
$n = 700$, so the median is half the sum of 350th and 351st observations.
The 350th and 351st observations are in the 100–119 class, so this is the median class.
b is lower class boundary = 99.5
f is sum of frequencies below median class = 258
f_m is frequency of median class = 214
w is width of median class = 20
median is 108.098

(c) The law firm should use the median value in its recruitment campaign because it is the larger of the two values and therefore represents the annual salary of the lawyers most favourably.

21 (a) males: managers

(b) females: administrative

22 (a) 213 shoppers used the high-street car park on that day.

(b) The mode is 3, with the largest frequency of 83.

(c) $n = 213$, so the median is the 107th observation, which is 3.

(d) $\sum fx = 609$, $\sum f = 213$; mean is 2.859

23 (a) The modal class is 100–129, with the largest frequency of 35.

(b) $\sum fx = 9062$, $\sum f = 90$; mean is 100.689

(c) $n = 90$, so the median is half the sum of the 45th and 46th observations.
The 45th and 46th observations are in the 100–129 class, so this is the median class.
b is lower class boundary = 99.5
f is sum of frequencies below median class = 39
f_m is frequency of median class = 35
w is width of median class = 30
median is 104.643

24 (a) $\sum x = 4265$, $n = 8$; mean is £533.125

(b) $n = 8$, so the median is half the sum of the 4th and 5th observations.
The 4th observation is 560 and the 5th observation is 565, so the median is £562.50.

(c) The mode is £575, which occurs twice.

(d) It will increase the mean value because 555 > 533.13.
new $\sum x = 4465$, $n = 8$; new mean is £558.125
The median remains unchanged.
The mode remains unchanged.

25 The numerator is $(5 \times 21712) + (16 \times 23160) + (2 \times 18933) = 516986$; the denominator is $5 + 16 + 2 = 23$.
The combined mean is £22477.65.

26 (a) $18/60 = 30\%$ of companies employ more than 150 people.
(b) The modal class is 51–150, with the largest frequency of 21.
(c) $\sum fx = 6260$, $\sum f = 60$; mean is 104.333
$n = 60$, so the median is half the sum of the 30th and 31st observations. The 30th and 31st observations are in the 51–150 class, so this is the median class.
b is lower class boundary = 50.5
f is sum of frequencies below median class = 21
f_m is frequency of median class = 21
w is width of median class = 100
median is 93.357
The difference between the mean and median is $104.333 - 93.357 = 10.976$.

27 (a) The frequency distribution is as follows:

Monthly rent (x)	Frequency (f)	Cumulative frequency	fx
1250	7	7	8750
1500	4	11	6000
1750	6	17	10500
2000	4	21	8000
2250	3	24	6750
2500	4	28	10000
	$\sum f = 28$		$\sum fx = 50000$

(b) $\sum fx = 50,000$, $\sum f = 28$; mean is £1785.71
(c) 11 flats have a higher monthly rental than the mean amount.
(d) The mode is £1250, with the largest frequency of 7, so the mean is greater than the mode,
(e) $n = 28$, so the median is half the sum of the 14th and 15th observations.
The 14th observation is 1750 and the 15th observation is 1750, so the median is £1750.

28 The numerator is $(1560 \times 32) + (1240 \times 28) + (985 \times 25) = 109,265$; denominator is $1560 + 1240 + 985 = 3785$. The combined mean is 28.868.

29 Option (a). The mode because the data are qualitative.

30 $\sum x = 20.7$, $n = 5$; mean is 4.14

31 (a) $\sum fx = 6816$, $\sum f = 148$; mean is 46.054
   (b) The modal class is 40–49, with the largest frequency of 57.
   (c) $n = 148$, so the median is half the sum of the 74th and 75th observations.
       The 74th and 75th observations are in the 40–49 class, so this is the median class.
       b is lower class boundary $= 39.5$
       f is sum of frequencies below median class $= 37$
       f_m is frequency of median class $= 57$
       w is width of median class $= 10$
       median is 45.991

32

   males : $\sum fx = 133$, $\sum f = 55$; mean is 2.418
   females : $\sum fx = 63$, $\sum f = 55$; mean is 1.145

   On average, females have the lower number of average late arrivals in a week.

33 (a) gas: $\sum x = 321$, $n = 6$; mean is 53.5
   (b) electricity: $\sum x = 2589$, $n = 6$; mean is 431.5
   (c) $n = 6$, so the median is half the sum of 3rd and 4th observations.
       For gas, the 3rd observation is 49 and the 4th observation is 56, so the median is 52.5.
       For electricity, the 3rd observation is 430 and the 4th observation is 436, so the median is 433.
   (d) For gas, the owners should use the median value for prospective buyers because it is the smaller of the two values and therefore represents the gas payments most favourably.
       For electricity, the owners should use the mean value for prospective buyers because it is the smaller of the two values and therefore represents the electricity payments most favourably.

34 (a) The modal class is 201–300, with the largest frequency of 161.
   (b) $\sum fx = 162444$, $\sum f = 488$; mean is 332.877
   (c) $n = 488$, so the median is half the sum of the 244th and 245th observations.
       The 244th and 245th observations are in the 201–300 class, so this is the median class.
       b is lower class boundary $= 200.5$
       f is sum of frequencies below median class $= 87$
       f_m is frequency of median class $= 161$
       w is width of median class $= 100$
       median is 298.016

35 Option (c). The average value of the two middle items when the data are arranged in ascending numerical order.

36 (a) The mode is 32 mph, with the largest frequency of 26.
   (b) $\sum fx = 4488$, $\sum f = 137$; mean is 32.759 mph
       $n = 137$, so the median is the 69th observation, which is 33 mph.
   (c) The next car would be expected to be travelling at 33 mph, because this is the value closest to the mean and the median.

37 (a) $n = 20$, so the median is half the sum of the 10th and 11th observations.
The 10th observation is 361 and the 11th observation is 365, so the median is £363.

(b) $\sum x = 7375$, $n = 20$; mean is £368.75

(c) The insurance company should use the median value in their advertising campaign because it is the smaller of the two values and therefore represents the online quotation rate most favourably.

38 (a) $50/118 = 42\%$ of customers spent less than 15 minutes with a sales assistant.

(b) The modal class is 15–19, with the largest frequency of 39.

(c) $\sum fx = 1781$, $\sum f = 118$; mean is 15.093 minutes
$n = 118$, so the median is half the sum of the 59th and 60th observations.
The 59th and 60th observations are in the 15–19 class, so this is the median class.
b is lower class boundary $= 14.5$
f is sum of frequencies below median class $= 50$
f_m is frequency of median class $= 39$
w is width of median class $= 5$
median is 15.654 minutes
The difference between the mean and median is $15.654 - 15.093 = 0.561$ minutes.

39 (a) A: $\sum x = 1048$, $n = 12$; mean is 87.333
B: $\sum x = 1067$, $n = 12$; mean is 88.917

(b) For A the mode is 79, which occurs twice; for B the mode is 98, which occurs twice.

(c) $n = 12$, so the median is half the sum of the 6th and 7th observations.
For A, the 6th observation is 79 and the 7th observation is 79, so the median is 79.
For B, the 6th observation is 98 and the 7th observation is 98, so the median is 98.

(d) Party B should use the median value to demonstrate its popularity because it is greater than the mean and therefore represents the number of votes most favourably.

40 (a) There were 119 transactions in which four or more seats were booked.

(b) $n = 235$, so the median is the 118th observation, which is 4.
$\sum fx = 861$, $\sum f = 235$; mean is 3.664

(c) The mode is 2, with the largest frequency of 75.

CHAPTER 6

Measures of Dispersion

OBJECTIVES

This chapter explains how to:

- calculate and interpret
  - range, quartiles and interquartile range
  - a five-number summary
  - variance, standard deviation and coefficient of variation
- identify outliers and construct a box plot
- understand when it is appropriate to use each measure of dispersion

KEY TERMS

box-and-whisker plot
box plot
coefficient of variation
deviation
first quartile
five-number summary

interquartile range
lower quartile
measure of dispersion
modified box plot
outlier
quartiles

range
standard deviation
third quartile
upper quartile
variance

Introduction

As we have seen in the previous chapter, measures of central tendency – such as the mode, mean and median – describe a set of data by identifying a 'typical value' that is representative of the set. Moving forward in our statistical analysis, we are now interested in describing the variation of the individual values within the data set.

Consider the following example. Suppose we recorded the number of televisions sold during one week in two large department stores. One store has a city-centre location; the other is located on a retail park.

	Monday	Tuesday	Wednesday	Thursday	Friday	Saturday	Sunday
City-centre store	24	28	24	21	29	23	26
Retail park store	8	12	5	24	24	52	50

The measures of central tendency for the number of televisions sold during this week are the same for both stores: mode = 24, mean = 25 and median = 24.

However, it can be seen from the two data sets that the variation in the number of sales each day is quite different, which may have an impact on staffing levels. For the city-centre store, a similar number of televisions are sold each day, indicating that the same number of sales assistants would be required throughout the week. At the retail park, the store is quieter on the weekdays but very busy at the weekends; perhaps the store manager would need to consider employing additional members of staff on Saturdays and Sundays.

When describing a data set, it is therefore important to provide information about the variation of individual values as well as defining a single representative value. A **measure of dispersion** allows us to quantify this variability for a set of data.

Range

The simplest measure of dispersion to calculate and interpret is the **range**. It is defined as the difference between the largest value and the smallest value in a data set. The formula for the range can be written as

$$\text{range} = \text{maximum value} - \text{minimum value}$$

When comparing two sets of data, a larger range is associated with the data set which shows more variation from the centre value. A data set which shows less variation among its values will have a smaller range.

Consider again the daily sales of televisions in our two department stores:

	Monday	Tuesday	Wednesday	Thursday	Friday	Saturday	Sunday
City-centre store	24	28	24	21	29	23	26
Retail park store	8	12	5	24	24	52	50

For the city-centre store, the largest data value is 29 and the smallest is 21. Therefore, the range for this store is 29 − 21 = 8. Between 21 and 29 televisions were sold on each day of the week.

Similarly, the range for the store located on the retail park is 52 − 8 = 44 televisions. There is more variation in this data set, as indicated by a greater difference between the highest and lowest number of daily sales.

Although the range is easy to calculate and interpret, it is not the most useful measure of dispersion because it only uses two of the data values in its calculation: the largest and the smallest. It ignores all of the other values in a data set. Consequently, the range is strongly influenced by extreme values because these values will naturally occur at the lower and/or higher end of a data set.

Returning to our television sales, suppose that the city-centre store had a half-price sale on the Wednesday of the week in which the data were recorded. If 74 televisions were sold rather than 24, then the range for this store becomes $74 - 21 = 53$, which is a considerable increase from the original range of 8 televisions. The range is influenced strongly in the direction of the high number of sales recorded on the Wednesday and we can see that the range is not a very satisfactory measure of dispersion for a data set that contains extreme values.

Quartiles and the Interquartile Range

Quartiles are values that divide an ordered set of data into four equal parts, or quarters. We can use quartiles to calculate a measure of dispersion that is more resistant to extreme values than the range: it is called the interquartile range.

Three quartiles – denoted as Q_1, Q_2 and Q_3 – are required to divide a set of data into four equal parts. Q_1, also known as the first quartile or lower quartile, is the value which separates the smallest 25% of the values from the remaining data set. The second quartile, Q_2, is the median, which we discussed in the previous chapter. We know already that the median is the middle value which divides the set into two halves. Q_3 separates the smallest 75% of the values from the remaining data set; it is also known as the third quartile or upper quartile.

A graphical representation of the quartiles is shown below.

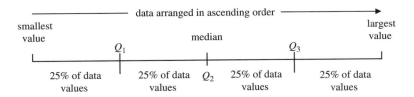

Several different techniques can be used to identify the quartiles for a data set, but the resulting values will be very similar, particularly when there are a large number of data values in the set. Here we will use a series of steps based on the methods for finding the median value.

1. Arrange the data in numerical order, from the smallest value to the largest.
2. Identify the median value using the methods already described in Chapter 5.
3. Use the median value to separate the data set into two halves.
4. The lower quartile or Q_1 is the median of the set of data values that are less than the median of the entire data set.
5. The upper quartile or Q_3 is the median of the set of data values that are greater than the median of the entire data set.

Using the two examples below, we demonstrate how to identify the quartiles for an even number of data values, and for an odd number of data values.

The number of complaints emailed to the customer services team at a theme park were recorded during the 12-week summer period. The data are shown in the table below.

Week	1	2	3	4	5	6	7	8	9	10	11	12
Number of complaints	214	189	152	206	237	158	192	146	203	177	165	221

Putting the data in numerical order, we have:

146	152	158	165	177	189	192	203	206	214	221	237

There is an even number of values in the data set, 12, so the median is calculated as the average of the two values closest to the middle. Using $\frac{1}{2}(12)$ and $\frac{1}{2}(12) + 1$ identifies the 6th and 7th data values; the 6th value is 189 and the 7th value is 192, so the median or Q_2 is calculated as

$$Q_2 = \frac{189 + 192}{2} = 190.5$$

Using the median to separate the data into two halves, we can then identify the lower and upper quartiles as the median of the lower half and the median of the upper half:

data values less than the median   data values greater than the median

146	152	158	165	177	189

192	203	206	214	221	237

$$Q_1 = \frac{158 + 165}{2} = 161.5 \qquad\qquad Q_3 = \frac{206 + 214}{2} = 210$$

We can interpret the lower and upper quartiles as follows:

- in approximately 25% of the weeks, the customer services team received less than 161.5 emails;
- in approximately 75% of the weeks, 210 emails or fewer were received from customers.

The number of books ordered by 13 families using an online store was recorded for a year. The data collected are:

6	14	51	3	17	22	29	40	35	11	23	9	32

Putting the data in numerical order, we have:

3	6	9	11	14	17	22	23	29	32	35	40	51

There is an odd number of values in the data set, 13, so the median is the middle data value. Using $\frac{1}{2}(13 + 1)$ identifies the 7th data value as the middle one:

$$Q_2 = 22$$

Using the median to separate the data into two halves, we can then identify the lower and upper quartiles as the median of the lower half and the median of the upper half.

data values less than the median

3	6	9	11	14	17

data values greater than the median

23	29	32	35	40	51

$$Q_1 = \frac{9 + 11}{2} = 10$$

$$Q_3 = \frac{32 + 35}{2} = 33.5$$

We can interpret the lower and upper quartiles as follows:

- approximately 25% of the families ordered 10 books or fewer;
- approximately 75% of the families ordered fewer than 33.5 books.

The quartiles are resistant to extreme values which may occur within the data set: Q_1 and Q_3 are not influenced by these values. Returning to the previous examples, we can see that if the smallest number of complaints emailed by customers was 6 rather than 146, the value of the lower quartile would remain unchanged at 161.5 complaints. Similarly, the upper quartile would still be 33.5 books even if the largest number of books ordered by a family was actually 251 rather than 51.

The difference between the upper and lower quartiles provides us with a measure of dispersion known as the interquartile range, sometimes abbreviated to IQR. It is calculated as follows:

$$\text{interquartile range} = \text{upper quartile } Q_3 - \text{lower quartile } Q_1$$

The interquartile range is defined as the range of the central 50% of the values in a data set. It is interpreted in a similar way to the range: a data set with a large interquartile range will have greater variation than a data set with a smaller interquartile range.

Using our examples again, for the number of complaints emailed to the theme park, we can calculate the interquartile range as $Q_3 - Q_1 = 210 - 161.5 = 48.5$ and for the number of books ordered using the online store, the corresponding result is $Q_3 - Q_1 = 33.5 - 10 = 23.5$.

Compared to the range, the interquartile range is preferred as a measure of dispersion when a data set contains extreme values. The interquartile range is resistant to extreme values because it is calculated using the quartiles. However, a disadvantage of the interquartile range is that it ignores 50% of the data values, only using the middle section of the set.

Five-Number Summary

To provide a numerical description of our data set which includes both a measure of central tendency and an indication of variation, we can use a **five-number summary**. This consists of the minimum and maximum data values, the lower and upper quartiles and the median, listed in ascending order, as follows:

$$\text{minimum} \quad Q_1 \quad \text{median} \quad Q_3 \quad \text{maximum}$$

Consider the data below which show the ages of the top ten wealthiest male and female billionaires.

males

45	64	66	69	72	73	77	78	83	85

females

51	51	58	59	63	64	70	74	91	94

The five-number summary for each gender is:

males

minimum	Q_1	median	Q_3	maximum
45	66	72.5	78	85

females

minimum	Q_1	median	Q_3	maximum
51	58	63.5	74	94

Comparing the five-number summary for the two data sets, we can see that the median age for females is lower than the median age for males; and the interquartile range for males $(78 - 66 = 12)$ is lower than the interquartile range for females $(74 - 58 = 16)$.

Box Plots

Based on a five-number summary, a **box plot** is a graphical display which tells us about the average value and variability of a data set. A box plot is a very useful way to visually summarise and compare data sets; it is sometimes known as a **box-and-whisker plot**. There are several steps involved in constructing a box plot:

1. Create a horizontal axis with a scale that allows the smallest and largest data values to be included on the diagram.
2. Draw a box above the axis; the left-hand vertical side of the box should be located at the position of the lower quartile, and the right-hand side at the position of the upper quartile.
3. Inside the box, draw a vertical line at the position of the median on the axis scale.
4. Draw a line that extends from the left-hand side of the box at Q_1 to the smallest value in the data set, marked by a small vertical line. Create a corresponding line that joins the right-side of the box at Q_3 to the largest value in the data set.

To demonstrate the construction of a box plot, we will return to our example about the ages of the wealthiest billionaires, choosing to focus only on males at this stage. The five-number summary for males is:

males

minimum	Q_1	median	Q_3	maximum
45	66	72.5	78	85

Step 1. The minimum age for the males is 45 and the maximum value is 85, so our horizontal axis could be drawn as follows:

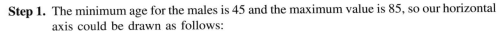
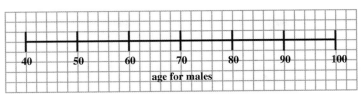

Step 2. We locate the position of our box using the lower quartile, 66, and the upper quartile, 78.

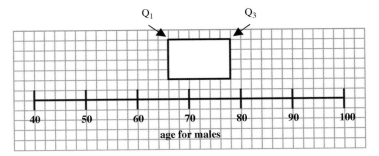

Step 3. Using the median value, 72.5, we draw a vertical line inside the box.

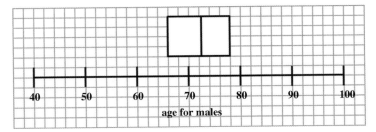

Step 4. We complete the box plot by drawing lines that extend from the sides of the box to the minimum and maximum values. These lines are sometimes known as 'whiskers', giving the alternative name for the diagram: box-and-whisker plot.

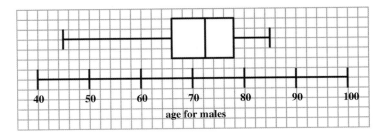

Box plots are most useful for visually comparing two or more data sets side by side on a single diagram using the same scale.

If we show the five-number summary for male and female ages for the wealthiest billionaires on the same box plot, the following points can easily be noted:

- The median age for the males is greater than the median age for the females, shown by comparing the position on the axis scale of the vertical line drawn inside each box.
- Comparing the length of each box plot from minimum to maximum values shows that the range for each gender is fairly similar.
- The interquartile range for males is smaller than that for females; this is seen on the diagram by comparing the length of each box.
- The males have a smaller minimum value and a smaller maximum value when compared to the data for females.

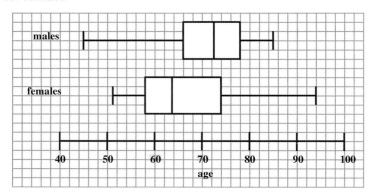

Box plots can alternatively be drawn with a vertical axis rather than a horizontal axis. Our example box plot could be drawn vertically as follows:

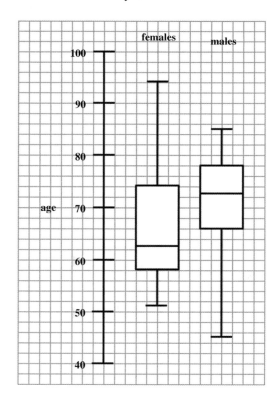

In addition to a five-number summary, a box plot can also be used to highlight any extreme values, or outliers, in a data set. In this case, the diagram is known as a **modified box plot**.

We can identify outliers using a rule-based technique, which is preferable to relying on subjective judgement. A value in the data set is classified as an **outlier** if it is positioned less than 1.5 times the interquartile range below the first quartile or more than 1.5 times the interquartile range above the third quartile.

As part of the method for constructing a modified box plot, we determine the lower and upper limits for a data set as follows:

$$\text{lower limit} = \text{lower quartile } Q_1 - 1.5 \times \text{IQR}$$
$$\text{upper limit} = \text{upper quartile } Q_3 + 1.5 \times \text{IQR}$$

Any data values that are positioned below the lower limit or above the upper limit are then identified as outliers; these values are highlighted on a box plot using an asterisk (*) or an equivalent symbol.

The horizontal extension lines, or whiskers, are shortened on the modified box plot. If there are outliers in the lower data values, the extension line on the left-hand side of the box is shortened so that it reaches the smallest data value that is not an outlier, rather than the smallest value in the data set. Similarly, if outliers are identified in the upper part of the data set, the line on the right-hand side is shortened to the largest data value that is not an outlier, rather than the largest value in the data set.

We can identify outliers and construct modified box plots for our example data about the ages of male and female billionaires. Recall the data set and five-number summary for each gender:

males

45	64	66	69	72	73	77	78	83	85

minimum	Q_1	median	Q_3	maximum
45	66	72.5	78	85

females

51	51	58	59	63	64	70	74	91	94

minimum	Q_1	median	Q_3	maximum
51	58	63.5	74	94

The limits for each data set are calculated below:

for males,

$$\text{lower limit} = \text{lower quartile } Q_1 - 1.5 \times \text{IQR} = 66 - (1.5 \times (78 - 66)) = 66 - 18 = 48$$
$$\text{upper limit} = \text{upper quartile } Q_3 + 1.5 \times \text{IQR} = 78 + (1.5 \times (78 - 66)) = 78 + 18 = 96$$

and for females,

$$\text{lower limit} = \text{lower quartile } Q_1 - 1.5 \times \text{IQR} = 58 - (1.5 \times (74 - 58)) = 58 - 24 = 34$$
$$\text{upper limit} = \text{upper quartile } Q_3 + 1.5 \times \text{IQR} = 74 + (1.5 \times (74 - 58)) = 74 + 24 = 98$$

Examining the values in the lower part of the data set for each gender, it can be seen that the data value 45 is below the lower limit for the males of 48, and therefore we identify this age as an outlier. In the data for the females, the smallest value, 51, is not below the female lower limit of 34 and so we can conclude that there are no outliers in the lower part of the data set for females. Considering the upper part of the data sets, we can see that the largest data value for each gender is not above the corresponding upper limit; there are no further outliers to be identified.

As we have not identified any outliers in our female ages, our box plot for females remains unchanged, but we can draw a modified box plot for the males. The outlier is represented using an asterisk and the line on the left-side of the box is shortened so that it now extends only to the data value 64 rather than the minimum value in the data set.

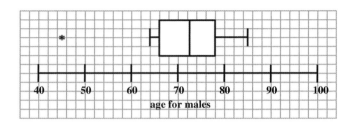

Variance and Standard Deviation

The range and the interquartile range are useful measures of dispersion because they are easy to calculate and interpret. However, both measures are limited in use because they do not take into account all of the individual values in a data set: the range uses only the smallest and largest values, and the interquartile range ignores 50% of the data values, only using the middle section of the set.

Alternatively, we can use a measure of dispersion known as the **variance**, which incorporates all of the individual data values in its calculation. The variance provides an indication of variability by considering the distance of each data value from the mean of the data set; this distance is called the **deviation**.

As a starting point, we may choose to calculate the total deviation of the individual values from the mean. However, this calculation will equal zero for every set of data: the totals of the positive and negative deviations – caused by data values larger and smaller than the mean – will exactly cancel each other because the mean is a measure of the centre of the set. This 'zero' property of the total deviation is illustrated in the example below.

This table shows the number of miles driven by car for a family over a two-week period. The mean for the data set is 79 miles.

55	92	58	96	102	98	110	37	67	22	89	97	78	108

The deviations are calculated by subtracting each data value from the mean. Here we can see that the total deviation is zero.

Number of miles	Data value – mean
55	$55 - 79 = -24$
92	$92 - 79 = 13$
58	-21
96	17
102	23
98	19
110	31
37	-42
67	-12
22	-57
89	10
97	15
78	-1
108	29
	Total: $157 - 157 = 0$

Since the total deviation is unhelpful, our variance calculation actually involves squaring each deviation and then finding the average of these squared values. Using this method, we are provided with a measure of dispersion in which each individual data value contributes to the final result.

It is necessary to distinguish between the variance calculated for population data, denoted as σ^2, and the variance calculated for sample data, denoted as s^2.

The population variance is the sum of squared deviations from the population mean, divided by the population size, N:

$$\sigma^2 = \frac{\sum (x - \mu)^2}{N}$$

The sample variance is the sum of the squared deviations from the sample mean, divided by the sample size, n, minus 1:

$$s^2 = \frac{\sum (x - \bar{x})^2}{n - 1}$$

Although N is used in the denominator for the population formula, we use $n - 1$ in the formula for the sample because this provides a more accurate estimation of the population variance.

The formulae stated above are sometimes known as the *conceptual* formulae: they help us to understand the way in which the variance is derived using the squared deviations from the mean. In practice, we generally prefer to use the equivalent *computational* formulae because they reduce the amount of arithmetic work.

The computational formulae for population data and sample data are:

$$\sigma^2 = \frac{\sum x^2 - \frac{\left(\sum x\right)^2}{N}}{N}$$

$$s^2 = \frac{\sum x^2 - \frac{\left(\sum x\right)^2}{n}}{n - 1}$$

The final result for the variance is the same regardless of whether we use the conceptual or computational formulae.

Since the calculation for the variance of a data set involves squaring the deviations, the units of measurement are also squared. For example, if our data are recorded in kilograms then the units of measurement for the variance will be kilograms squared (kg^2), which is meaningless. We can return to the units of measurement of the original data by taking the positive square root of the variance: this measure of dispersion is known as the **standard deviation**.

Taking the positive square root of the population variance gives the standard deviation formula for population data as

$$\sigma = \sqrt{\sigma^2}$$

For the sample standard deviation we use the positive square root of the sample variance,

$$s = \sqrt{s^2}$$

In terms of interpretation, the variance and standard deviation provide us with a measure of variability in relation to the mean of the data set. A large value indicates that the data values are spread out from the mean, whereas if a data set contains many values that are close to the mean, then its variance and standard deviation will be small.

EXAMPLES: POPULATION DATA

A civil engineering consultancy advertised eight vacancies on a recruitment website in a month. The human resources department recorded the number of people who applied for each position.

45	12	37	21	9	18	27	11

For this population data (with $N = 8$ and $\mu = 22.5$), the variance can be calculated using the *conceptual* formulae as follows:

Number of people x	Deviation $x - \mu$	Squared deviation $(x - \mu)^2$
45	22.5	506.25
12	−10.5	110.25
37	14.5	210.25
21	−1.5	2.25

(*Continued*)

Number of people x	Deviation $x - \mu$	Squared deviation $(x - \mu)^2$
9	-13.5	182.25
18	-4.5	20.25
27	4.5	20.25
11	-11.5	132.25
		$\sum (x - \mu)^2 = 1184$

We obtain

$$\sigma^2 = \frac{\sum (x - \mu)^2}{N} = \frac{1184}{8} = 148$$

Using the *computational* formula, the population variance can also be calculated as shown below.

Number of people x	x^2
45	2025
12	144
37	1369
21	441
9	81
18	324
27	729
11	121
$\sum x = 180$	$\sum x^2 = 5234$

We then have

$$\sigma^2 = \frac{\sum x^2 - \frac{(\sum x)^2}{N}}{N} = \frac{5234 - \frac{180^2}{8}}{8} = \frac{1184}{8} = 148$$

We can see from these examples that the conceptual formula and the computational formula give the same value for the population variance.

Taking the positive square root of the population variance provides us with the standard deviation for these population data:

$$\sigma = \sqrt{\sigma^2} = \sqrt{148} = 12.166$$

EXAMPLE: SAMPLE DATA

A coffee shop owner decided to investigate the popularity of a new variety of muffin by running a trial for one month. He recorded the number of people who purchased this variety of muffin on a sample of eight days:

6	7	9	2	3	5	3	5

The variance can be calculated for these sample data (with $n = 8$ and $\bar{x} = 5$) using the *conceptual* formula as follows:

Number of people x	Deviation $x - \bar{x}$	Squared deviation $(x - \bar{x})^2$
6	1	1
7	2	4
9	4	16
2	−3	9
3	−2	4
5	0	0
3	−2	4
5	0	0
		$\sum (x - \bar{x})^2 = 38$

We obtain

$$s^2 = \frac{\sum (x - \bar{x})^2}{n - 1} = \frac{38}{7} = 5.429$$

Using the *computational* formula, the sample variance can also be calculated as shown below.

Number of people x	x^2
6	36
7	49
9	81
2	4
3	9
5	25
3	9
5	25
$\sum x = 40$	$\sum x^2 = 238$

We then have

$$s^2 = \frac{\sum x^2 - \frac{(\sum x)^2}{n}}{n-1} = \frac{238 - \frac{40^2}{8}}{7} = \frac{38}{7} = 5.429$$

Thus the same result is obtained for the sample variance using the conceptual formula and the computational formula.

The standard deviation for these sample data can be found by taking the positive square root of the sample variance:

$$s = \sqrt{s^2} = \sqrt{5.429} = 2.330$$

The variance and standard deviation are useful measures of dispersion because the calculations involve using all of the values within the data set. However, both measures are strongly influenced by extreme values because these values are numerically 'far away' from the mean.

Considering our sample data again, suppose the coffee shop owner decided to reduce the price of the muffins for one of the days when he recorded the number of people making a purchase. If 89 customers rather than 9 customers purchased the new variety of muffin, then the effect on the variance and standard deviation can be seen using the conceptual formula. With the increased purchases on the third day, the data set becomes:

| 6 | 7 | 89 | 2 | 3 | 5 | 3 | 5 |

The sample mean is now 15, and the values in the table change as shown below.

Number of people x	Deviation x^2	Squared deviation $(x - \bar{x})^2$
6	−9	81
7	−8	64
89	74	5476
2	−13	169
3	−12	144
5	−10	100
3	−12	144
5	−10	100
		$\sum (x - \bar{x})^2 = 6278$

We obtain

$$s^2 = \frac{\sum (x - \bar{x})^2}{n-1} = \frac{6278}{7} = 896.857$$

$$s = \sqrt{s^2} = \sqrt{896.857} = 29.948$$

So the sample variance has increased from 5.429 to 896.857, and the standard deviation for the sample has increased from 2.330 to 29.948. Both measures of dispersion have been strongly affected by the extreme data value of 89.

If our data set has already been summarised as a frequency distribution, then our formulae for the population and sample variance are adjusted. This is the same principle we applied to the calculations for measures of central tendency in Chapter 5. The conceptual and computational formulae are shown below:

$$\sigma^2 = \frac{\sum f(x - \mu)^2}{\sum f} \quad \sigma^2 = \frac{\sum fx^2 - \frac{(\sum fx)^2}{\sum f}}{\sum f}$$

$$s^2 = \frac{\sum f(x - \bar{x})^2}{(\sum f) - 1} \quad s^2 = \frac{\sum fx^2 - \frac{(\sum fx)^2}{\sum f}}{(\sum f) - 1}$$

The same formulae can be applied to a grouped frequency distribution, but in this case each class mid-point must be used to represent the value of x because the individual data values are not available to us.

Coefficient of Variation

When we want to compare two data sets to decide which set has more variability in its values, we cannot use the standard deviation if the data sets have different units of measurement. The standard deviation is a measure of absolute variability and therefore its magnitude is affected by the size of the data values.

The example given below demonstrates the way in which the standard deviation is affected by a change to the units of measurements. Choosing a sample of cars classified as luxury vehicles, the overall length was recorded in inches for each car as follows:

car length in inches

167.4	188.8	192.0	191.6	162.8	182.6	189.1	190.8	183.9	173.4

The sample mean and sample standard deviation for these data are:

$$\bar{x} = \frac{\sum x}{n} = \frac{1822.4}{10} = 182.24$$

$$s = \sqrt{\frac{\sum x^2 - \frac{(\sum x)^2}{n}}{n - 1}} = \sqrt{\frac{333139.6 - \frac{1822.4^2}{10}}{9}} = \sqrt{\frac{1025.424}{9}} = \sqrt{113.936} = 10.674$$

If we now convert the car lengths from inches into metres, the new data and calculations are shown below.

car length in metres

| 4.25 | 4.80 | 4.88 | 4.87 | 4.14 | 4.64 | 4.80 | 4.85 | 4.67 | 4.40 |

$$\bar{x} = \frac{\sum x}{n} = \frac{46.3}{10} = 4.63$$

$$s = \sqrt{\frac{\sum x^2 - \frac{(\sum x)^2}{n}}{n-1}} = \sqrt{\frac{215.034 - \frac{46.3^2}{10}}{9}} = \sqrt{\frac{0.665}{9}} = \sqrt{0.074} = 0.272$$

We can see from this example that although our sample of cars is the same, the change in units of measurement has resulted in a changed standard deviation. In the first instance, the standard deviation is measured in inches, whereas following the change of units, it is measured in metres. It is meaningless to compare the magnitude of these standard deviation results and conclude that the first data set has more variation because the standard deviation is the largest value.

In this situation, the **coefficient of variation** is a measure of dispersion that can be used as an alternative because it expresses the standard deviation as a percentage of the mean: it relates the variability of the data values to the mean of the data set.

For population data, the coefficient of variation is calculated as

$$CV = \frac{\sigma}{\mu} \times 100\%$$

The sample coefficient of variation is

$$CV = \frac{s}{\bar{x}} \times 100\%$$

Returning to our sample of cars, we will see that using the coefficient of variation as a measure of dispersion shows that the variability is the same for both data sets.

car length in inches

| 167.4 | 188.8 | 192.0 | 191.6 | 162.8 | 182.6 | 189.1 | 190.8 | 183.9 | 173.4 |

$$CV = \frac{10.674}{182.24} \times 100\% = 5.9\%$$

car length in metres

| 4.25 | 4.80 | 4.88 | 4.87 | 4.14 | 4.64 | 4.80 | 4.85 | 4.67 | 4.40 |

$$CV = \frac{0.272}{4.63} \times 100\% = 5.9\%$$

When comparing two sets of data, a smaller coefficient of variation is associated with the data set which shows less variation from the mean. A data set which shows more variation among its values will have a larger coefficient of variation.

HINTS AND TIPS

IDENTIFYING OUTLIERS

When you are calculating the lower and upper limits to identify outliers for a modified box plot, it is essential that the correct order of precedence is used.

Recall the five-number summary for the ages of the wealthiest male billionaires.

minimum	Q_1	median	Q_3	maximum
45	66	72.5	78	85

The limits used for identifying outliers were calculated as follows:

lower limit = lower quartile $Q_1 - 1.5 \times \text{IQR} = 66 - (1.5 \times 12) = 66 - 18 = 48$
upper limit = upper quartile $Q_3 + 1.5 \times \text{IQR} = 78 + (1.5 \times 12) = 78 + 18 = 96$

You can see from the positioning of the brackets that the multiplication has been performed first in each calculation, before the addition or subtraction. If, in error, the order of precedence was reversed then the resulting limits would be $(66 - 1.5) \times 12 = 774$ and $(78 + 1.5) \times 12 = 954$, which would clearly be incorrect for this data set with its maximum age of 85.

VARIANCE CALCULATIONS

The value of the variance is always positive because the numerator of the formula, conceptual or computational, should never produce a negative result. If you have calculated the variance for a data set and the final result is negative, you will need to go through your procedure again and check the individual components you have used in the formula.

Use of the computational formula can sometimes lead to a negative value for the variance if you have confused $\sum x^2$ and $\left(\sum x\right)^2$, which give very different results for a data set:

- $\sum x^2$ means 'square each x-value and then add them all together'.
- $\left(\sum x\right)^2$ means 'add together all of the x-values and then square the result'.

For our example data about the wealthiest male billionaires, the ages were:

45	64	66	69	72	73	77	78	83	85

So we have

$$\sum x^2 = 45^2 + 64^2 + 66^2 + 69^2 + 72^2 + 73^2 + 77^2 + 78^2 + 83^2 + 85^2 = 51878$$
$$\left(\sum x\right)^2 = (45 + 64 + 66 + 69 + 72 + 73 + 77 + 78 + 83 + 85)^2 = 712^2 = 506944$$

WHICH MEASURE?

Choosing the most appropriate measure of dispersion to use for your situation can be a complex decision. It can depend on the whether your data set contains any extreme values and whether you prefer a simple calculation or one which uses all of the data values.

Remember that a five-number summary and modified box plot can also provide useful information about the variability in a data set.

The following table shows the advantages and disadvantages of each measure of dispersion discussed in this chapter.

	Range	Interquartile range	Variance	Standard deviation	Coefficient of variation
Easy to calculate and interpret	yes	yes	no	no	no
Uses all of the data values in the set	no	no	yes	yes	yes
Is influenced by extreme values	yes	no	yes	yes	yes
Useful for comparing data sets	yes	yes	no	no	yes

Using Excel

RANGE

To find the range of a data set using Excel, it is necessary to create a formula that uses two of the built-in statistical functions, **MAX** and **MIN**.

Function	Description	Syntax
MAX	displays the largest value in a set of data	MAX(number1, number2, . . .)
MIN	displays the smallest value in a set of data	MIN(number1, number2, . . .)1

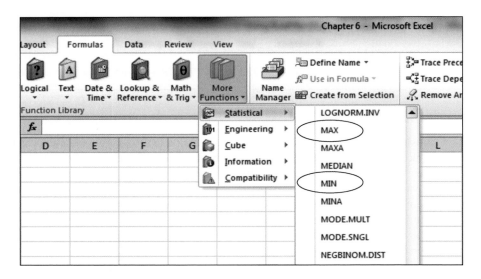

We will use the data collected about the number of televisions sold during one week in two large department stores. One store has a city centre location; the other is located on a retail park.

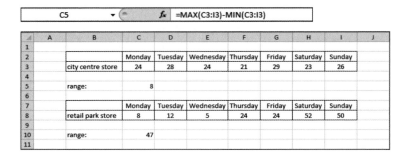

VARIANCE AND STANDARD DEVIATION

There are built-in statistical functions that allow us to use Excel to calculate the variance and standard deviation for sample data and also for population data.

Function	Description	Syntax
VAR.P	calculates the variance based on the entire population	VAR.P(number1, number2, . . .)
STDEV.P	calculates the standard deviation based on the entire population	STDEV.P(number1, number2, . . .)
VAR.S	calculates the variance based on a sample	VAR.S(number1, number2, . . .)
STDEV.S	calculates the standard deviation based on a sample	STDEV.S(number1, number2, . . .)

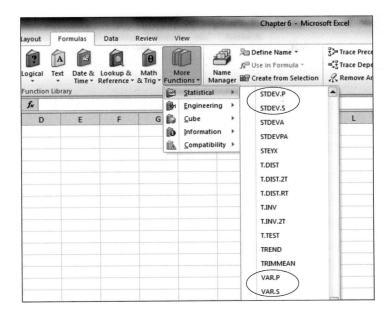

Returning to our earlier examples:

Population Data

A civil engineering consultancy advertised eight vacancies on a recruitment website for a month. The human resources department recorded the number of people who applied for each position.

| D4 | ▼ | f_x | =VAR.P(B2:I2) |

| D5 | ▼ | f_x | =STDEV.P(B2:I2) |

▲	A	B	C	D	E	F	G	H	I	J
1										
2		45	12	37	21	9	18	27	11	
3										
4		variance:		148						
5		standard deviation:		12.166						
6										

Sample Data

A coffee shop owner decided to investigate the popularity of a new variety of muffin by running a trial for one month. He recorded the number of people who purchased this variety of muffin on a sample of eight days.

	D4		▼	⦿	f_x	=VAR.S(B2:I2)			

	D5		▼	⦿	f_x	=STDEV.S(B2:I2)			

	A	B	C	D	E	F	G	H	I	J
1										
2		6	7	9	2	3	5	3	5	
3										
4		variance:		5.429						
5		standard deviation:		2.330						
6										

COEFFICIENT OF VARIATION

Excel does not provide a built-in function to calculate the coefficient of variation directly, but we can use **STDEV.S** or **STDEV.P** and **AVERAGE** in a formula to produce the required result.

Returning to our sample of cars classified as luxury vehicles, the overall length was recorded in inches for each car.

standard deviation:		=STDEV.S(B3:K3)	
mean:		=AVERAGE(B3:K3)	
coefficient of variation:		=E5/E6	

	A	B	C	D	E	F	G	H	I	J	K	L
1												
2		car length in inches										
3		167.4	188.8	192	191.6	162.8	182.6	189.1	190.8	183.9	173.4	
4												
5		standard deviation:			10.674							
6		mean:			182.24							
7		coefficient of variation:			5.9%							
8												

Practice Exercises

1 The cost of a treatment session was recorded for eight physiotherapy centres; the figures are shown below to the nearest pound (£). Describe these data using a five number summary.

42	35	40	65	48	52	57	38

2 In a survey, a sample of 340 tourists from overseas were asked how long they had queued for entry to a major attraction in London.

The responses given were rounded to the nearest 5 minutes, and a frequency distribution was created as shown in the table below:

Waiting time (nearest 5 mins)	Number of tourists (f)
5	9
10	11
15	17
20	29
25	47
30	42
35	36
40	32
45	30
50	51
55	20
60	16

(a) To calculate the variance for this data set, should we use $\sum f$ or $\left(\sum f\right) - 1$ in the denominator for the formula? Give a reason for your answer.

(b) Use the computational formula to calculate the variance for the frequency distribution.

3 The stem and leaf diagram below records the length (in minutes) of weekly meetings for the senior management team of an international shipping company.

length of meeting   3|2 means 32 minutes

3	2	6	7	9				(4)
4	6	6	8	8				(4)
5	0	1	1	1	3	8		(6)
6	1	2	5	5	5	7	9	(7)
7	3	4	6	6	9			(5)
8	4							(1)

What is the range for this data set?

4 Explain how to determine whether there are any outliers in a data set.

5 Which measures of dispersion use all of the values in a data set?
   (a) interquartile range and standard deviation
   (b) range and variance
   (c) variance and coefficient of variation

6 Two students completed a series of five controlled assessments during a business studies course at school. Their marks were as follows:

Student 1	53	56	58	51	62
Student 2	70	22	79	75	34

(a) Calculate the population mean for each student. What do you notice about your results?

(b) Compare the variation in the marks for each student using the population standard deviation. Interpret your results.

(c) When comparing two data sets, why is it important to provide information about the variation of individual values as well as defining a single representative value for each set?

7 A practice manager at a doctors' surgery decided to record the number of appointments cancelled by patients on a sample of 16 days throughout the year. A table was produced for the collected data as follows:

12	9	6	16	11	14	12	8
2	20	6	18	14	7	13	11

Calculate the coefficient of variation for the number of cancelled appointments.

8 Describe one advantage and two disadvantages of using the range as a measure of dispersion?

9 Decide whether the following statements are TRUE or FALSE. Explain your response for any FALSE statements.

(a) The calculation for the interquartile range does not use all of the values in a data set.

(b) The interquartile range is influenced by extreme values.

(c) It is preferable to use the interquartile range rather than the variance when the variation in two data sets is being compared.

10 The age of every person who attended a private viewing at an art gallery was written down as follows:

45	67	42	68	67	38	45	49
57	52	68	63	61	54	39	57
68	44	41	47	27	26	48	51

(a) Use the computational formula to calculate the variance for this population.

(b) Repeat the variance calculation using the conceptual formula.

(c) Compare your results from parts (a) and (b).

11 A media website reported on the number of pages that contained advertisements in the magazines for 15 leading publishers during the first half of the year. The following summary was provided:

Minimum number of pages	347
Lower quartile	512.5
Upper quartile	828
Maximum number of pages	1261

(a) Calculate the interquartile range for this data set.
(b) Determine the lower and upper limits.
(c) Are there any outliers? Support your answer with an explanation.

12 What are the components provided in a five-number summary?
(a) minimum, interquartile range, median, range, maximum
(b) minimum, lower quartile, mean, upper quartile, maximum
(c) minimum, lower quartile, median, upper quartile, maximum

13 The amount of vitamin C (in milligrams) was measured in 100 g of 29 different types of fruit. The lower and upper quartiles were found to be $Q_1 = 8.5$ mg and $Q_3 = 47.5$ mg. Calculate the interquartile range.

14 Construct a modified box plot for the data given in the table below representing the monthly mortgage payments (to the nearest £50) for 40 members of the same fitness centre. Summary statistics are provided as follows:

lower quartile = 1400
upper quartile = 2000
median = 1650
lower limit = 500
upper limit = 2900

1550	1800	1800	1400	1400	1400	2250	2300
1250	2500	1350	1950	1900	1250	650	1400
2300	1450	1500	1400	1400	1500	2450	1750
1250	450	2100	1900	2050	2400	2250	1350
1350	1700	1750	1500	1600	2600	1850	1700

15 The table shows the frequency distribution for the number of songs on the albums released by a singer-songwriter over two decades.

Number of songs	Frequency
5–9	5
10–14	12
15–19	5
20–24	1
25–29	1
30–34	1
35–39	1

Calculate μ and σ^2 for this distribution.

16 As part of a customer satisfaction questionnaire, day guests at a health spa were asked to record how many minutes they spent in the pools and the distance they travelled (in miles) to reach the venue.

The coefficient of variation for each data set is shown below.
minutes spent in the pools: 36.25%
distance travelled in miles: 14.73%

Using this information, decide whether the time spent in the pools varied more or less than the distance travelled to the venue. Give a reason to support your answer.

17 Sales figures (in thousands) for some of the UK's best-selling cars in 2010 were recorded as follows:

121.9	87.4	84.3	68.1	65.0	50.2	43.5	42.6	41.9	38.6

The variance for the sample of cars is 725.652.
(a) The sales figure for the first car was incorrectly recorded and should have been 221.9 rather than 121.9. Do you think the variance will be affected by this change? Give a reason for your answer.
(b) Check your response to part (a) by recalculating the variance for the data set with the corrected value using the computational formula.

18 Calculate the range for the following set of data, which shows the number of staff employed at 30 hotels.

44	36	21	65	22	20
36	41	40	42	36	20
51	39	28	29	26	19
35	39	37	41	46	34
45	32	27	21	25	34

19 The table below shows the new car prices (in thouands of pounds (£)) for a sample of 36 luxury cars.

32	144	75	73	108	65
93	146	52	57	44	156
113	70	56	91	117	152
130	131	150	138	162	84
82	86	144	123	112	107
58	156	90	113	159	151

Work out the five-number summary for these data and provide a graphical representation of the information.

20 Taking a sample of 32 vacuum cleaners, a distribution company recorded the weight (in kilograms) and price (in pounds (£)) of each product.
The following statistics have already been calculated:

	Weight	Price
Mean	4.3	120
Standard deviation	2.4	55.1

Using the coefficient of variation, decide whether the weights of the vacuum cleaners vary more or less than the prices.

21 The box plots below show the age distribution for males and females who submitted their application for a sales assistant vacancy at a clothing store based in a shopping centre.

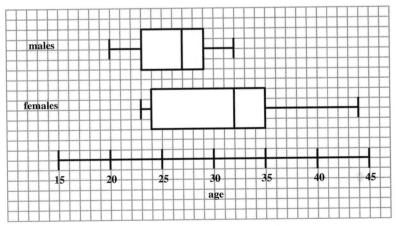

(a) Work out the range and interquartile range for each gender.
(b) Which gender has more variation in its data set? Support your answer with a suitable explanation.

22 (a) Explain why using the standard deviation as a measure of dispersion may be preferable to calculating the interquartile range.

(b) State one disadvantage of the standard deviation.

23 The table shows the unemployment total (in millions) in the UK as recorded every January between 2002 and 2012.

Year	Unemployment total (in millions)
2002	1.51
2003	1.52
2004	1.44
2005	1.45
2006	1.59
2007	1.71
2008	1.62
2009	2.12
2010	2.49
2011	2.47

Calculate the mean and standard deviation for these population data.

24 The number of hours spent reading by 25 teenagers during one week is shown in the table.

10	8	12	8	11
5	9	14	5	9
13	2	5	16	11
11	4	9	3	11
12	17	9	17	13

For these data:

(a) Write down the five-number summary.

(b) Draw a box plot with a vertical axis.

25 Use the words provided to fill in the blank spaces in the following statements about measures of dispersion.

difference	mean	percentage	more

(a) When comparing two sets of data, a larger range is associated with the data set which shows _____ variation.

(b) The _____ between the upper and lower quartiles provides us with a measure of dispersion known as the interquartile range.

(c) The variance provides an indication of variability by considering the distance of each data value from the _____ of the data set.

(d) The coefficient of variation expresses the standard deviation as a _____ of the mean.

26 The transfer fees (in millions of pounds (£)) paid for a sample of 20 football players by English football clubs during summer 2013 are shown in the table below.

30	18	2	17
6.5	9	7	2
15.5	12	2	6
35	2.5	5.4	12
7	2.6	12	12.5

(a) Identify the outliers in this data set.

(b) Draw a modified box plot to display the distribution of transfer fees.

(c) Should the lower and upper limit be shown on the box plot? Explain your response.

27 Explain why the variance for a set of data can never be negative.

28 Calculate the variance for this frequency distribution, which shows the tuition fees for undergraduate home students at a sample of 66 UK institutions.

Tuition fee £000s	Frequency
6	4
6.5	2
7	5
7.5	4
8	5
8.5	12
9	34

29 A researcher calculates the standard deviation for two sets of data. For data set A she finds a standard deviation of 6.398 centimetres, and for data set B she finds a standard deviation of 8.971 litres. She concludes that the values in data set B show more variability than those in data set A because it has a larger standard deviation. Is this conclusion appropriate? Give an explanation with your answer.

30 Decide whether the following statements are TRUE or FALSE. Explain your response for any FALSE statements.
(a) The quartiles divide a set of data into three equal parts.
(b) The second quartile, Q_2, is the median.
(c) Q_1, also known as the first quartile, is the value which separates the smallest 25% of the values from the remaining data set.
(d) The upper quartile is the mean of the set of data values that are greater than the median of the entire data set.

31 In a survey, people living in Manchester were asked to calculate the distance (to the nearest 10 km) between their current residence and the place of their birth. The data are shown in the table below:

280	110	60	280	300	10	50
10	90	10	20	140	40	80
100	30	140	120	50	70	160
130	20	80	20	10	10	10

Find the lower and upper quartiles for this data set.

32 For a sample of 25 employees, the data in the following table shows the number of days absent from work for health reasons in a year.

12	29	16	18	17
25	20	2	24	21
18	12	28	10	22
21	24	10	17	10
7	21	15	45	5

Which of these statements is true? Explain how you reached your conclusion.
(a) There are no outliers.
(b) 45 is the only outlier.
(c) 29 and 45 are both outliers.

33   The television viewing figures for the programmes of two rival channels are represented using the box plots shown below.

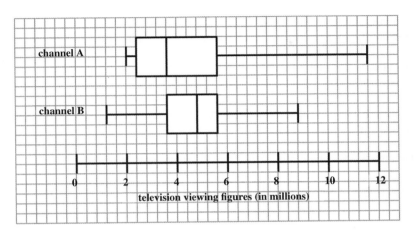

Use the diagram to complete the statements below, inserting 'larger' or 'smaller' in the blank spaces.

The median for channel A is _____ than the median for channel B.

Channel B has the _____ minimum value.

The range for channel A is _____ than the range for channel B.

Channel A has the _____ maximum value.

34   The box plots below represent the number of customers served per hour in three different departments within a store. The data were collected in a sample of 30 hours selected on different days during April and May.

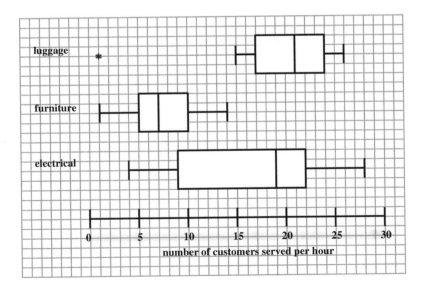

Use this information to answer the following questions. In each case, explain which aspect of the diagram helped you to reach your conclusion.

(a) Which department has the largest interquartile range?
(b) Is the median of the furniture department larger or smaller than the median of the luggage department?
(c) Which departments do not have outliers in their data sets?
(d) Does the luggage department have the largest number of customers per hour as one of its data values?
(e) What is the range of the number of customers served per hour in the electrical department?

35 A data set has a mean of 59.217 metres. What are the units of measurement for the variance and standard deviation of the data set?

36 The annual percentage rate (APR) for 20 credit cards is recorded below.

18.9	18.9	17.9	16.9	25.0	18.9	18.9	17.9	16.9	25.0
18.9	18.9	17.9	16.9	25.0	29.7	59.8	22.4	17.9	25.0

(a) Calculate the interquartile range.
(b) The data value 59.8% has been incorrectly recorded. The actual APR for this credit card is 29.8%. Recalculate the interquartile range using the corrected value.
(c) Based on the answers to parts (a) and (b), state an important advantage of using the interquartile range as a measure of variation.

37 Two hospitals recorded the length of time that a sample of 105 patients waited for the start of their appointment in an outpatient clinic.

Waiting time in minutes	Number of patients	
	Hospital 1	Hospital 2
0–9	2	19
10–19	9	16
20–29	14	15
30–39	27	18
40–49	30	12
50–59	15	14
60–69	8	11

(a) Estimate the variance for each distribution.
(b) Compare the variation in waiting time at the hospitals.

38 The variance for the annual salary (recorded in thousands of pounds (£)) for all of the water treatment engineers employed by a building services company is found to be

23.806. Using the correct notation, calculate the standard deviation for the recorded salaries. Explain the reason for your choice of notation.

39 The table below shows the price (to the nearest pound (£)) of a return flight with 12 different airlines from London to New York on a specific day in February.

513	428	345	998	503	431	622	476	520	749	857	564

For these data, $Q_1 = 453.50$, $Q_2 = 516.50$, and $Q_3 = 685.5$. Interpret these quartiles.

40 The length of each Underground train line in London is shown below:

Underground train line	Length in miles
Bakerloo Line	14.5
Central Line	46
Circle Line	17
Hammersmith & City Line	16
District Line	40
Jubilee Line	22.5
Metropolitan Line	41.5
Northern Line	36
Piccadilly Line	44.3
Victoria Line	13.3
Waterloo and City Line	1.5

(a) Do these data values represent a population or a sample? Explain your response.
(b) Calculate the mean and standard deviation for the line length. Use the conceptual formula for the standard deviation.
(c) What are the units of measurement for the standard deviation?

Solutions to Practice Exercises

1 The minimum value is 35; the maximum value is 65.
$n = 8$, so the median is half the sum of 4th and 5th observations.
The 4th observation is 42 and the 5th observation is 48, so the median is 45.
Q_1 is half the sum of the 2nd and 3rd observations $= \frac{1}{2}(38 + 40) = 39$.
Q_3 is half the sum of the 6th and 7th observations $= \frac{1}{2}(52 + 57) = 54.5$.
The five-number summary is:

minimum	Q_1	median	Q_3	maximum
35	39	45	54.5	65

2 (a) We should use $(\sum f) - 1$ in the denominator for the formula because the data set represents a sample of tourists rather than a population.
   (b) Using the computational formula:

$$s^2 = \frac{\sum fx^2 - \frac{(\sum fx)^2}{\sum f}}{(\sum f) - 1} = \frac{485575 - \frac{142205625}{340}}{340 - 1} = 198.593$$

3 The range is largest value – smallest value $= 84 - 32 = 52$ minutes.

4 Outliers should be identified using a rule-based technique, which is preferable to relying on subjective judgement. A value in the data set is classified as an outlier if it is positioned less than 1.5 times the interquartile range below the first quartile or more than 1.5 times the interquartile range above the third quartile.

5 Option (c). The calculations for the variance and coefficient of variation use all of the values in a data set.

6 (a) student 1: $\sum x = 280$, $N = 5$; population mean is 56
   student 2: $\sum x = 280$, $N = 5$; population mean is 56
   The mean mark for each student is the same.
   (b) student 1
   population standard deviation

$$\sigma = \sqrt{\frac{\sum x^2 - \frac{(\sum x)^2}{N}}{N}} = \sqrt{\frac{15754 - \frac{280^2}{5}}{2}} = \sqrt{\frac{74}{5}} = \sqrt{14.8} = 3.847$$

   student 2
   population standard deviation

$$\sigma = \sqrt{\frac{\sum x^2 - \frac{(\sum x)^2}{N}}{N}} = \sqrt{\frac{18406 - \frac{280^2}{5}}{5}} = \sqrt{\frac{2726}{5}} = \sqrt{545.2} = 2.350$$

The standard deviation calculations show that the marks for student 2 are more spread out from the mean whereas the marks for student 1 are close to the mean.

(c) When comparing two data sets, it is important comment on variation because a single representative value may give the impression that the data sets contain similar values; whereas a measure of dispersion will confirm which contains more varied values.

7   sample mean

$$\bar{x} = \frac{\sum x}{n} = \frac{179}{16} = 11.1875$$

sample standard deviation

$$s = \sqrt{\frac{\sum x^2 - \frac{(\sum x)^2}{n}}{n-1}} = \sqrt{\frac{2341 - \frac{179^2}{16}}{15}} = \sqrt{\frac{338.4375}{15}} = \sqrt{22.5625} = 4.75$$

The coefficient of variation for the number of cancelled appointments is $4.75/11.1875 \times 100 = 42.46\%$.

8   Disadvantage: the range only uses two values from the data set for its calculation. Disadvantage: the range is affected by extreme values because these are used in the calculation.
Advantage: the range is easy to calculate and interpret.

9   (a) TRUE
   (b) FALSE
      The interquartile range is defined as the range of the central 50% of the values in a data set so the extreme values in a data set are not involved in the calculations.
   (c) TRUE

10   (a) using the computational formula:

$$\sigma^2 = \frac{\sum x^2 - \frac{(\sum x)^2}{N}}{N} = \frac{65974 - \frac{1498176}{24}}{24} = 147.917$$

   (b) using the conceptual formula:

$$\mu = \frac{\sum x}{N} = \frac{1224}{24} = 51$$

$$\sigma^2 = \frac{\sum (x - \mu)^2}{N} = \frac{3550}{24} = 147.917$$

   (c) The results from parts (a) and (b) are the same.

11   (a) The interquartile range is $Q_3 - Q_1 = 828 - 512.5 = 315.5$ pages.
   (b) lower limit $= Q_1 - 1.5 \times IQR = 512.5 - (1.5 \times 315.5) = 512.5 - 473.25 = 39.25$
      upper limit $= Q_3 + 1.5 \times IQR = 828 + (1.5 \times 315.5) = 828 + 473.25 = 1301.25$
   (c) There are no outliers in the data set because the minimum value, 347, is larger than the lower limit of 39.25, and the maximum value, 1261, is smaller than the upper limit of 1301.25.

12 Option (c). Minimum, lower quartile, median, upper quartile, maximum are the components provided in a five-number summary.

13 The interquartile range is $Q_3 - Q_1 = 47.5 - 8.5 = 39$ mg.

14

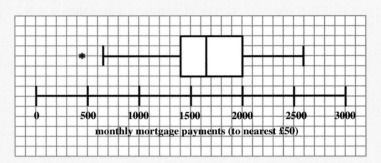

monthly mortgage payments (to nearest £50)

15

$$\mu = \frac{\sum x}{N} = \frac{382}{26} = 14.692$$

$$\sigma^2 = \frac{\sum fx^2 - \frac{(\sum fx)^2}{\sum f}}{\sum f} = \frac{7024 - \frac{145924}{26}}{26} = \frac{1411.538}{26} = 54.290$$

16 When comparing two sets of data, a larger coefficient of variation is associated with the data set that shows more variation from the mean, so the time spent in the pools varied more than the distance travelled to the venue because its coefficient of variation is larger.

17 (a) Yes, the variance will be affected by this change because the calculation uses all of the data values and involves squaring their differences from the mean; therefore it is strongly influenced by extreme values.
  (b) using the computational formula:

$$s^2 = \frac{\sum x^2 - \frac{(\sum x)^2}{n}}{n - 1} = \frac{82320.09 - \frac{552792.3}{10}}{10 - 1} = 3004.54$$

This confirms our response to part (a) because the sample variance has increased from 725.652 to 3004.54.

18 The range is largest value – smallest value $= 51 - 19 = 32$ employees.

19 The minimum value is 32; the maximum value is 156.
  $n = 36$, so the median is half the sum of 18th and 19th observations.
  The 18th observation is 108 and the 19th observation is 112, so the median is 110.
  Q_1 is half the sum of the 9th and 10th observations $= \frac{1}{2}(73 + 75) = 74$.
  Q_3 is half the sum of the 27th and 28th observations $= \frac{1}{2}(144 + 144) = 144$.
  The five-number summary is:

minimum	Q_1	median	Q_3	maximum
32	74	110	144	156

The resulting box plot is:

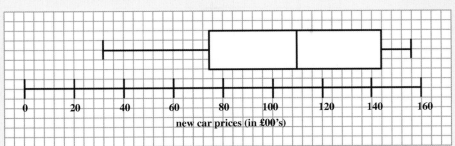

new car prices (in £00's)

20 The coefficient of variation for weight is $2.4/4.3 \times 100 = 55.81\%$.
The coefficient of variation for price is $55.1/120 \times 100 = 45.92\%$.
The weights of the vacuum cleaners vary more than the prices for this data set.

21 (a) males: range $= 32-20 = 12$; interquartile range $= 29-23 = 6$
        females: range $= 44-23 = 21$; interquartile range $= 35-24 = 11$
     (b) Female applicants have more variation in their ages than male applicants because
          the range and interquartile range is larger when compared to males.

22 (a) The standard deviation may be preferred as a measure of dispersion because it
          uses all of the values in the data set, whereas the interquartile range does not.
     (b) A disadvantage of the standard deviation it is influenced by extreme values that
          occur in the data set.

23 population mean

$$\mu = \frac{\sum x}{N} = \frac{17.92}{10} = 1.792$$

population standard deviation

$$\sigma = \sqrt{\frac{\sum x^2 - \frac{(\sum x)^2}{N}}{N}} = \sqrt{\frac{33.639 - \frac{321.126}{10}}{10}} = \sqrt{\frac{3.3639}{10}} = 0.391$$

24 (a) The minimum value is 2; the maximum value is 17.
        $n = 25$, so the median is the 13th observation which is 10.
        Q_1 is half the sum of the 6th and 7th observations $= \frac{1}{2}(5 + 8) = 6.5$.
        Q_3 is half the sum of the 19th and 20th observations $= \frac{1}{2}(12 + 13) = 12.5$.
        The five-number summary is:

minimum	Q_1	median	Q_3	maximum
2	6.5	10	12.5	17

(b)

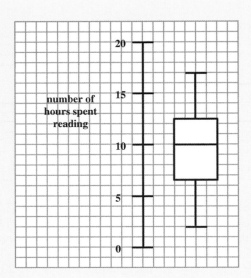

25   (a) more
     (b) difference
     (c) mean
     (d) percentage

26   (a) $n = 20$, so the median is half the sum of 10th and 11th observations.
         The 10th observation is 7 and the 11th observation is 9, so the median is 8.
         Q_1 is half the sum of the 5th and 6th observations $= \frac{1}{2}(2.6 + 5.4) = 4$.
         Q_3 is half the sum of the 15th and 16th observations $= \frac{1}{2}(12.5 + 15.5) = 14$.
         The interquartile range is $Q_3 - Q_1 = 14 - 4 = 10$.

    $$\text{lower limit} = Q_1 - 1.5 \times \text{IQR} = 4 - (1.5 \times 10) = 4 - 15 = -11$$
    $$\text{upper limit} = Q_3 + 1.5 \times \text{IQR} = 14 + (1.5 \times 10) = 14 + 15 = 29$$

     The outliers in the data set are the data values 30 and 35.
     (b) modified box plot

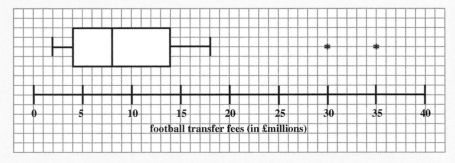

     (c) No, the limits should not be shown on the box plot because they are only used to
         help us identify any outliers in the data set.

27   Considering the conceptual formula:
     • the value of the numerator is always positive because it is the total of the squared
       deviations of the individual values from the mean, and squared values are always
       positive;

- the value of the denominator is N or $n-1$ depending on whether the data set represents a population or a sample, but both of these values are always positive.

28 sample variance

$$s^2 = \frac{\sum fx^2 - \frac{(\sum fx)^2}{\sum f}}{(\sum f) - 1} = \frac{4639.5 - \frac{302500}{66}}{66 - 1} = 0.864$$

29 The researcher's conclusion is not appropriate because we cannot use the standard deviation for comparison if the data sets have different units of measurement; standard deviation is a measure of absolute variability and therefore its magnitude is affected by the size of the data values.

30 (a) FALSE
The values in a data set are divided into four equal parts by the three quartiles.
   (b) TRUE
   (c) TRUE
   (d) FALSE
The upper quartile is the median of the set of data values that are greater than the median of the entire data set.

31 Q_1 is half the sum of 7th and 8th observations $= \frac{1}{2}(20 + 20) = 20$.
Q_3 is half the sum of 21st and 22nd observations $= \frac{1}{2}(120 + 130) = 125$.

32 Q_1 is half the sum of 6th and 7th observations $= \frac{1}{2}(10 + 12) = 11$.
Q_3 is half the sum of 19th and 20th observations $= \frac{1}{2}(22 + 24) = 23$.
The interquartile range is $Q_3 - Q_1 = 23 - 11 = 12$ days.

$$\text{lower limit} = Q_1 - 1.5 \times \text{IQR} = 11 - (1.5 \times 12) = 11 - 18 = -7$$
$$\text{upper limit} = Q_3 + 1.5 \times \text{IQR} = 23 + (1.5 \times 12) = 23 + 18 = 41$$

Option (b) is true: 45 is the only outlier.
There are no data values smaller than the lower limit of –7, and only the maximum value 45 is larger than the upper limit of 41.

33 (a) smaller
   (b) smaller
   (c) larger
   (d) larger

34 (a) The electrical department has the largest interquartile range; this can be concluded by comparing the length of each box, that is, the distance between the left-hand vertical side and the right-hand side.
   (b) Using the position on the scale of the vertical line drawn inside each box, it can be seen that the median of the furniture department is smaller than the median of the luggage department.
   (c) The furniture and electrical departments do not have outliers in their data sets because there are no asterisks shown on their box plots.
   (d) The luggage department does not have the largest number of customers per hour as one of its data values; using the lines which extend from the right-hand side of each box, we can see that its largest data value is 26 customers, whereas the electrical department has a maximum of 28 customers.

(e) The range for the electrical department is $28 - 4 = 24$ customers; the largest and smallest data values are obtained using the position of the ends of the lines extending from the sides of the box.

35 The units of measurement would be metres squared for the variance, and metres for the standard deviation.

36 (a) Q_1 is half the sum of the 5th and 6th observations $= \frac{1}{2}(17.9 + 17.9) = 17.9$.
Q_3 is half the sum of the 15th and 16th observations $= \frac{1}{2}(25 + 25) = 25$.
IQR is $Q_3 - Q_1 = 25 - 17.9 = 7.1\%$.

(b) Q_1 is half the sum of the 5th and 6th observations $= \frac{1}{2}(17.9 + 17.9) = 17.9$.
Q_3 is half the sum of the 15th and 16th observations $= \frac{1}{2}(25 + 25) = 25$.
IQR is $Q_3 - Q_1 = 25 - 17.9 = 7.1\%$.

(c) The IQR remains unchanged, showing that this measure of variation is not affected by extreme values in the data set.

37 (a) Using the computational formula for hospital 1:

$$s^2 = \frac{\sum fx^2 - \frac{\left(\sum fx\right)^2}{\sum f}}{\left(\sum f\right) - 1} = \frac{179716.3 - \frac{16666806}{105}}{105 - 1} = 201.777$$

Using the computational formula for hospital 2:

$$s^2 = \frac{\sum fx^2 - \frac{\left(\sum fx\right)^2}{\sum f}}{\left(\sum f\right) - 1} = \frac{145286.3 - \frac{10972656}{105}}{105 - 1} = 392.162$$

(b) The variation in waiting time at hospital 2 is larger than at hospital 1 because the estimate of the variance is a larger value.

38
$$\sigma = \sqrt{\sigma^2} = \sqrt{23.806} = 4.879$$

This is a population standard deviation because the data set represents all of the water treatment engineers employed by the building services company; therefore we use σ rather than s.

39 Q_1: approximately 25% of the airline tickets cost less than £453.50.
Q_2: approximately 50% of the ticket prices are less than £516.50 and approximately 50% are more than £516.50.
Q_3: approximately 75% of the airline tickets cost less than £685.50.

40 (a) The data values represent a population because all of the Underground train lines are listed in the table.

(b) $\sum x = 292.6$, $N = 11$; population mean is 26.6 population standard deviation

$$\sigma = \sqrt{\frac{\sum (x - \mu)^2}{N}} = \sqrt{\frac{2354.22}{11}} = \sqrt{214.02} = 14.629$$

(c) The standard deviation is measured using the same units as the original data set, so the units would be miles.

Correlation

This chapter explains how to:

- use scatter diagrams to describe a linear relationship
- calculate and interpret
  - correlation coefficient
  - rank correlation coefficient
- understand the limitations of correlation
- describe the difference between correlation and causation

KEY TERMS

bivariate data	linear relationship	positive correlation
cause-and-effect	lurking variable	qualitative variable
relationship	negative correlation	quantitative variable
correlation coefficient		

Introduction

In statistics, we are often interested in analysing potential relationships in bivariate data, that is, data in which two variables have been measured or observed for each individual in our sample. This relationship can be described using graphical methods such as a scatter diagram, but a numerical technique is also required so that we can quantify the association.

Correlation allows us to investigate the extent to which two numerical variables are related to each other. The correlation coefficient is a measure of the strength and direction of their linear relationship, indicating positive correlation or negative correlation between the variables. Rank correlation is used as an alternative method when both of the variables are ranked.

In this chapter, we will begin by exploring how scatter diagrams can be used to describe the linear relationship between two variables, and then move on to learning how to calculate and interpret the correlation coefficient and rank correlation. Finally, we will highlight some important limitations of correlation.

Scatter Diagrams

A scatter diagram provides us with a visual representation of the relationship between two quantitative variables.

Although there are many different ways in which two variables can be related, here we are primarily interested in looking for evidence of a linear association; in this case, the arrangement of x-values and y-values plotted on the scatter diagram would resemble a straight line.

The interpretation of a scatter diagram for two variables that have a linear association involves observing overall patterns in the data that show the direction and the strength of their relationship. The direction is indicated by a positive or negative slope, and the strength depends on how closely the data points are scattered about a straight line.

This scatter diagram indicates that there is a positive linear relationship between the plotted x-values and the y-values.

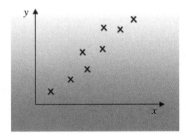

A positive linear relationship means that as the x-values increase, the y-values increase as well. The data points resemble a line with a positive slope from the lower left of the diagram to the upper right.

The data points in this scatter diagram have a negative linear relationship. The overall pattern shows a negative slope from the upper left of the diagram to the lower right.

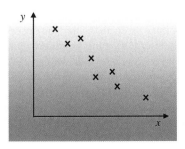

A negative linear relationship means that the data values 'move' in opposite directions. As the x-values increase, the y-values decrease; whereas as the x-values decrease, the y-values increase.

The scatter diagrams below show two different levels of strength in the positive linear relationship between the x-values and y-values.

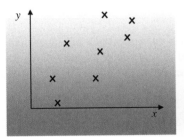 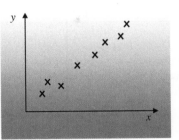

This linear relationship is weak because the data points are widely scattered about a straight line.

The data points lie close to a straight line, indicating a strong linear relationship between the variables.

Although a scatter diagram is a very effective way of representing bivariate data visually, sometimes it can be difficult to determine the strength of the relationship between the variables.

The diagrams below show exactly the same set of x-values with their corresponding y-values, but the scale has been changed on both axes. The overall linear pattern of the plotted data points appears to show a stronger relationship in the first plot because of the amount of white space on the diagram.

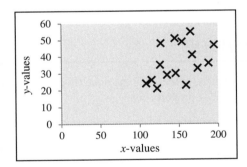 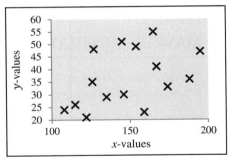

In general, observing the pattern of data values in a scatter diagram is not a reliable way of measuring the strength of their association. It is therefore necessary to use a calculation-based method to produce a numerical value that adds to the information obtained by visually inspecting the diagram.

Correlation Coefficient

For sample data, the correlation coefficient, denoted by r, provides us with a numerical measure of the strength and direction of the linear relationship between two quantitative variables. It is also known as the Pearson product-moment correlation coefficient, named after Karl Pearson (1857–1936), and is often abbreviated to PMCC.

If we have a set of n pairs of data values, the correlation coefficient is calculated using

$$r = \frac{\sum x_i y_i - \dfrac{\sum x_i \sum y_i}{n}}{\sqrt{\left(\sum x_i^2 - \dfrac{\left(\sum x_i\right)^2}{n}\right)\left(\sum y_i^2 - \dfrac{\left(\sum y_i\right)^2}{n}\right)}}$$

where (x_1, y_1) is the first pair of values, (x_2, y_2) is the second pair of values, and (x_n, y_n) is the final pair in the data set. It is sensible to round the calculated correlation coefficient to three decimal places. The formula can also be expressed as

$$r = \frac{S_{xy}}{\sqrt{S_{xx}S_{yy}}}$$

where

$$S_{xy} = \sum x_i y_i - \frac{\sum x_i \sum y_i}{n}$$

$$S_{xx} = \sum x_i^2 - \frac{\left(\sum x_i\right)^2}{n}$$

$$S_{yy} = \sum y_i^2 - \frac{\left(\sum y_i\right)^2}{n}$$

EXAMPLE – CORRELATION COEFFICIENT

The table below shows the length of the kitchen (in feet) and the price (in thousands of pounds) of ten houses advertised for sale on a property website.

Kitchen length (feet) x	13	13	17	17	10	12	16	11	14	11
Price (£000s) y	375	650	525	500	390	320	275	205	300	425

Kitchen length x	Price y	x^2	y^2	xy
13	375	169	140625	4875
13	650	169	422500	8450
17	525	289	275625	8925
17	500	289	250000	8500
10	390	100	152100	3900
12	320	144	102400	3840

(*Continued*)

Kitchen length x	Price y	x^2	y^2	xy
16	275	256	75625	4400
11	205	121	42025	2255
14	300	196	90000	4200
11	425	121	180625	4675
$\sum x = 134$	$\sum y = 3965$	$\sum x^2 = 1854$	$\sum y^2 = 1731525$	$\sum xy = 54020$

The correlation coefficient for this data is

$$r = \frac{54020 - \dfrac{134 \times 3965}{10}}{\sqrt{\left(1854 - \dfrac{134^2}{10}\right)\left(1731525 - \dfrac{3965^2}{10}\right)}} = \frac{889}{\sqrt{58.4 \times 159402.5}} = 0.291$$

INTERPRETATION

After the correlation coefficient has been calculated for bivariate sample data, it is important that this numerical value is correctly interpreted so that we can draw conclusions about the linear relationship between the two variables.

Direction

The sign of r tells us about the direction of the linear relationship.

If r is a positive value then this shows that the two variables are positively correlated, that is, they have a positive linear relationship. Here the scatter diagram would show a positive slope in the pattern of plotted data points: as the x-values increase, the y-values increase as well.

A negative value for r indicates that the variables have a negative linear relationship. In this case, there would be a negative slope in the pattern of plotted data points and we would say that the variables are negatively correlated. As the x-values increase, the y-values decrease; whereas as the x-values decrease, the y-values increase.

The following table summarises the interpretation for the sign of r.

Sign of r	Correlation	Scatter diagram	Relationship
positive	positively correlated	positive slope	As the x-values increase, the y-values increase as well; and as the x-values decrease, the y-values decrease
negative	negatively correlated	negative slope	As the x-values increase, the y-values decrease; whereas as the x-values decrease, the y-values increase

Strength

The correlation coefficient is always a number between -1 and 1 inclusive. The strength of the linear relationship is measured by the magnitude of this value.

If r is close to zero, we would describe the linear relationship as very weak. The strength of the association between the two variables increases as r moves away from zero, approaching either -1 or 1.

A correlation coefficient of exactly zero indicates that there is no linear relationship at all. A value of r calculated to be exactly -1 or 1 shows perfect correlation; in this case, the data points plotted on the scatter diagram would lie exactly on a straight line. Sample data values observed in a real-world situation rarely result in a correlation coefficient of exactly zero, -1 or 1.

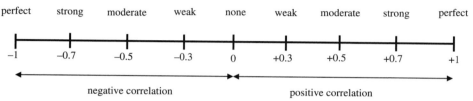

The scatter diagrams in Figure 7.1 provide a visual representation of different strengths of the linear relationship between two variables. Each diagram has a corresponding value of r.

EXAMPLE – INTERPRETING THE CORRELATION COEFFICIENT

In the previous example involving the length of the kitchen (in feet) and the price (in thousands of pounds) of ten houses advertised for sale on a property website, we calculated the value of the correlation coefficient as 0.291. From this value, we can conclude:

- direction: 0.291 is a positive number, and therefore we know that the two variables are positively correlated;
- strength: 0.291 indicates that the two variables have a weak linear relationship.

Overall, there is only a weak association between the variables; as the length of the kitchen increases, the house price also increases, and as the kitchen length decreases, the house price also decreases.

UNITS

The correlation coefficient does not have any units of measurement – its value is independent of the scale of each variable. Changing the units of one or both of the variables will not have any effect on the sign or magnitude of the value of r.

Returning to the example involving the length of kitchens and house prices, we could change the units of measurement of kitchen length from feet to metres as follows:

Kitchen length (metres) x	4.0	4.0	5.2	5.2	3.1	3.7	4.9	3.4	4.3	3.4
Price (£000s) y	375	650	525	500	390	320	275	205	300	425

For the new data, we can calculate:

$$S_{xy} = 16602.5 - \frac{41.2 \times 3965}{10} = 266.700$$

$$S_{xx} = 175 - \frac{41.2^2}{10} = 5.256$$

$$S_{yy} = 1731525 - \frac{3965^2}{10} = 159402.500$$

The correlation coefficient has the same result as before:

$$r = \frac{S_{xy}}{\sqrt{S_{xx}S_{yy}}} = \frac{266.700}{\sqrt{5.256 \times 159402.5}} = 0.291$$

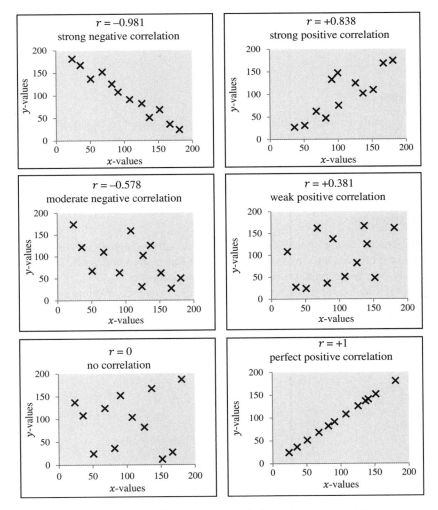

FIGURE 7.1   Different strengths of linear relationship between two variables

LIMITATIONS

When we are interpreting the value of the correlation coefficient, there are several limitations that should be considered before final conclusions are made.

Extreme Values

If there is an observation in your data set that does not follow the same general pattern as the rest of the values, then correlation should be used with caution – it is not resistant to extreme values and therefore may be adversely affected by an unusual observation. It is a good idea to check your scatter diagram for extreme values before continuing with the calculations.

Suppose we had made a mistake in the data taken from the property website about the length of kitchens and sale prices, recording the length of the kitchen as 130 feet instead of 13 feet for the house priced at £650,000. The resulting correlation coefficient would increase from 0.291 using the correct data values to 0.690 incorporating the error. Our interpretation about the linear relationship between kitchen length and sale price would change from finding weak correlation to concluding that there is evidence of a strong association.

Variable Type

Correlation can only be used for quantitative variables; it cannot be calculated if either of the variables are qualitative. For example, it is not possible to measure the linear relationship between the sale price of a house and the name of the town in which it is located because town name is a **qualitative variable** and therefore cannot be described numerically.

Linear Relationship

The correlation coefficient should only be used if a scatter diagram of your bivariate data indicates that the plotted data values follow a straight-line pattern. It describes the strength and direction only of a linear relationship between the variables.

The data represented on this scatter diagram would have a correlation coefficient near to zero, indicating very little evidence of a linear relationship between the two variables. However, as we can see from the diagram, the x-values and corresponding y-values are strongly related but in a pattern which is not linear.

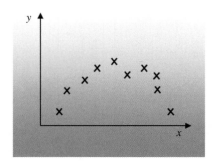

It is therefore essential that whenever you calculate the correlation coefficient for some sample data, you also provide a visual representation of the data values in a scatter diagram so that you can report and intepret your results fully.

Rank Correlation Coefficient

We can investigate the linear relationship between two sets of ranked data using the rank correlation coefficient. This value is denoted as r_s and is sometimes known as Spearman's rank correlation coefficient because it was developed by Charles Spearman (1863–1945). The formula used for calculation is

$$r_s = 1 - \frac{6 \sum d_i^2}{n(n^2 - 1)}$$

where n is the number of pairs of data values, and d_i represents the difference in ranks for each pair.

The direction and strength of the linear relationship between the ranks can be interpreted from the value of r_s by applying the same analysis that was used for the correlation coefficient. So, if the rank correlation coefficient is a positive value, then the ranks are positively correlated. In this case, when the ranking of one variable is high, so is that of the other variable. For negative correlation, we would have higher rankings in one variable measured against lower rankings in the other variable and vice versa; the sign of r_s would be negative. Our scale for interpreting the strength of the correlation would remain the same, although now we are measuring the strength of the linear relationship between the rankings rather than the actual data values.

EXAMPLE – RANK CORRELATION COEFFICIENT

Two house buyers were asked to rank the ten houses advertised for sale on a property website. Their order of preference is recorded below:

House code	A	B	C	D	E	F	G	H	I	J
House buyer 1	2	1	3	4	5	10	8	7	9	6
House buyer 2	3	1	4	2	8	9	6	5	10	7

House code	House buyer 1	House buyer 2	d	d^2
A	2	3	−1	1
B	1	1	0	0
C	3	4	−1	1
D	4	2	2	4
E	5	8	−3	9

(*Continued*)

House code	House buyer 1	House buyer 2	d	d^2
F	10	9	1	1
G	8	6	2	4
H	7	5	2	4
I	9	10	−1	1
J	6	7	−1	1
				$\sum d^2 = 26$

The rank correlation coefficient for this data is

$$r_s = 1 - \frac{6 \times 26}{10(100 - 1)} = 0.842$$

In interpreting the value of r_s we can see that there is a strong linear relationship between the rankings of the two house buyers and that they are in agreement about which houses they preferred and which ones they liked least.

Cause and Effect

Correlation provides us with information about the strength and direction of a linear relationship, but it is not able to explain why or how that relationship exists.

Although our calculations may lead us to conclude that two variables are correlated, this does not indicate that there is a **cause-and-effect relationship**, that is, that a change in one variable *causes* a change in the other variable. We can use our knowledge of the two variables to consider the likelihood of a causal association, but this analysis cannot be confirmed by the correlation coefficient.

Sometimes there might be an obvious causal association between the variables being observed. For example, suppose we use the property website as before to select ten houses in the same geographical area, all with gas-powered central heating. We could measure total square footage to provide a numerical value for the size of each house and then measure the amount of gas consumption for the houses. Common sense tells us that increasing total square footage will cause an increase in gas consumption because more gas is required to heat a larger space to a fixed temperature.

However, often we will find that there is an additional factor which influences the observed x-values and y-values. Rather than the existence of a cause-and-effect relationship between our two variables, a change in this third variable, sometimes called a **lurking variable**, causes a change in the sample data. For example, suppose that the sale price of the properties in our sample is positively correlated with the number of television sets owned by the people buying those houses. We might incorrectly conclude that an increase in sale price causes a rise in the number of television sets owned. In this case, the increase in both of the observed variables is likely to be caused by an increase in a third factor, annual income.

HINTS AND TIPS

DIFFERENCE BETWEEN $\sum x^2$ AND $\left(\sum x\right)^2$

Make sure that you understand the difference between $\sum x^2$ and $\left(\sum x\right)^2$ in preparation for calculating S_{xx} (and similarly for S_{yy}):

- $\sum x^2$ means 'square each x-value and then add them all together';
- $\left(\sum x\right)^2$ means 'add together all of the x-values and then square the result'.

So, for the x-values 3, 7, 12, 19, and 26:

$$\sum x^2 = 3^2 + 7^2 + 12^2 + 19^2 + 26^2 = 1239$$

$$\left(\sum x\right)^2 = (3 + 7 + 12 + 19 + 26)^2 = 67^2 = 4489$$

You can see that the two expressions give very different results.

VALUES GREATER THAN 1 AND LESS THAN −1

Remember that the numerical value for the correlation coefficient and the rank correlation coefficient must lie between −1 and 1 inclusive. If your calculations result in a number outside this range, then you must check each step until you find the mistake.

CAUSALITY

When you are interpreting your value of r or r_s it is important to recall that correlation is limited to describing the direction and strength of a linear relationship rather than any additional information about the two variables.

Returning to our original example about kitchen lengths and house prices, we cannot conclude that an increase in kitchen length causes an increase in sale price, because the measurement of correlation does not provide any information about why the relationship between the two variables exists. There may be a lurking variable, such as location, which affects both sets of data values.

Using Excel

CORRELATION COEFFICIENT

There is a built-in statistical function in Excel for calculating the correlation coefficient for data collected about two quantitative variables.

Function	Description	Syntax
CORREL	calculates the correlation coefficient between two sets of data (also known as arrays)	CORREL(array1,array2)

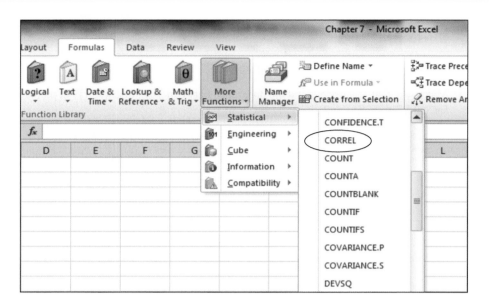

Returning to our earlier example about the length of the kitchen (in feet) and the price (in thousands of pounds) of ten houses advertised for sale on a property website:

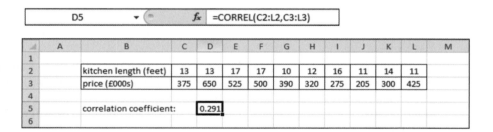

RANK CORRELATION COEFFICIENT

To use Excel for investigating the linear relationship between two sets of ranked data using the rank correlation coefficient, it is necessary to create a formula.

Consider our previous example in which two house buyers were asked to rank the ten houses advertised for sale on a property website.

| F14 | | | f_x | =1-(6*SUM(F3:F12))/(10*(100-1)) | | |

◢	A	B	C	D	E	F	G
1							
2		house code	house-buyer 1	house-buyer 2	d	d^2	
3		A	2	3	-1	1	
4		B	1	1	0	0	
5		C	3	4	-1	1	
6		D	4	2	2	4	
7		E	5	8	-3	9	
8		F	10	9	1	1	
9		G	8	6	2	4	
10		H	7	5	2	4	
11		I	9	10	-1	1	
12		J	6	7	-1	1	
13							
14		rank correlation coefficient:				0.842	
15							

Practice Exercises

1 Decide whether the following statements are TRUE or FALSE. Explain your response for any FALSE statements.
(a) The value of the correlation coefficient is always greater than zero.
(b) A correlation coefficient of exactly zero means that two variables have no relationship.
(c) If there is a negative linear relationship between two variables, this means that as the x-values increase, the y-values increase as well.
(d) A value of r close to 1 would indicate a strong positive linear association between two variables.
(e) The correlation coefficient is a numerical measure of the strength and direction of the linear relationship between two quantitative variables.

2 The number of employed males (in thousands) and the number of unemployed males (in thousands) were recorded each month for a geographical region in the UK over a ten-month period. The following information was then calculated:

$$\sum x = 2007 \quad \sum y = 16163, \quad \sum x^2 = 1854 \quad \sum y^2 = 1731525 \quad \sum xy = 54020$$

Work out the value of r for the number of employed and unemployed men in this region.

3 Which of the PMCC values 0.067, −0.742, 1, 0.988, 0.871, −0.255 indicates:
(a) perfect correlation?
(b) weak negative correlation?

4   The following table shows the number of peak morning arrivals and peak afternoon departures for rail passengers at six city-based train stations on a typical autumn weekday.

Peak morning arrivals (thousands)	6.4	5.4	11.0	7.9	4.2	3.9
Peak afternoon departures (thousands)	8.6	6.1	12.1	8.9	5.7	4.6

(a) Draw a scatter diagram showing the data values provided.
(b) Use your scatter diagram to work out the sign of the PMCC.
(c) Calculate the PMCC for this data set.

5   Using appropriate graphs, give a possible visual representation for each of the following:
(a) no correlation
(b) weak positive correlation
(c) strong negative correlation

6   For ten office buildings in London, the table below shows the height of the building above ground level and number of floors.

Building	Height in metres	Number of floors
Heron Tower	242	46
Beaufort House	63.0	14
Plantation Place	73.2	16
Bastion House	69.2	21
The Willis Building	125.6	26
City Point	125.0	35
Moor House	81.4	18
Dashwood House	73.4	19
The Broadgate Tower	164.0	35
Lloyds Building	84.0	12

(a) Use this data set to determine the value of r for the height of the buildings and the number of floors.
(b) If you changed the units of the building height to feet and re-calculated r, would you expect the new value to be the same as the result in part (a). Give a reason for your answer.
(c) Change the units of the building height to feet (rounding to the nearest whole number) and recalculate r. Comment on your result.

7   The table below shows the number of items bought and the total amount of money spent (to the nearest pound) during 11 consecutive shopping trips to a supermarket.

Number of items bought	40	87	18	9	61	91	80	65	7	4	77
Total spent (to nearest £)	49	109	37	10	76	117	89	71	10	3	91

(a) Calculate the value of r for this data set.

(b) Use your results in part (a) to describe the relationship between the variables.

8 At a busy petrol station, the average price of petrol per litre and the amount of petrol sold each month were recorded over a one-year period. The data are plotted in the following scatter diagram:

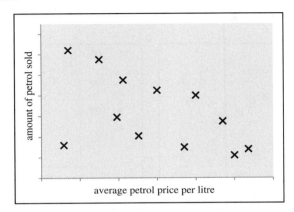

(a) What does the scatter diagram indicate about a possible linear relationship between these two variables?

(b) There would appear to be an unusual observation in the data set. If this observation is included in calculations, then the value of r is -0.536, whereas if it is excluded, then $r = -0.777$. Would you expect this change in the value of r? Give a reason for your answer.

9 New employees joining the London branch of an international organisation are sent on a numerical skills training course after working for one month. Their percentage score in an online test was recorded before and after the training course, as follows.

Employee	Score before training course	Score after training course
1	35	61
2	74	76
3	52	43
4	67	82
5	25	37
6	44	68
7	92	89
8	65	74
9	39	42
10	57	60

(a) Show the percentage scores recorded before and after the training course using a scatter diagram.
(b) Calculate the rank correlation coefficient.

10 Match each scatter diagram to its corresponding value of the correlation coefficient from the following list: 0.788, −0.962, 0.511, −0.174.

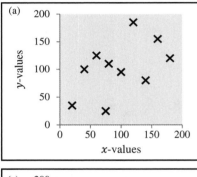

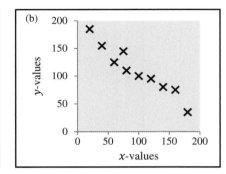

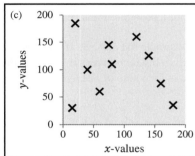

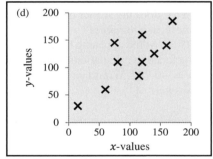

11 For each pair of variables listed below, decide whether they are likely to have positive, negative or no correlation.
(a) price of a dictionary
number of copies of the dictionary sold in a bookshop
(b) annual salary of a job advertised in the newspaper
number of applicants for the job
(c) number of adults in each household
number of cars owned by the household
(d) number of overseas visitors to the UK
number of home visits made by a doctor

12 Explain two limitations of the correlation coefficient.

13 For a research project investigating the relationship between intelligence and employment, ten females and ten males, all aged 30, were asked to take an IQ test and to state their current annual salary. The results are shown below:

Females		Males	
IQ test score	Annual salary (£000s)	IQ test score	Annual salary (£000s)
81	25	110	66
72	56	96	124
103	31	93	35
89	94	122	19
94	107	79	105
76	18	86	47
71	24	89	39
79	38	90	64
94	21	104	17
82	45	118	26

(a) Draw a multiple scatter diagram to show IQ test score and annual salary for females and also for males. Use two different colours when plotting the data sets to distinguish between males and females.
(b) Comment on any major differences in the pattern of plotted points for females when compared to males.
(c) Calculate the correlation coefficient for females and also for males. Compare your results to the differences found in part (b).

14 During his campaign, a politician believes that there is negative correlation between the length of his speech (in minutes) and the number of people who vote for him. He thinks that reducing his speech length to 5 minutes will cause a large increase in voters. Explain why he has misunderstood the interpretation of correlation.

15 The table below shows the life expectancy at birth (in years) and the carbon dioxide emissions per capita (in tonnes) for nine countries.

Life expectancy at birth (in years)	Carbon dioxide emissions per capita (in tonnes)
80.1	10.6
72.4	1.5
68.8	7
79.3	2.8

(*Continued*)

Life expectancy at birth (in years)	Carbon dioxide emissions per capita (in tonnes)
59.7	0.1
77	5
80	8.7
81.2	6.7
66.9	0.1

Calculate the correlation coefficient for these data and interpret its value in terms of the linear relationship between the variables.

16 How would you describe the correlation between two variables if $r = -0.892$? When the data values for one variable increase, what happens to the data values of the other variable?

17 The number of mortgage approvals and the average house price for a detached house in the UK were recorded each year for a decade. The data are plotted on the scatter diagram below.

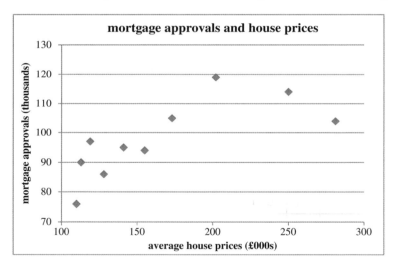

(a) Looking at the scatter diagram above, would you expect these variables to be positively or negatively correlated? Estimate the magnitude of the correlation coefficient.
(b) Given that $S_{xx} = 31995.6$, $S_{yy} = 1500$, $S_{xy} = 5117$, find the correlation coefficient. Compare the calculated value to your estimate made in part (a).

18 Answer YES or NO to each question and give an explanation for your response.
(a) Is the value of the PMCC affected if the units of measurement are changed for one of the data sets?
(b) If there is a strong positive relationship between two variables, does this mean that a change in one variable causes a change in the other variable?
(c) Can a value of r be calculated if the variables are qualitative?

19 A secondary school analysed the number of hours of absence from lessons and the examination scores for 25 pupils in the same class.

Absence hours	2	5	2	17	11	10	14	6	6	13
Examination score	87	91	67	42	52	64	23	84	75	41

Absence hours	7	7	7	8	15	19	9	10	3	10
Examination score	69	74	89	80	47	49	74	12	65	56

Absence hours	4	13	13	0	20
Examination score	59	46	68	79	23

Plot the data values for absence hours and examination scores on a scatter diagram. Does there appear to be a linear relationship between the variables?

20 If two variables have a correlation coefficient of 0.314, does this suggest that they might have a linear association? Explain their relationship in more detail.

21 The correlation coefficient for the length of a ferry journey (in hours) and the price of a ticket for a foot passenger (in pounds (£)) is 0.724. Can you conclude that an increase in journey time causes a corresponding increase in ticket price? Give a reason to support your answer.

22 If two variables have a correlation coefficient close to zero, what could this mean about their relationship? Draw two different scatter diagrams that could represent the data values.

23 Two customers were asked to give nine department stores a score (1 to 20) for customer service. Calculate and interpret the rank correlation coefficient for the data.

Store	A	B	C	D	E	F	G	H	I
Customer 1	15	6	19	7	12	2	16	10	5
Customer 2	13	4	19	9	10	3	12	14	8

24 Explain what is wrong with each of the following statements.
   (a) A three-year study revealed evidence of negative correlation between interest rates and the number of applications for a mortgage. The calculated value of r was -1.921, showing a very strong linear relationship.
   (b) An audit of company records indicated that the colour of a car was positively correlated with the monthly sales figures.
   (c) A correlation coefficient of 0.293 was calculated in a research project investigating the association between the number of years spent in education and annual salary (in euros). When the annual salary figures were converted to dollars, a much stronger correlation of 0.786 was reported.

25 A scatter diagram suggests that two variables have a strong negative linear relationship. Which of the following statements describes the overall pattern of the plotted points?
(a) a positive slope from the lower left of the diagram to the upper right
(b) a negative slope from the upper-left of the diagram to the lower right
(c) the points could be positioned with a negative or positive slope

26 The table below shows the sales and production of passenger cars in Italy over a six-year period.

	Year 1	Year 2	Year 3	Year 4	Year 5	Year 6
Cars produced (millions)	0.893	0.911	0.659	0.661	0.573	0.486
Cars sold (millions)	2.3	2.5	2.1	2.2	2.0	1.7

(a) Plot the data on a scatter diagram and work out the value of the PMCC.
(b) Use your results from part (a) to describe the type of relationship between the number of cars produced and sold in Italy over the six-year period.
(c) Can you conclude that an increase in production causes a corresponding increase in sales? Give a reason to support your response.

27 (a) Using the data in the table below, calculate the correlation coefficient for the average daily sunshine hours and the average rainfall (in millimetres) in New York during the year.

Month	Average daily sunshine hours	Average rainfall in mm
January	6	94
February	6	97
March	7	91
April	8	81
May	9	81
June	11	84
July	11	107
August	10	109
September	9	86
October	7	89
November	6	76
December	5	91

(b) Explain what your correlation coefficient means in terms of the relationship between average daily sunshine hours and average rainfall.

(c) A new set of data has been produced by converting the sunshine data to minutes.

Month	Average daily sunshine minutes	Average rainfall in mm
January	360	94
February	360	97
March	420	91
April	480	81
May	540	81
June	660	84
July	660	107
August	600	109
September	540	86
October	420	89
November	360	76
December	300	91

Recalculate the correlation coefficient. Did the unit conversion have an effect on the correlation coefficient?

28 This scatter diagram indicates that there is positive correlation between the number of solicitors' offices in a town and the number of crimes committed.

number of crimes

number of solicitors offices

(a) Does the diagram show that reducing the number of solicitors offices will reduce the number of crimes committed?

(b) Suggest a lurking variable that might affect both of these variables.

29 Suppose a new observation (5.9, 1.3) was added to the data set given in Exercise 4.
(a) Plot and label this observation on the existing scatter diagram.
(b) Recalculate the PMCC and comment on the effect of the inclusion of this observation in the data set.

30 Would it be appropriate to investigate the correlation between gender and the amount of money spent every year on clothes? Give a reason for your viewpoint.

31 At a leading supermarket, the weight and price of ten boxes of chocolates was recorded as follows:

Weight (grams)	350	400	380	70	165	360	250	407	165	214
Price (£s)	3	5	3	1	4	8	4	6	5	7

(a) Plot these data values on a scatter diagram and comment on the direction and strength of any straight-line patterns you observe.
(b) Calculate the PMCC and compare the result to the observations you made in part (a).

32 The scatter diagram below shows data collected about age and monthly expenditure during a national survey.

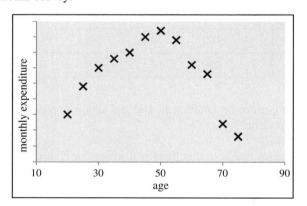

(a) From a visual inspection of the scatter diagram, do you think that the relationship between these two variables is weak or strong?
(b) Would calculating the correlation coefficient be a useful way of describing the relationship? Give a reason for your response.

33 The frequency of Internet use was investigated during the years 2006–2012. The resulting data set below shows:
• the number of people aged 16+ (in millions) who use the Internet every day;
• the number of people aged 16+ (in millions) who never use the Internet.

Year	Every day	Never
2006	16.2	16.3
2007	20.7	12.6

(*Continued*)

Year	Every day	Never
2008	23.0	11.4
2009	26.6	9.9
2010	29.2	8.9
2011	31.4	8.1
2012	33.2	7.6

(a) Would you expect these variables to have a positive or negative linear relationship?
(b) Calculate the correlation coefficient. Was your expectation for part (a) correct?

34 Describe the relationship between two quantitative variables which have a PMCC close to 1. Draw a scatter diagram that could represent this relationship.

35 Fill in the blank spaces in the following statements about correlation.
(a) The correlation coefficient is a measure of the _____ and direction of the linear relationship between two variables.
(b) If two variables are negatively correlated, then the x-values _____ as the y-values decrease, whereas as the x-values _____, the y-values increase.
(c) The _____ of r tells us about the direction of the linear relationship.
(d) A value of r calculated to be exactly -1 or 1 shows _____ correlation.

36 In a survey of eight UK universities, study information about their degree course in Tourism Management was obtained as follows:

Percentage time spent in lectures in year 1	Percentage coursework assessment in year 1	Percentage of students who left before completion
26	32	18
16	86	5
23	52	5
24	83	8
25	37	5
17	87	10
29	47	10
24	75	17

Calculate the correlation coefficient between:
(a) percentage time spent in lectures in year 1 and percentage coursework assessment in year 1

(b) percentage time spent in lectures in year 1 and percentage of students who left before completion

(c) percentage coursework assessment in year 1 and percentage of students who left before completion

Interpret all of your results.

37 From the annual reports of six clothing companies, the number of stores worldwide and the number of employees was recorded.

Calculations obtained from data are: $S_{xx} = 14499.133$, $S_{yy} = 8.495$, $S_{xy} = 320.660$. Find the value of r and interpret its meaning.

38 This scatter diagram shows the data collected during an investigation into the relationship between the length of a train journey (in miles) and the price of the train ticket (in pounds (£)).

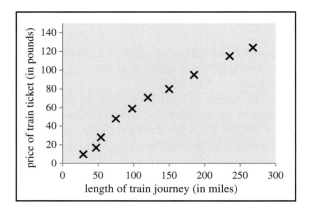

(a) Does the scatter diagram indicate that there is positive or negative correlation between these two variables?

(b) From the following list, choose which value of r is most likely to be correct for this relationship: 0.267, −0.986, 0.689, 0.981 or −0.627.

(c) Does the strength of the linear relationship imply that an increase in the length of the train journey would cause an increase in the price of the ticket?

(d) If we converted the journey lengths from miles to kilometres, would the value of the correlation coefficient be increased, decreased or remain the same?

39 A hospital decides to investigate whether there is an association between the number of nights a patient spends in hospital and the number of weeks it takes them to make a full recovery.

(a) Write a sentence to describe the relationship between the two variables if they were found to be positively correlated.

(b) If there was negative correlation, how would you describe their relationship?

(c) Do you think it is more likely that the number of nights a patient spends in hospital and the number of weeks it takes them to make a full recovery would have a positive or a negative relationship? Explain your answer.

(d) The investigation found that there was evidence of strong positive correlation. Would this mean that reducing the number of nights in hospital reduces the recovery time for patients? Describe two possible lurking variables that might affect the data.

40 For 14 secondary schools in the same county, it was found that the number of students aged 16–18 and the average point score per A-level entry had a correlation coefficient of exactly zero. Does this result indicate that the variables are not related? Give a reason for your answer.

Solutions to Practice Exercises

1 (a) FALSE

The correlation coefficient is always a number between −1 and 1 inclusive.

(b) FALSE

A correlation coefficient of exactly zero indicates that there is no linear relationship. However, the x-values and corresponding y-values might be strongly related in a pattern which is not linear. A scatter diagram should always be drawn so that results can be fully interpreted.

(c) FALSE

A negative linear relationship means that as the x-values increase, the y-values decrease; whereas as the x-values decrease, the y-values increase.

(d) TRUE

(e) TRUE

2

$$r = \frac{3241993 - \dfrac{2007 \times 16163}{10}}{\sqrt{\left(408621 - \dfrac{2007^2}{10}\right)\left(26125307 - \dfrac{16163^2}{10}\right)}} = \frac{-1921.1}{\sqrt{5816.1 \times 1050.1}} = -0.777$$

3 (a) 1

(b) −0.255

4 (a)

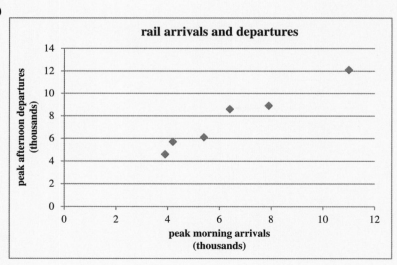

(b) The scatter diagram shows that the data points resemble a line with a positive slope from the lower left of the diagram to the upper right. This means that the sign of the PMCC will be positive.

(c) x = peak morning arrivals in thousands; y = peak afternoon departures in thousands

	x	y	x^2	y^2	xy		
	6.4	8.6	40.96	73.96	55.04		
	5.4	6.1	29.16	37.21	32.94	S_{xy}	35.803
	11	12.1	121.00	146.41	133.10	S_{xx}	35.473
	7.9	8.9	62.41	79.21	70.31	S_{yy}	37.773
	4.2	5.7	17.64	32.49	23.94	PMCC	**0.978**
	3.9	4.6	15.21	21.16	17.94		
Totals	38.8	46.0	286.38	390.44	333.27		

5 (a)
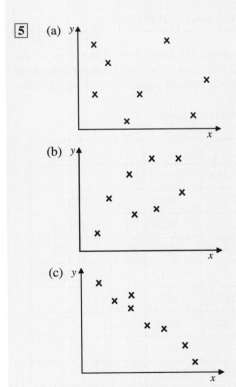
(b)

(c)

6 (a) x = height of building in metres; y = number of floors

Metres	x	y	x^2	y^2	xy		
	242	46	58564.00	2116	11132.0		

(Continued)

Metres	x	y	x^2	y^2	xy		
	63	14	3969.00	196	882.0	S_{xy}	5247.440
	73.2	16	5358.24	256	1171.2	S_{xx}	28869.696
	69.2	21	4788.64	441	1453.2	S_{yy}	1107.600
	125.6	26	15775.36	676	3265.6	r	**0.928**
	125	35	15625.00	1225	4375.0		
	81.4	18	6625.96	324	1465.2		
	73.4	19	5387.56	361	1394.6		
	164	35	26896.00	1225	5740.0		
	84	12	7056.00	144	1008.0		
Totals	**1100.8**	**242**	**150045.76**	**6964**	**31886.8**		

(b) We would expect the value of r to remain the same even if the units of the building height were changed from metres to feet. Its value is independent of the scale of each variable, and so changing the units of one or both of the variables will not have any effect.

(c) x = height of building in feet; y = number of floors

Feet	x	y	x^2	y^2	xy		
	794	46	630436	2116	36524		
	207	14	42849	196	2898	S_{xy}	17207.6
	240	16	57600	256	3840	S_{xx}	310593.6
	227	21	51529	441	4767	S_{yy}	1107.6
	412	26	169744	676	10712	r	**0.928**
	410	35	168100	1225	14350		
	267	18	71289	324	4806		
	241	19	58081	361	4579		
	538	35	289444	1225	18830		
	276	12	76176	144	3312		
Totals	**3612**	**242**	**1615248**	**6964**	**104618**		

As expected, changing the units of one of the variables has not affected the value of r, which remains at 0.928.

7 (a) x = number of items bought; y = total spent (to nearest £)

	x	y	x^2	y^2	xy		
	40	49	1600	2401	1960		
	87	109	7569	11881	9483	S_{xy}	13868.000
	18	37	324	1369	666	S_{xx}	11784.000
	9	10	81	100	90	S_{yy}	16727.636
	61	76	3721	5776	4636	r	**0.988**
	91	117	8281	13689	10647		
	80	89	6400	7921	7120		
	65	71	4225	5041	4615		
	7	10	49	100	70		
	4	3	16	9	12		
	77	91	5929	8281	7007		
Totals	539	662	38195	56568	46306		

(b) The value of r shows us that the number of items bought and the total amount spent have a strong positive correlation, meaning that when more items are bought, the amount spent increases, and when fewer items are bought, the amount spent is low.

8 (a) The overall pattern in the scatter diagram shows that the variables have a negative linear relationship; the spacing of the plotted points indicates that the relationship is not very strong.

(b) Correlation is not resistant to extreme values and therefore may be adversely affected by an unusual observation, so the change in value of r is expected when the observation is excluded from the data set.

9 (a)

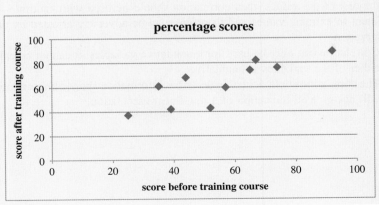

(b) x = score before training course; y = score after training course

Employee	x ranked	y ranked	$x_r - y_r$	$(x_r - y_r)^2$		
1	9	6	3	9		
2	2	3	−1	1	numerator	144
3	6	8	−2	4	denominator	990
4	3	2	1	1	r_s	**0.855**
5	10	10	0	0		
6	7	5	2	4		
7	1	1	0	0		
8	4	4	0	0		
9	8	9	−1	1		
10	5	7	−2	4		
Totals				24		

10 (a) $r = 0.511$
(b) $r = -0.962$
(c) $r = -0.174$
(d) $r = 0.788$

11 (a) negative correlation
(b) positive correlation
(c) positive correlation
(d) no correlation

12 If there is an observation in your data set that does not follow the same general pattern as the rest of the values, then correlation should be used with caution – it is not resistant to extreme values and therefore may be adversely affected by an unusual observation.
• Correlation can only be used for quantitative variables; it cannot be calculated if either of the variables is qualitative.
• The correlation coefficient only describes information about a linear relationship; it will not give an indication of a non-linear association.

13 (a)

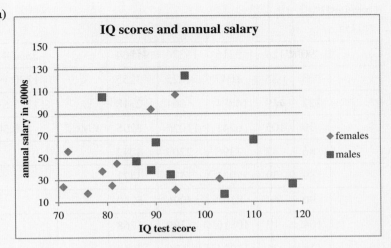

(b) From the scatter diagram, we can see that the overall pattern of plotted points for females shows an upward slope indicating positive correlation, whereas the male data points appear to show a negative linear relationship.

(c) x = IQ test score; y = annual salary in £000s

Females	x	y	x^2	y^2	xy		
	81	25	6561	625	2025		
	72	56	5184	3136	4032	S_{xy}	810.1
	103	31	10609	961	3193	S_{xx}	1000.9
	89	94	7921	8836	8366	S_{yy}	8748.9
	94	107	8836	11449	10058	PMCC	**0.274**
	76	18	5776	324	1368		
	71	24	5041	576	1704		
	79	38	6241	1444	3002		
	94	21	8836	441	1974		
	82	45	6724	2025	3690		
Totals	**841**	**459**	**71729**	**29817**	**39412**		

Males	x	y	x^2	y^2	xy		
	110	66	12100	4356	7260		

(*Continued*)

Males	x	y	x^2	y^2	xy		
	96	124	9216	15376	11904	S_{xy}	−2354.4
	93	35	8649	1225	3255	S_{xx}	1830.1
	122	19	14884	361	2318	S_{yy}	11757.6
	79	105	6241	11025	8295	PMCC	−0.508
	86	47	7396	2209	4042		
	89	39	7921	1521	3471		
	90	64	8100	4096	5760		
	104	17	10816	289	1768		
	118	26	13924	676	3068		
Totals	987	542	99247	41134	51141		

The results of the calculations agree with the observations made in part (b) indicating positive correlation for females and negative correlation for males.

14 The politician thinks that the negative correlation indicates a cause-and-effect relationship between the two variables: that a change in one will cause a change in the other. This is incorrect because the correlation describes the strength and magnitude of a linear relationship between the length of his speech and the number of voters, but does not provide evidence of cause.

15 x = life expectancy at birth (in years); y = carbon dioxide emissions per capita (in tonnes)

	x	y	x^2	y^2	xy		
	80.1	10.6	6416.010	112.36	849.060		
	72.4	1.5	5241.760	2.25	108.600	S_{xy}	156.833
	68.8	7	4733.440	49.00	481.600	S_{xx}	446.600
	79.3	2.8	6288.490	7.84	222.040	S_{yy}	116.356
	59.7	0.1	3564.090	0.01	5.970	PMCC	0.688
	77	5	5929.000	25.00	385.000		
	80	8.7	6400.000	75.69	696.000		
	81.2	6.7	6593.440	44.89	544.040		
	66.9	0.1	4475.610	0.01	6.690		
Totals	665.4	42.5	49641.840	317.05	3299.000		

The value of the PMCC shows us that the life expectancy at birth and the carbon dioxide emissions per capita have a fairly strong positive correlation, meaning that the data values increase and decrease together.

16 The variables have a strong negative correlation, meaning that as the data values for one variable increase, the data values for the other variable decrease.

17 (a) From the scatter diagram, we would expect the variables to be positively correlated because the overall pattern of plotted points shows an upward slope. The magnitude of the correlation coefficient should be estimated around 0.750 because the spacing of the data points indicates that the relationship is moderately strong.

(b) $r = \dfrac{5117}{\sqrt{31955.6 \times 1500}} = 0.739$

This value of 0.739 fits with our estimate made in part (a). The sign is positive, indicating a positive linear association, and the magnitude shows a moderately strong relationship.

18 (a) NO
The correlation coefficient does not have any units of measurement – its value is independent of the scale of each variable. Changing the units of one or both of the variables will not have any effect on the value of the PMCC.

(b) NO
Correlation provides us with information about the strength and direction of a linear relationship but it is not able to explain why or how that relationship exists. Although our calculations may lead us to conclude that two variables are correlated, this does not indicate that there is a cause-and-effect relationship: that a change in one variable causes a change in the other variable.

(c) NO
Correlation can only be used for quantitative variables; it cannot be calculated if either of the variables is qualitative.

19

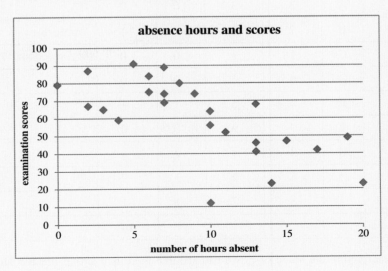

The scatter diagram shows that the data points form a pattern with a negative slope from the upper left of the diagram to the lower right, giving an indication of a negative linear relationship between number of hours of absence from lessons and examination score.

20 Yes, the correlation coefficient suggests that the two variables have a weak positive linear relationship. This means that as the x-values increase, the y-values also increase.

21 We cannot conclude that an increase in journey time causes a corresponding increase in ticket price, because the correlation coefficient describes the strength and magnitude of a linear relationship between the journey time and ticket price, but does not provide evidence of cause.

22 A correlation coefficient close to zero may mean that the two variables are related but not in a linear way or could indicate that they are not related at all. Scatter diagrams representing these two interpretations are as follows:

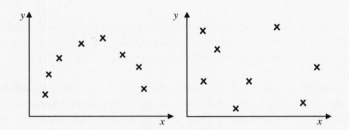

23 x = score from customer 1; y = score from customer 2

Store	x ranked	y ranked	$x_r - y_r$	$(x_r - y_r)^2$		
A	3	3	0	0		
B	7	8	−1	1	numerator	96
C	1	1	0	0	denominator	720
D	6	6	0	0	r_s	**0.867**
E	4	5	−1	1		
F	9	9	0	0		
G	2	4	−2	4		
H	5	2	3	9		
I	8	7	1	1		
Totals				**16**		

In interpreting the value of r_s we can see that there is a strong linear relationship between the rankings of the two customers and that they are in agreement about which department stores provide the best and worst customer service.

24 (a) The correlation coefficient must have been calculated or reported incorrectly because the value can only be in the range of −1 to 1 inclusive, whereas −1.921 is outside this range.

(b) The colour of a car is a qualitative variable and therefore is it not possible to assess the correlation or linear relationship between the colour and the monthly sales figures; correlation can only be used for quantitative variables.

(c) Changing the units of measurement from euros to dollars will not change the value of the correlation coefficient because it is independent of the scale of both of the variables.

25 Option (b). A negative linear relationship is represented by plotted points that show a negative slope from the upper left of the diagram to the lower right.

26 (a)

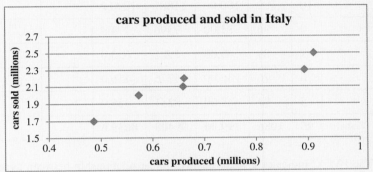

x = cars produced in millions; y = cars sold in millions

	x	y	x^2	y^2	xy		
	0.893	2.3	0.797	5.29	2.054		
	0.911	2.5	0.830	6.25	2.278	S_{xy}	0.218
	0.659	2.1	0.434	4.41	1.384	S_{xx}	0.147
	0.661	2.2	0.437	4.84	1.454	S_{yy}	0.373
	0.573	2.0	0.328	4.00	1.146	PMCC	0.931
	0.486	1.7	0.236	2.89	0.826		
Totals	4.183	12.8	3.063	27.68	9.142		

(b) The PMCC indicates a strong positive linear relationship between production and sales of cars in Italy over the six-year period. This means that as production increases, sales increase, and as production decreases, sales also decrease.

(c) We cannot conclude that an increase in production causes a corresponding increase in sales because the PMCC describes the strength and magnitude of a linear relationship between the production and sales of cars, but does not provide evidence of cause.

27 (a) x = average daily sunshine hours; y = average rainfall in mm

Hours	x	y	x^2	y^2	xy		
	6	94	36.00	8836	564.0		

(*Continued*)

Hours	x	y	x^2	y^2	xy		
	6	97	36.00	9409	582.0	S_{xy}	61.500
	7	91	49.00	8281	637.0	S_{xx}	46.917
	8	81	64.00	6561	648.0	S_{yy}	1125.000
	9	81	81.00	6561	729.0	PMCC	**0.268**
	11	84	121.00	7056	924.0		
	11	107	121.00	11449	1177.0		
	10	109	100.00	11881	1090.0		
	9	86	81.00	7396	774.0		
	7	89	49.00	7921	623.0		
	6	76	36.00	5776	456.0		
	5	91	25.00	8281	455.0		
Totals	95	1086	799.00	99408	8659.0		

(b) The PMCC indicates a weak positive linear relationship between average daily sunshine hours and average rainfall in millimetres. This means that as sunshine hours increase, rainfall also increases, but the linear relationship is rather weak.

(c) x = average daily sunshine minutes; y = average rainfall in mm

Minutes	x	y	x^2	y^2	xy		
	360	94	129600	8836	33840		
	360	97	129600	9409	34920	S_{xy}	3690.000
	420	91	176400	8281	38220	S_{xx}	168900.000
	480	81	230400	6561	38880	S_{yy}	1125.000
	540	81	291600	6561	43740	PMCC	**0.268**
	660	84	435600	7056	55440		
	660	107	435600	11449	70620		
	600	109	360000	11881	65400		
	540	86	291600	7396	46440		
	420	89	176400	7921	37380		
	360	76	129600	5776	27360		
	300	91	90000	8281	27300		
Totals	5700	1086	2876400	99408	519540		

As expected, changing the units of one of the variables has not affected the value of r which remains at 0.268.

28 (a) Although our diagram may lead us to conclude that two variables are positively correlated, it does not indicate that there is a cause-and-effect relationship: that a reduction in the number of solicitors offices will reduce the number of crimes committed.

(b) A lurking variable might be the size of population in the town. Larger towns are likely to have more solicitors' offices and a higher crime rate, whereas small towns might have fewer solicitors' offices and a smaller number of crimes committed.

29 (a)

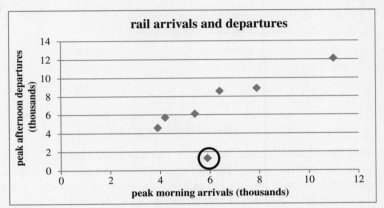

(b) $x =$ peak morning arrivals in thousands; $y =$ peak afternoon departures in thousands

x	y	x^2	y^2	xy		
6.4	8.6	40.96	73.96	55.04		
5.4	6.1	29.16	37.21	32.94	S_{xx}	38.896
11	12.1	121.00	146.41	133.10	S_{xx}	35.749
7.9	8.9	62.41	79.21	70.31	S_{yy}	72.517
4.2	5.7	17.64	32.49	23.94	PMCC	**0.764**
3.9	4.6	15.21	21.16	17.94		
5.9	1.3	34.81	1.69	7.67		
Totals	**44.7**	**47.3**	**321.19**	**392.13**	**340.94**	

The inclusion of this observation in the data set has reduced the strength of the correlation between the peak morning arrivals and the peak afternoon departures for rail passengers. Correlation is not resistant to extreme values and therefore can be adversely affected by an unusual observation, so the change in value of the PMCC is expected when the new observation is added to the original data set.

30   It would not be appropriate to investigate the correlation between gender and the amount of money spent every year on clothes because gender is a qualitative variable. Correlation can only be calculated for quantitative bivariate data.

31   (a)

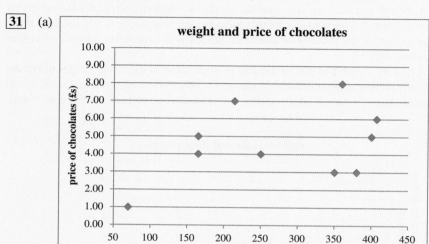

From the scatter diagram, we can see that the overall pattern of plotted points shows an upward slope. The spacing of the data points indicates that the relationship between weight and price for the boxes of chocolates is fairly weak.

(b) x = weight of chocolates in grams; y = price of chocolates in pounds

	x	y	x^2	y^2	xy		
	350	3.00	122500	9.00	1050		
	400	5.00	160000	25.00	2000	S_{xx}	864.40
	380	3.00	144400	9.00	1140	S_{xx}	127482.90
	70	1.00	4900	1.00	70	S_{yy}	38.40
	165	4.00	27225	16.00	660	PMCC	**0.391**
	360	8.00	129600	64.00	2880		
	250	4.00	62500	16.00	1000		
	407	6.00	165649	36.00	2442		
	165	5.00	27225	25.00	825		
	214	7.00	45796	49.00	1498		
Totals	2761	46.00	889795	250.00	13565		

This value of 0.391 fits with our observations made in part (a). The sign is positive, indicating a positive linear association, and the magnitude shows a fairly weak relationship between the variables.

32 (a) The scatter diagram indicates that there is a strong relationship between age and monthly expenditure.

(b) The correlation coefficient would not be a useful way of describing the relationship because it is a measure of linear association, whereas the scatter diagram shows that the variables are not linearly related.

33 (a) We would expect these variables to have a negative linear relationship so that the number of people who never use the Internet decreases as the number of people who use the Internet every day increases.

(b) x = number of people who use the Internet every day
y = number of people who never use the Internet

	x	y	x^2	y^2	xy		
	16.2	16.3	262.44	265.69	264.06		
	20.7	12.6	428.49	158.76	260.82	S_{xx}	-109.674
	23.0	11.4	529.00	129.96	262.20	S_{xx}	224.317
	26.6	9.9	707.56	98.01	263.34	S_{yy}	55.709
	29.2	8.9	852.64	79.21	259.88	PMCC	-0.981
	31.4	8.1	985.96	65.61	254.34		
	33.2	7.6	1102.24	57.76	252.32		
Totals	180.3	75	4868.33	855	1816.96		

As expected, the sign of the correlation coefficient is negative, indicating negative correlation between the variables.

34 A PMCC close to 1 indicates a strong positive linear relationship between the variables. This means that as the x-values increase, the y-values also increase. A scatter diagram representing this relationship is as follows:

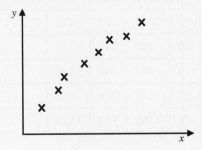

35 (a) strength
(b) increase, decrease
(c) sign
(d) perfect

36 x = percentage time spent in lectures in year 1
y = percentage coursework assessment in year 1
z = percentage of students who left before completion

(a)

x	y	x^2	y^2	xy		
26	32	676	1024	832		
16	86	256	7396	1376	S_{xx}	−514.000
23	52	529	2704	1196	S_{xx}	136.000
24	83	576	6889	1992	S_{yy}	3659.875
25	37	625	1369	925	PMCC	**−0.729**
17	87	289	7569	1479		
29	47	841	2209	1363		
24	75	576	5625	1800		
Totals	**184**	**499**	**4368**	**34785**	**10963**	

The PMCC of −0.729 indicates a strong negative linear relationship between percentage time spent in lectures in year 1 and percentage coursework assessment in year 1.

(b)

x	z	x^2	z^2	xz		
26	18	676	324	468		
16	5	256	25	80	S_{xz}	54.000
23	5	529	25	115	S_{xx}	136.000
24	8	576	64	192	S_{zz}	191.500
25	5	625	25	125	PMCC	**0.335**
17	10	289	100	170		
29	10	841	100	290		
24	17	576	289	408		
Totals	**184**	**78**	**4368**	**952**	**1848**	

The PMCC of 0.335 shows that there is weak positive correlation between percentage of time spent in lectures in year 1 and percentage of students who left before completion.

(c)

	y	z	y^2	z^2	yz		
	32	18	1024	324	576		
	86	5	7396	25	430	S_{yz}	−135.250
	52	5	2704	25	260	S_{yy}	3659.875
	83	8	6889	64	664	S_{zz}	191.500
	37	5	1369	25	185	PMCC	−0.162
	87	10	7569	100	870		
	47	10	2209	100	470		
	75	17	5625	289	1275		
Totals	499	78	34785	952	4730		

The PMCC of −0.162 is interpreted as a weak negative linear relationship between percentage coursework assessment in year 1 and percentage of students who left before completion.

37

$$r = \frac{320.660}{\sqrt{14499.133 \times 8.495}} = 0.914$$

The value of r indicates a strong positive linear relationship between number of stores worldwide and number of employees. This means that when the number of stores is high, the number of employees is high.

38 (a) The scatter diagram indicates that there is positive correlation between the length of a train journey (in miles) and the price of the train ticket (in pounds).
(b) r is most likely to be 0.981.
(c) No – the strength of the linear relationship does not imply that an increase in the length of the train journey would cause an increase in the price of the ticket because correlation does not indicate whether there is a cause-and-effect relationship between two variables.
(d) If we converted the journey lengths from miles to kilometres, the value of the correlation coefficient would remain the same because it is independent of the scale of both of the variables.

39 (a) If the two variables were found to be positively correlated, it would mean that as the number of nights a patient spends in hospital increases, the number of weeks it takes them to make a full recovery also increases.
(b) For negative correlation, it would mean that as the number of nights a patient spends in hospital increases, the number of weeks it takes them to make a full recovery decreases.

(c) Positive – patients who spend a longer time in hospital might have a more severe illness and therefore also might require a longer recovery time.

Negative – patients who spend longer in hospital have more treatment given to them and so perhaps the recovery time afterwards is reduced because they have already made good progress towards full health.

(d) Correlation does not give us any information about a cause-and-effect relationship between two variables, so a strong positive correlation does not mean that a reduction in one variable will cause a reduction in the other one. Possible lurking variables might be the age of the patient and the number of days that the patient had already been ill. Both of these factors could affect the variables and be the root cause of the relationship.

40 A PMCC value of exactly zero indicates that there is no linear relationship. However, the variables might be strongly related, but in a pattern which is not linear. A scatter diagram should always be drawn so that results can be fully interpreted.

CHAPTER 8

Simple Linear Regression

OBJECTIVES

This chapter explains how to:

- distinguish between independent and dependent variables
- understand a simple linear regression model
- find the equation of a line of best fit
- use a regression equation to
  - calculate predicted values
  - interpret the y-intercept and gradient

KEY TERMS

dependent variable	interpolation	residual
explanatory variable	least squares method	response variable
extrapolation	line of best fit	simple linear regression
gradient	linear equation	y-intercept
independent variable	regression line	

Introduction

In the previous chapter, we explored the way in which correlation can be used to describe the linear relationship between two quantitative variables, but we found that it is limited to describing the direction and strength of the relationship.

Using simple linear regression, we can investigate the relationship between the two variables in more detail by determining how a change in the value of one variable affects the value of the other variable. Most importantly, we can use this regression model to form an equation that allows us to predict the value of one variable for a known value of the other.

Before introducing the concepts that result in creating a simple linear regression model, we will review linear equations as a reminder about the meaning of the y-intercept and the gradient. Later in the chapter, you will learn how to determine the equation of the line of best fit for a data set, and gain an understanding of the interpretation and use of the equation.

Independent and Dependent Variables

In the context of regression, we need to distinguish between independent and dependent variables.

An **independent variable**, or **explanatory variable**, is used to predict the value of a **dependent variable**. We sometimes use the term 'explanatory variable' because a change in this variable helps to explain a change in a dependent variable. The values of a dependent variable can be predicted by an independent variable. An alternative name for a dependent variable is **response variable**, because its value changes in response to changes in an independent variable.

In a business scenario, we would consider the volume of sales of a retail organisation to be a dependent variable. The number of product sales might be affected by a wide range of independent variables such as:

- number of retail units rented;
- number of sales assistants employed;
- retail price of the product;
- total opening hours of the retail units;
- amount of money spent on advertising.

If we are interested in analysing the effect of many independent variables on a dependent variable, then we would use a multiple regression model. However, in simple linear regression, the focus of this chapter, we are limited to investigating the relationship between a single independent variable and its effect on a dependent variable. For a pair of variables with measured or recorded numerical values (x, y), we always denote the independent variable as x and the dependent variable as y.

Linear Equations

Every straight line on a graph can be described by a **linear equation** in the general form of $y = a + bx$, where x is the independent variable and is plotted using the x-axis, and y is the dependent variable plotted on the y-axis.

The constants a and b can be positive or negative, integers or decimal numbers, and each pairing of values provides the linear equation for a different straight line. Consider these examples:

	Value of a	Value of b	Linear equation
(i)	1	0.5	$y = 1 + 0.5x$
(ii)	-1	-2	$y = -1 - 2x$
(iii)	4	-2	$y = 4 - 2x$

The line represented by each linear equation in the table above can be drawn on a graph as follows:

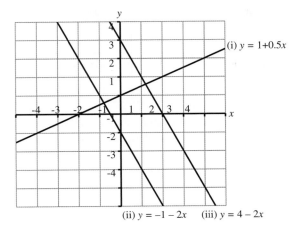

(i) $y = 1 + 0.5x$

(ii) $y = -1 - 2x$ (iii) $y = 4 - 2x$

At the point where a straight line crosses the y-axis, the constant a, also known as the **y-intercept**, is equal to the y-value of the coordinate; this is the value of the dependent variable when the value of the independent variable is zero.

The constant b is called the **gradient** and represents the slope of a straight line. The gradient is a measure of the amount by which the dependent variable changes for every one-unit increase in the independent variable. If b is negative, the line slopes downwards and it is the decrease in the value of y, each time the value of x increases by one unit; a graph sloping upwards has a positive gradient which represents an increase in y for every unit increase in x.

A visual representation of the y-intercept and the gradient is shown on the following graph:

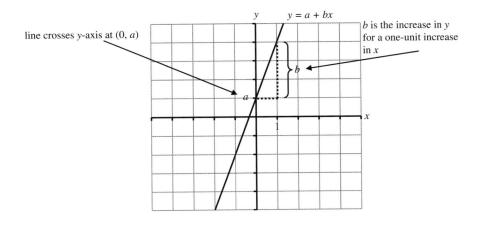

line crosses y-axis at $(0, a)$

$y = a + bx$

b is the increase in y for a one-unit increase in x

The table below shows the meaning of the constants a and b for our example lines.

	Value of a	Line crosses y-axis at:	Value of b	Every time x increases by 1:	Linear equation
(i)	1	$(0, 1)$	0.5	y increases by 0.5	$y = 1 + 0.5x$
(ii)	-1	$(0, -1)$	-2	y decreases by 2	$y = -1 - 2x$
(iii)	4	$(0, 4)$	-2	y decreases by 2	$y = 4 - 2x$

Regardless of the maximum and minimum values shown on the axes of a graph, we can use a linear equation to calculate the value of the dependent variable, y, for any given value of the independent variable, x.

Using our example equations, we can substitute different values of x to provide the corresponding y-values, as follows:

	Linear equation	Given value of x	Calculation	Calculated value of y
(i)	$y = 1 + 0.5x$	7	$y = 1 + (0.5 \times 7)$	4.5
(ii)	$y = -1 - 2x$	-16	$y = -1 - (2 \times -16)$	31
(iii)	$y = 4 - 2x$	112	$y = 4 - (2 \times 112)$	-220

Simple Linear Regression Model

In the previous section, we recalled how a linear equation could be used to describe the relationship between two variables where the value of y depends directly on the value of x, and where the data values of the variables would lie exactly on a straight line if they were plotted on a graph.

In many situations, the nature of the relationship between two variables is not sufficiently straightforward that it can be exactly described by a linear equation, meaning that we are not able to make predictions about the dependent variable based solely on the value of the independent variable. Here we need to develop and use an alternative model to take into account any additional complexities in the relationship.

As an example, consider the sales and advertising figures for a company that sells televisions. It is likely that these two variables have a linear relationship where the number of televisions sold depends on the amount of money spent on advertising by the company. However, we know from experience that human behaviour (including spending habits) is unpredictable and so this introduces some random variation into the relationship between volume of sales and advertising expenditure.

In this case, it would not be possible to describe the relationship directly using a linear equation; consequently, if we used the company's historical records to draw a scatter diagram then we would find that the data points do not lie exactly on a straight line. Most importantly, we are not able to use a linear equation to predict the number of televisions sold given a known amount of money spent on advertising.

As described in Chapter 7, we can establish that two quantitative variables have a linear relationship by drawing a scatter diagram and calculating the correlation coefficient. If we discover that the data points do not lie exactly on a straight line and therefore the correlation coefficient is not equal to 1 or −1, then we are able to use regression to provide a model for predicting the value of y, given a known value of x.

When we plot data values on a scatter diagram, it is possible to draw many, many different lines through some of the data points, as follows:

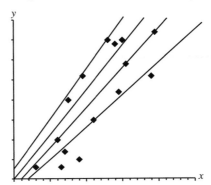

If the data points in a scatter diagram do not lie on a straight line, then it will not be possible to draw a single line that passes exactly through every point.

We are specifically interested in the line that will give the best description of the linear relationship between the two variables. Simple linear regression involves finding the equation of this line which will provide the best possible prediction for the dependent variable based on the independent variable; it is known as the **regression line** or the **line of best fit**.

Finding the Line of Best Fit

For any straight line that we choose to draw on a scatter diagram, there will be differences between each data point and the corresponding position on the straight line. These differences, also known as **residuals**, can be positive or negative values depending on whether the data point lies above or below the straight line. A graphical representation of this concept is shown below.

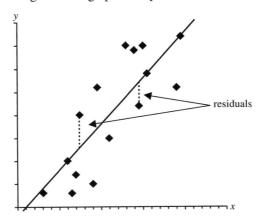

Each residual is the difference between the actual y-value of the data point and the y-value that we would predict if we used the linear equation of this line for the prediction. These differences represent the random variation that occurs in the relationship between an independent and a dependent variable, as we described in the previous section. The total magnitude of the residuals, regardless of whether the residual is positive or negative, is a measure of the effectiveness of the line we have chosen in terms of how well it fits the data points.

In finding the line of best fit, our aim is to draw the line which best fits the data points and so minimises these differences. This line will provide us with the best prediction for the dependent variable based on the values of the independent variable. To be able to identify this line, we need to calculate the gradient and y-intercept; this is achieved using the **least squares method** which was developed by Adrien-Marie Legendre (1752–1833).

If we have a set of n pairs of data values, the least squares method uses the following formulae to calculate the constants a and b for the line of best fit, $y = a + bx$. As before, b is the gradient of the line and a is the y-intercept:

$$b = \frac{S_{xy}}{S_{xx}} \quad a = \bar{y} - b\bar{x}$$

where

$$S_{xy} = \sum x_i y_i - \frac{\sum x_i \sum y_i}{n} \quad S_{xx} = \sum x_i^2 - \frac{\left(\sum x_i\right)^2}{n}$$

As in Chapter 7, (x_1, y_1) is the first pair of values, the second pair of values is (x_2, y_2), and (x_n, y_n) is the final pair in the data set. It is sensible to round the values of a and b to three decimal places.

EXAMPLE – FINDING THE LINE OF BEST FIT

The table below shows the number of televisions sold and the amount of money spent on advertising (in thousands of pounds (£)) for a company as recorded over a ten-month period. The number of televisions sold is the dependent variable because its value depends on the amount of money spent on advertising, the independent variable.

Advertising expenditure (£000s) x	16	19	12	16	13	17	19	15	17	21
Number of televisions sold y	370	410	205	320	290	455	300	280	375	420

Plotting the data on a scatter diagram and calculating the correlation coefficient will help us to check for any linear relationship between x and y.

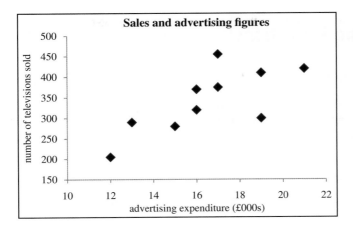

The correlation coefficient for these data is

$$r = \frac{57890 - \dfrac{165 \times 3425}{10}}{\sqrt{\left(2791 - \dfrac{165^2}{10}\right)\left(1225975 - \dfrac{3425^2}{10}\right)}} = \frac{1377.5}{\sqrt{68.5 \times 52912.5}} = 0.724$$

The scatter diagram and the value of the correlation coefficient show us that there is a linear relationship between the two variables, even though the data points do not lie on a straight line. It is therefore reasonable to use the least squares method to find the line of best fit.

The gradient for the line of best fit is

$$b = \frac{57890 - \dfrac{165 \times 3425}{10}}{2791 - \dfrac{165^2}{10}} = \frac{1377.5}{68.5} = 20.109$$

The y-intercept for the line of best fit is:

$$a = \frac{3425}{10} - \left(\frac{1377.5}{68.5} \times \frac{165}{10}\right) = 10.693$$

So the equation for the regression line is written as:

$$y = 10.693 + 20.109x$$

Making Predictions

When the least squares method has been used to find the line of best fit, then we can predict the value of the dependent variable, y, for any specific value of the independent variable, x.

It is possible to find the corresponding value of y, known as $\hat{y}$ (pronounced 'y-hat'), using a graphical method by drawing the line of best fit on our scatter diagram, as illustrated in the graph below.

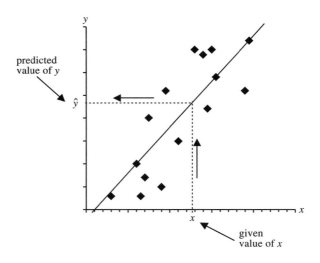

However, a more precise method is preferable and so instead we substitute the given value of x into the regression equation to provide a predication for y.

It is important to remember that any prediction we make is only an estimate of the value of y; we cannot know the exact value if the given value of x was not in the original data set.

EXAMPLE – PREDICTION

In the previous example involving the number of televisions sold and the amount of money spent on advertising (in thousands of pounds (£)) for a company as recorded over a ten-month period, we found the equation of the regression line to be $y = 10.693 + 20.109x$.

Suppose we want to know how many televisions will be sold when the advertising expenditure is £14,000. Here, we would substitute $x = 14$ into the regression equation, giving a predicted value of y as

$$\hat{y} = 10.693 + (20.109 \times 14) = 292.219$$

So we estimate that 292 televisions will be sold when the company spends £14,000 on advertising.

Interpolation and Extrapolation

Although it is possible to predict the value of the dependent variable for any specific value of the independent value, the predicted value might not always be reliable.

The calculations for the gradient and y-intercept of the regression line are based entirely on the data values that have been observed or measured. Therefore, we can only use the regression equation to provide a reliable prediction if the given value for x fits within the range of the x-values in the original data set; this is known as interpolation. If we use an x-value that is outside the range of the data, then this procedure is called extrapolation, and our predicted value, $\hat{y}$, may not be reliable because the linear relationship observed between the two variables may no longer be valid. Values of the dependent variable predicted using extrapolation should be used with caution.

EXAMPLE – INTERPOLATION AND EXTRAPOLATION

Returning to the example about televisions, recall that the data set contained the following values:

Advertising expenditure (£000s) x	16	19	12	16	13	17	19	15	17	21
Number of televisions sold x	370	410	205	320	290	455	300	280	375	420

The prediction that we have already made is reliable because the given x-value, £14,000, fits within the range of the original data set which has a minimum of £12,000 and a maximum of £21,000.

Suppose we now wanted to know how many televisions will be sold when the advertising expenditure is £55,000. Here, we would substitute $x = 55$ into the regression equation giving a predicted value of y as

$$\hat{y} = 10.693 + (20.109 \times 55) = 1116.688$$

We estimate that 1117 televisions will be sold when the company spends £55,000 on advertising. However, this might not be a reliable estimate because £55,000, the given value of x, does not fit within the range of the x-values in the data set; this is an example of extrapolation.

Interpretation

For a specific set of data, it is possible to interpret the meaning of the gradient and y-intercept for the regression equation in terms of the dependent and the independent variables.

During our earlier review of linear equations, we stated that:

- The constant *a*, or the *y*-intercept, is the value of the dependent variable when the value of the independent variable is zero.
- The constant *b*, or the gradient, is the amount by which the dependent variable changes for every one-unit increase in the independent variable. If *b* is negative, it represents a decrease in the value of *y*, whereas a positive gradient represents an increase in *y*.

Providing a practical interpretation of the gradient and *y*-intercept for a given scenario involves explaining these statements using the actual values of the constants and the names of the variables. The values of *a* and *b* are estimates calculated using a simple linear regression model. It is therefore important to include the words 'expected' and 'estimate' in our explanations.

EXAMPLE – INTERPRETATION

In the example used throughout this chapter, we defined the variables in the scenario as:

Variable	Denoted by	Defined as
independent	*x*	advertising expenditure (£000s)
dependent	*y*	number of televisions sold

From our calculations, we know that the gradient is 20.109 and the *y*-intercept is equal to 10.693. As a practical interpretation we can say the following:

- 10.693 is the expected number of televisions sold when the advertising expenditure is zero; we estimate that company sells approximately 11 televisions even when they do not spend any money on advertising.
- 20.109 is the expected amount by which the number of televisions sold increases for every one-unit increase in the advertising expenditure; we estimate that the company sells an additional 20 televisions every time they spend £1000 more on advertising.

HINTS AND TIPS

LINEAR RELATIONSHIP

A simple linear regression model should only be used in scenarios involving a single dependent variable and a single independent variable. Most importantly, we should be able to show that the two variables have a linear relationship by plotting the known data points on a scatter diagram or by calculating the correlation coefficient.

Once the existence of a linear relationship has been verified, then the equation of the regression line can be used to predict the value of the dependent variable for a given value of the independent variable.

ROUNDING ERRORS

Rounding errors should be avoided when calculating the gradient and y-intercept of the regression equation because too much rounding during the intermediate stages of the calculations will result in the equation of a slightly different line of best fit, and therefore affect the accuracy of any prediction for the dependent variable. There are two important guidelines with respect to rounding:

- Always ensure that the 'real' values of S_{xy} and S_{xx} are used in the calculation of b, rather than rounded values.
- Do not use a rounded value of the gradient when it is included in the calculation for the y-intercept of the regression line.

Returning to our earlier example, we found that $b = 20.109$ and $a = 10.693$. If we had rounded the values of S_{xy} and S_{xx} to 1378 and 69 respectively, our value of b would have been 19.971. The value of a would have increased to 12.500 if we had then used $b = 20$ in the subsequent calculation.

The effect of rounding in the gradient and y-intercept of the regression equation can be seen clearly in the table below:

	Denoted by	Value without rounding	Value with rounding applied
y-intercept	a	10.693	12.500
Gradient	b	20.109	19.971

PRACTICAL INTERPRETATION OF a

Recall that the constant a is the value of the dependent variable when the value of the independent variable is zero. Sometimes, where zero would not be a reasonable value for the independent variable, it does not make any logical sense to provide a practical interpretation of a.

In the example about television sales, zero could be a reasonable value for the independent variable: this would be the equivalent of no expenditure on advertising, which is plausible for this scenario.

Consider changing the independent variable to be defined as the retail price of a single television. This is reasonable because the volume of sales can still be said to depend on the unit price. However, it is extremely unlikely that the independent variable would ever be zero because this would mean that televisions are given away for free. In this situation, it does not make any sense to describe the volume of sales when the price of a television is zero and so we would choose not to provide a practical interpretation of a.

Using Excel

REGRESSION

You can find a line of best fit for data entered into an Excel spreadsheet by using two built-in statistical functions, **SLOPE** and **INTERCEPT**.

Function	Description	Syntax
SLOPE	calculates the slope of the regression line through the given data points (also known as arrays)	SLOPE (dependent array, independent array)
INTERCEPT	calculates the y-intercept for the regression line through the given data points (also known as arrays)	INTERCEPT (dependent array, independent array)

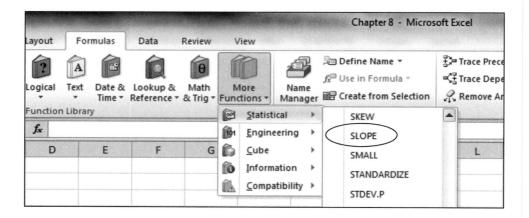

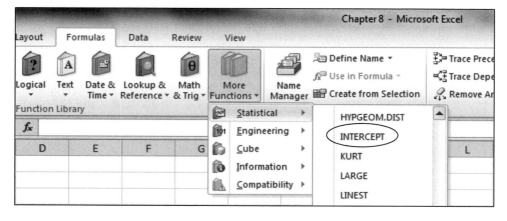

Using the example described earlier in this chapter, the table shows the number of televisions sold and the amount of money spent on advertising (in thousands of pounds (£)) for a company as recorded over a ten-month period. The number of televisions sold is the dependent variable because its value depends on the amount of money spent on advertising, the independent variable.

▲	A	B	C	D	E	F	G	H	I	J	K	L	M
1													
2		advertising expenditure (£000s) x	16	19	12	16	13	17	19	15	17	21	
3		number of televisions sold y	370	410	205	320	290	455	300	280	375	420	
4													
5		slope:	20.109										
6		intercept:	10.693										
7													

Using this information, we can write the equation for the regression line as: $y = 10.693 + 20.109x$.

Practice Exercises

1   Using an estate agent website, the following data were recorded for 12 houses in the same postal district:

Internal floor space square metres	Advertised sale price £000s
104.9	650
134.1	400
78.8	250
92.6	305
124.7	350
104.7	370
130.8	470
97.9	375

(*Continued*)

Internal floor space square metres	Advertised sale price £000s
64.5	240
75.8	270
77.5	300
122.4	420

(a) Calculate the gradient and the y-intercept of the line of best fit for these data.
(b) Explain why it would not be appropriate to use the line of best fit to predict the advertised sale price of a house with 570 square metres of internal floor space.

2 The number of rooms occupied and the number of empty car park spaces were recorded on the same day at each of 12 hotels owned by a large company. The following information was then calculated:

$$\sum x = 1900 \quad \sum y = 121 \quad \sum x^2 = 309950 \quad \sum xy = 17948$$

Find the equation of the regression line to predict number of empty car park spaces (y) from number of rooms occupied (x).

3 For each pair listed below, decide which variable is independent and which is dependent.
(a) distance between home and the workplace
   time taken for daily commute to work
(b) average daily temperature
   expenditure on household utilities bill for heating
(c) number of visitors to a tourist attraction
   price per person for entry to the attraction
(d) number of interviews to which a job-seeker is invited
   number of jobs applied for

4 For ten trains departing from Euston Station in London, the following table shows the number of stations at which each train stops and the time taken to reach its final destination.

Number of stations at which the train stops	17	14	7	2	6	3	4	7	9	11
Time taken to reach destination (minutes)	56	45	39	12	24	19	32	35	41	47

(a) Draw a scatter diagram showing the data values provided.
(b) Does the diagram show that the variables have a positive or negative linear relationship? Explain your answer.
(c) Find the equation of the line of best fit for the data points.
(d) Give a practical interpretation of the gradient of the regression line.

5   Without drawing any graphs, state whether the each of the following linear equations shows a negative or positive relationship between x and y; also interpret the gradient.
(a) $y = 9.5 + 24x$
(b) $y = 55 - 11.7x$

6   For 12 countries in the European Union, the table below shows the population (in millions) and the per capita GDP (in thousands of dollars ($)).

Population (millions)	Per capita GDP ($000s)
8.4	47
11.1	44
5.6	56
5.4	46
65.9	40
82.8	41
25.3	22
60.8	33
0.5	105
10.6	20
46.7	28
9.5	55

Use this data set to determine the regression equation where population is the independent variable and per capita GDP is the dependent variable.

7   A recruitment consultant records the number of years of work experience and the starting salary (in thousands of pounds (£)) for eight chartered accountants who have recently started working for a new company. The data are shown below.

Work experience (years)	5	8	2	16	3	7	4	10
Starting salary (£000s)	43.6	61.5	29.7	85.1	32.4	46.2	39.8	49.5

Using these data, the line of best fit is calculated as $y = 22.865 + 3.725x$.
(a) State the response variable and the explanatory variable in this scenario.
(b) In the context of the scenario, give a practical interpretation of the gradient and the y-intercept.
(c) Use the regression line to predict the starting salary for someone who has 12 years of work experience. Is this interpolation or extrapolation?
(d) Would it be appropriate to use the regression line to predict the starting salary for someone who has worked as a chartered accountant for 25 years? Fully explain the reason for your answer.

8   A market researcher is interested in calculating the regression equation for two variables: the number of visitors to a company's website and the number of products sold via their online store. Decide which variable should be denoted as x, and which should be denoted as y. Provide an explanation for your decision.

9   Considering the sale price of a residential property as a dependent variable, state three quantitative independent variables that might affect its value. What type of regression model would we use in this situation?

10   A company monitored the number of days (x) of business trips taken by executives of the company and the corresponding claims (£y) they submitted to cover the total expenditure of these trips. A random sample of ten trips gave the following results.

Number of days	10	3	8	17	5	9	14	16	21	13
Expenditure claim	116	39	85	159	61	94	143	178	225	134

(a) Obtain the equation of the least squares regression line.
(b) Use the equation from part (a) to predict the expenditure claim for a business trip that lasts 12 days.

11   Explain what is meant by the response variable and the explanatory variable in the context of simple linear regression.

12   Using an appropriate graph, draw a visual representation of the relationship between two variables where it would not be appropriate to apply a simple linear regression model.

13   For a research project investigating the relationship between income and holidays, ten families were asked to provide their annual income and the number of days they spent on holiday last year. The results are shown below:

Annual income (£000s)	Number of days spent on holiday
32.4	15
29.9	15
92.7	29
61	25
44.1	21
52.3	18
36.9	16
31.3	14
22.8	8
27.6	10

The regression equation for these data is $y = 4.855 + 0.284x$.

(a) Using the x-axis for annual income and the y-axis for number of days spent on holiday, plot the data values on a scatter diagram to verify that a simple linear regression model is appropriate in this scenario. Explain your response.

(b) Calculate the correlation between annual income and number of days spent on holiday. Does the value of r support your response in part (a)?

(c) For a family with an annual income of £165,000, how many days would you say that they spent on holiday last year? Why might this estimate be unreliable?

14 The technical director of a software development company has carried out an investigation to understand the relationship between the number of days taken off as sick leave by his team members and the number of days by which their project is delayed.

From the regression equation, $y = 2.536 + 6.966x$, he estimates that the number of days taken off as sick leave increases by approximately 7 each time the project is delayed by a day.

Explain the mistake he has made in interpreting the gradient of the regression equation and give the correct interpretation.

15 The table below shows the number of pages, x, and price, y, for ten business statistics textbooks available for sale from an online retailer.

Number of pages x	Purchase price (£) y
352	36.99
792	60.79
408	11.55
504	32.29
368	42.81
324	66.49
432	11.99
250	55.07
864	43.34
1016	58.89

(a) Find the equation for the line of best fit.

(b) Predict the price of a business statistics textbook that contains 375 pages.

(c) Explain why it would not make any logical sense to provide a practical interpretation of a in this context.

16 If we calculated the regression equation for the length of a taxi journey (in miles) and the cost of the journey, how would the gradient of the equation be interpreted in terms of the variables? Would the gradient be positive or negative? Give a reason for your answer.

17 Use the regression line $y = 152.248 - 13.626x$ to predict the value of y for the following values of x.
(a) $x = 3$
(b) $x = 10$

18 A retail company would like to determine predicted sales at stores in several new towns. The yearly sales (in thousands of pounds (£)) for their nine existing stores are known and they find out the size of the population (in thousands) for the town in which each store is located. The smallest town has a population of 16,000 and the largest population is 60,000. The regression line is found to be $y = 42.184 + 0.509x$. For a town with a population of 22,000, the company predicts that their sales will be £5338. What mistake has the company made in its prediction?

19 Explain why is would not be reasonable to apply a simple linear regression model to each of these sets of variables.
(a) number of cinema tickets sold and the genre of the film
(b) total price of a hotel bill and number of nights stayed, number of people, number of rooms booked and number of breakfasts ordered

20 Explain the purpose of finding the line of best fit for the data values of two quantitative variables.

21 The number of visitors and the average daily temperature were recorded for 9 days in June at an outdoor tourist attraction. Decide which variable is independent and which is dependent, and find the equation of the line of best fit for the data.

Average daily temperature (°C)	13.2	16.5	14.9	15.2	13.6	14.5	15.8	16.9	17.1
Number of visitors	1023	1362	1298	1369	986	1425	1459	1447	1698

22 Which type of diagram can be used to determine whether it is reasonable to use simple linear regression for predicting values of the dependent variable?
(a) pie chart
(b) times series graph
(c) scatter diagram

23 Explain what is meant by the terms 'interpolation' and 'extrapolation'.

24 During a local election, the number of public appearances and the votes received for each candidate were recorded. The data are represented on this scatter diagram.

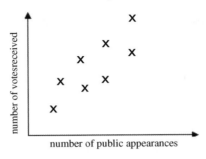

number of public appearances

(a) Would it be appropriate to apply a simple linear regression model to these data? Give a reason for your answer.

(b) Which is the response variable in this scenario?

25 Data were collected from residential customers by a home insurance company. They wanted to investigate the relationship between the number of claims made in a three-year period and the insurance premium offered for renewal of the policy. The line of best fit for the variables was calculated as $y = 157.23 + 29.5x$. What is the estimate of the change in insurance premium when the number of claims increases by one?

(a) £29.50

(b) we cannot calculate this estimate from the regression equation

(c) £157.23

26 (a) Using the data in the table below, calculate the regression equation for the number of people in a check-out queue and the time taken to be served (minutes) in a supermarket on a Saturday afternoon.

Number of people in the queue (x)	Time taken to be served (minutes) (y)
2	5
5	9
8	16
3	7
6	12
4	8

(b) Interpret the constants a and b.

27 On a scatter diagram, which axis should be used for plotting the values of the independent variable?

(a) x-axis

(b) y-axis

(c) either axis can be used

28 Would it be appropriate to use a line of best fit to predict the monthly income of a family from the amount that they spend on food each month? Give a reason for your viewpoint.

29 The owner of a second-hand car dealership records the following data for 12 cars brought in for part-exchange:

Age (years)	3	7	5	2	6	8	9	4	5	9	2	7
Mileage (000s miles)	29	48	39	25	38	55	62	37	41	59	23	50

(a) State the response variable in this scenario.
(b) Show that $S_{xx} = 68.917$ and $S_{xy} = 348.833$, rounded to three decimal places.
(c) Find the equation of the line of best fit in the form of $y = a + bx$.

30 For an online magazine article, the engine capacity (cc) and the top speed (km/hour) were measured for nine models of cars newly released for sale in 2013. The regression equation for these data was calculated as $y = 152.367 + 0.032x$. The reporter interpreted the y-intercept, stating that the top speed was approximately 152 km/hour for a car with an engine capacity of zero. What is wrong with the reporter's statement?

31 Fill in the blank spaces in the following statements about regression.
(a) An _____, or explanatory, variable is used to predict the value of a dependent value.
(b) The constant a, known as the _____, is the value of the dependent variable when the value of the independent variable is _____.
(c) The constant _____, or the gradient, is the amount by which the _____ variable changes for every _____ unit increase in the independent variable.
(d) For a pair of variables with measured or recorded numerical values (x, y), we always denote the independent variable as _____ and the _____ variable as y.

32 The least squares regression line for the amount of money spent on advertising (in thousands of pounds (£)) and the number of products sold (in thousands) was calculated for a clothing retailer as $y = 6.53 + 0.35x$. What is the estimate of the number of products sold when the company has no advertising expenditure?
(a) 653
(b) 350
(c) 6530

33 The table below shows the length of time spent in a supermarket (minutes) and the number of items purchased by 15 shoppers.

Length of time spent in store	Number of items purchased
30	12
12	2

(Continued)

Length of time spent in store	Number of items purchased
85	84
62	49
45	72
17	4
35	26
31	27
26	18
49	61
22	20
27	4
15	8
38	41
40	28

(a) Using the number of items purchased as the dependent variable, verify that the regression line is $y = 1.199x - 12.268$.

(b) Why would it be inappropriate to give a practical interpretation of a?

34 For each of the following linear equations, state the value of the y-intercept and the gradient:

(a) $y = 2 - 3x$

(b) $y = 14x - 8$

35 Explain what is wrong with each of the following statements:

(a) Every straight line on a graph can be described by a linear equation in the general form of $y = a + bx$ where x is the dependent variable and the independent variable is y.

(b) At the point where a straight line crosses the y-axis, the constant a, also known as the gradient, is equal to the y-value of the coordinate.

36 From the technical operations report of a manufacturing company, the age of its 20 machines (in years) and the number of breakdowns for each machine in the past year were recorded.

Calculations obtained from data are: $\bar{x} = 7.667$, $\bar{y} = 4.333$, $S_{xx} = 228$, $S_{xy} = 117$.

Find the regression equation and substitute $x = 4$ to find a value for $\hat{y}$.

37 Decide whether the following statements are TRUE or FALSE. Explain your response for any FALSE statements.
 (a) Too much rounding during the calculation of the gradient and y-intercept of the regression equation may result in inaccurate values.
 (b) It is reasonable to provide a practical interpretation of a for all scenarios.
 (c) When the least squares method has been used to find the line of best fit, the value of the y can be predicted for any value of x.
 (d) A simple linear regression model should only be used in scenarios involving a single dependent variable and a single independent variable.
 (e) The gradient of the regression equation is always a negative value.

38 A film production company has researched the relationship between the profit (in millions of dollars (\$)) and income (in millions of dollars (\$)) associated with making blockbuster movies. The regression equation was found to be $y = 128.374 + 0.537x$. Calculate the expected profit from a movie that generates \$600 million in income.

39 A bank manager recorded the monthly mortgage repayment (in thousands of pounds (£)) and the amount of disposable income (in thousands of pounds (£)) for eight customers. The following figures were worked out from the data:

$$\sum x = 10.37 \quad \sum y = 12.907 \quad \sum x^2 = 14.322 \quad \sum xy = 15.539$$

 (a) Find the equation of the line of best fit.
 (b) Use your answer to part (a) to predict the monthly disposable income for a family whose mortgage repayment is £1450 each month.

40 For each of the following linear equations, find the value of the y when $x = 9$ and when $x = 17$:
 (a) $y = 35 + 13x$
 (b) $y = 26x - 4$

Solutions to Practice Exercises

1 (a) x = internal floor space of the house; y = advertised sale price

	x	y	xy	x^2	n	$\bar{x}$	$\bar{y}$
	104.9	650	68185	11004.01	12	100.725	366.667
	134.1	400	53640	17982.81			
	78.8	250	19700	6209.44			
	92.6	305	28243	8574.76		S_{xx}	6123.842
	124.7	350	43645	15550.09		S_{xy}	1775405
	104.7	370	38739	10962.09		b	**2.899**
	130.8	470	61476	17108.64		a	**74.641**
	97.9	375	36712.5	9584.41			
	64.5	240	15480	4160.25			
	75.8	270	20466	5745.64			
	77.5	300	23250	6006.25			
	122.4	420	51408	14981.76			
Totals	**1208.7**	**4400**	**460944.5**	**127870.2**			

gradient is 2.899; y-intercept is 74.641

(b) It would not be appropriate to predict the advertised sale price for a house with 570 square metres of internal floor space. Our predicted value, $\hat{y}$, might not be reliable because the linear relationship observed between the two variables may no longer be valid outside the range of the independent variable ($x = 64.5$ to $x = 134.1$).

2

$$b = \frac{17948 - \dfrac{1900 \times 121}{12}}{\left(309950 - \dfrac{1900^2}{12}\right)} = \frac{-1210.333}{9116.667} = -0.133$$

$$a = \frac{121}{12} - \left(\frac{-1210.333}{9116.667} \times \frac{1900}{12}\right) = 131.104$$

regression line is $y = 31.104x - 0.133$

3 (a) independent: distance between home and the workplace
dependent: time taken for daily commute to work

(b) independent: average daily temperature
dependent: expenditure on household utilities bill for heating

(c) dependent: number of visitors to a tourist attraction
independent: price per person for entry to the attraction

(d) dependent: number of interviews to which a job-seeker is invited
independent: number of jobs applied for

4   (a)

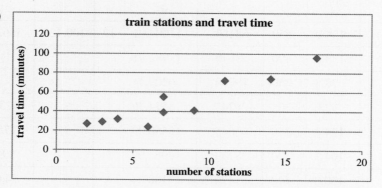

(b) The scatter diagram shows that the variables have a positive linear relationship because the data points resemble a line with a positive slope from the lower left of the diagram to the upper right.

(c) x = number of stations at which the train stops; y = time taken to reach destination

	x	y	xy	x^2	n	$\bar{x}$	$\bar{y}$
	17	96	1632	289	10	8.000	48.900
	14	74	1036	196			
	7	39	273	49			
	2	27	54	4	S_{xx}	210	
	6	24	144	36	S_{xy}	988	
	3	29	87	9	b	**4.705**	
	4	32	128	16	a	**11.262**	
	7	55	385	49			
	9	41	369	81			
	11	72	792	121			
Totals	**80**	**489**	**4900**	**850**			

regression line is $y = 11.262 + 4.705x$

(d) 4.705 is the expected amount by which the time to reach destination increases for every one-unit increase in the number of stations at which the a train stops; we estimate that the travel time takes an additional 5 minutes every time one more station is included in the route.

5 (a) There is a positive relationship between x and y because the gradient is a positive value, 24; each time the value of x increases by one unit, y increases by 24 units.

(b) There is a negative relationship between x and y because the gradient is a negative value, -11.7; each time the value of x increases by one unit, y decreases by 11.7 units.

6 $x =$ population; $y =$ per capita GDP

	x	y	xy	x^2	n	$\bar{x}$	$\bar{y}$
	8.4	47	394.8	70.56	12	21.717	47.75
	11.1	44	488.4	123.21			
	5.6	56	313.6	31.36			
	5.4	46	248.4	29.16		S_{xx}	8954.857
	65.9	40	2636	4342.81		S_{xy}	-2750.25
	82.8	41	3394.8	6855.84		b	**-0.307**
	25.3	22	556.6	640.09		a	**53.262**
	60.8	33	2006.4	3696.64			
	0.5	105	52.5	0.25			
	10.6	20	212	112.36			
Totals	**332.6**	**537**	**12133.6**	**18173.42**			

regression line is $y = 53.262 - 0.307x$

7 (a) response variable: starting salary
explanatory variable: number of years of work experience

(b) y-intercept
£22,865 is the expected starting salary when the number of years of work experience is zero;
we estimate that someone who does not have any work experience will receive a starting salary of £22,865.
gradient
£3725 is the expected amount by which the starting salary increases for every one-unit increase in the number of years of work experience; we estimate that the starting salary will increase by £3725 for each additional year of work experience as a chartered accountant.

(c) Substituting $x = 12$ in the regression equation gives: $\hat{y} = 22.865 + 3.725 \times 12 = 67.565$, so we estimate that a chartered accountant with 12 years' experience would receive a starting salary of £67,565. This is interpolation because the given value of x (12) is within the range of the data values recorded for the variable (2–16).

(d) It would not be appropriate to predict the starting salary for someone who has worked as a chartered accountant for 25 years. Our predicted value, $\hat{y}$, might not be reliable because the linear relationship observed between the two variables may no longer be valid outside the range of the explanatory variable ($x = 2$ to $x = 16$).

8 The number of visitors to the company's website should be denoted as x because it is the independent variable, and the number of products sold online should be denoted as y because it is the dependent variable.

9 Independent variables might include: number of bedrooms, amount of floor space and distance to town centre. If we are interested in analysing the effect of many independent variables on a dependent variable, then we would use a multiple regression model.

10 (a) $x =$ number of days for a business trip; $y =$ expenditure claim

	x	y	xy	x^2	n	$\bar{x}$	$\bar{y}$
	10	116	1160	100	10	11.6	123.4
	3	39	117	9			
	8	85	680	64			
	17	159	2703	289		S_{xx}	284.4
	5	61	305	25		S_{xy}	2813.6
	9	94	846	81		b	**9.893**
	14	143	2002	196		a	**8.640**
	16	178	2848	256			
	21	225	4725	441			
	13	134	1742	169			
Totals	**116**	**1234**	**17128**	**1630**			

least squares regression line is $y = 8.640 + 9.893x$

(b) Substituting $x = 12$ in the line of best fit gives: $\hat{y} = 8.640 + 9.893 \times 12 = 127.356$, so we estimate that a business trip lasting 12 days would result in an expenditure claim of £127.36.

11 An explanatory variable is used to predict the value of a response value. We use the term 'explanatory' because a change in this variable helps to explain a change in a response variable.

The values of a response variable can be predicted by an explanatory variable. The term 'response' is used because the value changes in response to changes in an explanatory variable.

12

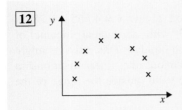

13 (a)

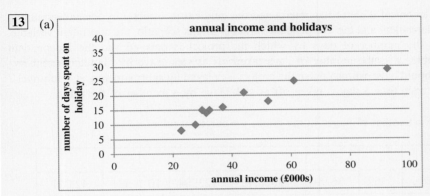

From the scatter diagram, we can see that the overall pattern of plotted points shows an upward slope, indicating positive linear relationship. It is therefore appropriate to use a simple linear regression model in this scenario.

(b) $x =$ annual income; $y =$ number of days spent on holiday

	x	y	x^2	y^2	xy		
	32.4	15	1049.76	225	486		
	29.9	15	894.01	225	448.5	S_{xy}	1132.2
	92.7	29	8593.29	841	2688.3	S_{xx}	3984.96
	61	25	3721	625	1525	S_{yy}	372.9
	44.1	21	1944.81	441	926.1	PMCC	**0.929**
	52.3	18	2735.29	324	941.4		
	36.9	16	1361.61	256	590.4		
	31.3	14	979.69	196	438.2		
	22.8	8	519.84	64	182.4		
	27.6	10	761.76	100	276		
Totals	**431**	**171**	**8502.3**	**22561.06**	**3297**		

The value of $r = 0.929$ supports the response made in part (a), indicating strong positive correlation for the variables.

(c) Substituting $x = 165$ in the regression equation gives: $\hat{y} = 4.855 + 0.284 \times 165 = 51.715$, so we estimate that a family with an annual income of £165,000 would spend approximately 52 days on holiday. This estimate might be unreliable because we have used extrapolation: the linear relationship observed between the two variables may not be valid outside the range of the independent variable ($x = 22.8$ to $x = 92.7$).

14 The technical director has interpreted the gradient incorrectly by misunderstanding the dependent and the independent variable. In this scenario, the dependent variable, y, is the number of days by which the project is delayed and the independent variable, x, is the number of days taken off as sick leave by his team members. He should have estimated that the project is delayed by approximately an additional 7 days each time a day is taken off as sick leave by a member of the team.

15 (a) x = number of pages in the book; y = purchase price

	x	y	xy	x^2	n	$\bar{x}$	$\bar{y}$
	352	36.99	13020.48	123904	10	531	42.021
	792	60.79	48145.68	627264			
	408	11.55	4712.4	166464			
	504	32.29	16274.16	254016		S_{xx}	620314
	368	42.81	15754.08	135424		S_{xy}	12543.23
	324	66.49	21542.76	104976		b	**0.020**
	432	11.99	5179.68	186624		a	**31.284**
	250	55.07	13767.5	62500			
	864	43.34	37445.76	746496			
	1016	58.89	59832.24	1032256			
Totals	**5310**	**420.21**	**235674.7**	**3439924**			

line of best fit is $y = 31.284 + 0.020x$

(b) Substituting $x = 375$ in the line of best fit gives $\hat{y} = 31.284 + 0.020 \times 375 = 38.784$, so we estimate that a business statistics textbook comprising 375 pages would have a purchase price of £37.78.

(c) The constant a is the value of the dependent variable when the value of the independent variable is zero. In this scenario, it does not make any sense to describe the purchase price of a book when the number of pages is zero, and so it would not make any logical sense to provide a practical interpretation of a.

16 The gradient is the expected amount by which the cost of the journey changes every time the length of the journey increases by 1 mile. The gradient would be positive because the cost would increase as the length of the journey increases.

17 (a) Substituting $x = 3$ in the regression equation gives

$$\hat{y} = 152.248 - 13.626 \times 3 = 111.370$$

(b) Substituting $x = 26$ in the regression equation gives

$$\hat{y} = 152.248 - 13.626 \times 10 = 15.988$$

18 Substituting $x = 22$ in the regression equation gives: $\hat{y} = 42.184 + 0.509 \times 22 = 53.382$, so we estimate that a town with a population of 22,000 would generate yearly sales of £53,382. The company has made a mistake when it stated the value of $\hat{y}$ using the units for the observed data (£000s); it has converted 53.382 into hundreds rather than thousands of pounds.

19 (a) Genre of the film is a qualitative variable and therefore is it not possible to apply a simple linear regression model to the film genre and the number of cinema tickets sold; a regression model can only be applied for quantitative variables.
(b) For a simple linear regression model, we are limited to investigating the relationship between a single independent variable and its effect on a dependent variable. There are multiple independent variables and so this model would not be appropriate.

20 In finding the line of best fit, the aim is to draw the line which best fits the data values on a scatter diagram so that the residuals are minimised. This line will provide the best prediction for the dependent variable based on the values of the independent variable.

21 number of visitors: dependent; average daily temperature: independent
$x =$ average daily temperature; $y =$ number of visitors

	x	y	xy	x^2	n	$\bar{x}$	$\bar{y}$
	13.2	1023	13503.6	174.24	9	15.3	1340.778
	16.5	1362	22473	272.25			
	14.9	1298	19340.2	222.01			
	15.2	1369	20808.8	231.04	S_{xx}	15.6	
	13.6	986	13409.6	184.96	S_{xy}	2114.9	
	14.5	1425	20662.5	210.25	b	135.571	
	15.8	1459	23052.2	249.64	a	−733.451	
	16.9	1447	24454.3	285.61			
	17.1	1698	29035.8	292.41			
Totals	137.7	12067	186740	2122.41			

line of best fit is $y = 135.571x - 733.451$

22 Option (c). A scatter diagram can be used to check for the existence of a linear relationship between two quantitative variables before applying a simple linear regression model.

23 We can only use the regression equation to provide a reliable prediction if the given value for x fits within the range of the x-values in the original data set; this is known as 'interpolation'. If we use an x-value that is outside the range of the data, then this procedure is called 'extrapolation', and our predicted value, $\hat{y}$, may not be reliable because the linear relationship observed between the two variables may no longer be valid.

24 (a) It would be appropriate to apply a simple linear regression model to these data because the scatter diagram verifies the existence of a linear relationship between the variables.
   (b) The response variable in this scenario is the number of votes received because it changes in response to the number of public appearances.

25 Option (a). An estimate of the change in insurance premium when the number of claims increases by one is the same as the gradient of the line of best fit, which is £29.50.

26 (a) $x =$ number of people in a supermarket queue; $y =$ time taken to be served

	x	y	xy	x^2	n	$\bar{x}$	$\bar{y}$
	2	5	10	4	6	4.667	9.500
	5	9	45	25			
	8	16	128	64			
	3	7	21	9		S_{xx}	23.333
	6	12	72	36		S_{xy}	42.000
	4	8	32	16		b	**1.800**
Totals	28	57	308	154		a	**1.100**

   regression line is $y = 1.100 + 1.800x$
   (b) constant a
   1.100 is the expected time taken to be served when the number of people in the queue is zero; we estimate that it will take 1.1 minutes to be served if there is no queue for the check-out.
   constant b
   1.800 is the expected amount by which the time taken to be served increases for every one unit increase in the number of people in the queue; we estimate that it takes an additional 1.8 minutes to be served every time one more person is in the queue.

27 Option (a). The independent variable should always be plotted using the x-axis.

28 It would not be appropriate to use a line of best fit to predict the monthly income of a family from the amount that they spend on food each month because monthly income is the independent variable and food expenditure is the dependent variable. A regression model is used to predict the value of the dependent variable for any specific value of the independent variable.

29 (a) the response variable is the mileage of the car
(b) $x=$ age of the car in years; $y=$ mileage in 000s miles

	x	y	xy	x^2	n	$\bar{x}$	$\bar{y}$
	3	29	87	9	12	5.583	42.167
	7	48	336	49			
	5	39	195	25			
	2	25	50	4		S_{xx}	68.917
	6	38	228	36		S_{xy}	348.833
	8	55	440	64		b	**5.062**
	9	62	558	81		a	**13.906**
	4	37	148	16			
	5	41	205	25			
	9	59	531	81			
	2	23	46	4			
	7	50	350	49			
Totals	67	506	3174	443			

As stated in the question, $S_{xy} = 68.917$ and $S_{xy} = 348.833$ rounded to three decimal places.

$$S_{xy} = \sum x_i y_i - \frac{\sum x_i \sum y_i}{n} = 3174 - \frac{67 \times 506}{12} = 348.833$$

$$S_{xx} = \sum x_i^2 - \frac{\left(\sum x_i\right)^2}{n} = 443 - \frac{67^2}{12} = 68.917$$

(c) The line of best fit is $y = 13.906 + 5.062x$.

30 The reporter has provided a practical interpretation of the y-intercept when it was not reasonable to do so. In this scenario, it does not make any sense to describe the top speed of a car when its engine capacity is zero because an engine capacity would never be zero.

31 (a) independent
(b) y-intercept, zero
(c) b, dependent, one
(d) x, dependent

32 Option (c). An estimate of the number of products sold when the company has no advertising expenditure is the same as the y-intercept of the line of best fit; this value is 6.53, which equates to 6530 products sold when the correct units are used.

33 (a) $x =$ time spent in supermarket (minutes); $y =$ number of items purchased

	x	y	xy	x^2	n	$\bar{x}$	$\bar{y}$
	30	12	360	900	15	35.6	30.4
	12	2	24	144			
	85	84	7140	7225			
	62	49	3038	3844		S_{xx}	5161.6
	45	72	3240	2025		S_{xy}	6186.4
	17	4	68	289		b	**1.199**
	35	26	910	1225		a	**–12.268**
	31	27	837	961			
	26	18	468	676			
	49	61	2989	2401			
	22	20	440	484			
	27	4	108	729			
	15	8	120	225			
	38	41	1558	1444			
	40	28	1120	1600			
Totals	**534**	**456**	**22420**	**24172**			

We can verify that the regression line is $y = 1.199x - 12.268$.
(b) A practical interpretation of a would be inappropriate because it would describe the number of items purchased when the shopper spends zero minutes – no time – in the supermarket.

34 (a) y-intercept is 2, gradient is -3
(b) y-intercept is -8, gradient is 14

35 (a) The dependent and independent variables are identified the wrong way round. The correct statement would be:
    Every straight line on a graph can be described by a linear equation in the general form of $y = a + bx$ where x is the *independent* variable and the *dependent* variable is y.
    (b) In this statement, the incorrect name is given to the constant a. It should say:
    At the point where a straight line crosses the y-axis, the constant a, also known as the *y-intercept*, is equal to the y-value of the coordinate.

36
$$b = \frac{117}{228} = 0.513$$

$$a = 4.333 - \left(\frac{117}{228} \times 7.667\right) = 0.399$$

The regression equation is $y = 0.399 + 0.513x$.
Substituting $x = 4$ in the regression equation gives $\hat{y} = 0.399 + 0.513 \times 4 = 2.451$.

37 (a) TRUE
    (b) FALSE
    Sometimes, where zero would not be a reasonable value for the independent variable, it does not make any logical sense to provide a practical interpretation of a.
    (c) TRUE
    (d) TRUE
    (e) FALSE
    The gradient of the regression equation can be negative or positive. If it is negative it represents a decrease in the value of y, whereas a positive gradient represents an increase in y for every one-unit increase in the independent variable.

38 Substituting $x = 600$ in the regression equation gives $\hat{y} = 128.374 + 0.537 \times 600 = 450.574$, so we estimate that a movie which generates \$600 million in income would result in a profit of approximately \$450.6 million.

39 (a)
$$b = \frac{15.539 - \dfrac{10.37 \times 12.907}{8}}{\left(14.322 - \dfrac{10.37^2}{8}\right)} = \frac{-1.192}{0.880} = -1.354$$

$$a = \frac{12.907}{8} - \left(\frac{-1.192}{0.880} \times \frac{10.37}{8}\right) = 3.369$$

regression line is $y = 3.369 - 1.354x$
    (b) Substituting $x = 1.450$ in the linear equation gives $\hat{y} = 3.369 - 1.354 \times 1.450 = 1.406$, so we estimate that the monthly disposable income is £1406 for a family whose mortgage repayment is £1450 each month.

40   (a) Substituting $x = 9$ in the linear equation gives

$$y = 35 + 13 \times 9 = 152$$

Substituting $x = 17$ in the linear equation gives

$$y = 35 + 13 \times 17 = 256$$

(b) Substituting $x = 9$ in the linear equation gives

$$y = 26 \times 9 - 4 = 230$$

Substituting $x = 17$ in the linear equation gives

$$y = 26 \times 17 - 4 = 438$$

Probability

OBJECTIVES

This chapter explains how to:

- distinguish between empirical, classical and subjective probability
- understand the meaning of
  - mutually exclusive events and independent events
  - intersection and union
  - conditional probability
- draw and interpret Venn diagrams
- calculate probabilities using
  - complement rule
  - addition rule
  - multiplication rule

KEY TERMS

addition rule
certain event
classical approach
complement event
compound event
conditional probability
empirical approach
equally likely outcomes
event

experiment
impossible event
independent events
intersection
multiplication rule
mutually exclusive events
outcome
probability
probability model

relative frequency
probability
sample space
simple event
subjective approach
union
Venn diagram

Introduction

In previous chapters, we have focused on presenting and summarising data that has been collected by taking measurements, asking questions or making observations in a specific situation. We have been certain about our data, mostly because they are based on occurrences that have already happened. For a company we could record with certainty the number of complaints from customers, the price of its products and the monthly profit; similarly, we could describe with certainty the way an employee travels to the office, their annual salary and how often they are absent from work. However, we are sometimes faced with situations in which there is some uncertainty, particularly if an occurrence has not yet taken place. For example, a company does not know exactly how many units of a product will be sold during the next summer sale; an employee cannot know with certainty that they will not be made redundant in the coming year.

Probability provides techniques that can be applied in situations where there is uncertainty and allows us to assign a numerical value to the likelihood of an occurrence. This chapter introduces basic terminology and notation, explains the underlying concepts and describes some rules for calculating probabilities.

Whilst explaining the concepts of probability, we will use two different types of example in this chapter. Sometimes, we will use simple and familiar activities such as rolling a die, whereas in other sections, business-based scenarios will be used to add context.

Terminology

In probability, we define an experiment, an outcome, the sample space and an event as follows:

Experiment
    An experiment is any action or process that can be repeated. We do not know the result of an experiment before it is carried out, but we can identify all of the results that could possibly occur.

Outcome
    An outcome is simply the result of an experiment.

Sample Space
    The sample space is the set of all possible outcomes of an experiment. Each possible result is represented by one and only one element in the sample space. We use S to denote the sample space of an experiment. The elements in the sample space are usually listed individually, but sometimes it can be more convenient to identify them with a descriptive statement. The order in which individual elements are listed in the sample space is unimportant.

Event
    An event is a collection of one or more outcomes of an experiment. It is always a subset of the sample space. A simple event consists of a single element in the sample space. An event which consists of more than one element in the sample space is called a compound event.

We usually denote an event with an uppercase letter. If we are discussing a scenario with one event, then A is often used, whereas if two events are involved, we would choose A and B. However, any uppercase letter would be acceptable. Sometimes we use descriptive text instead of a single letter. The probability that an event will occur is denoted by P(event), so the probability of event A occurring would be written as $P(A)$.

EXAMPLES – TERMINOLOGY

The table below demonstrates the use of this terminology using different scenarios.

Experiment	Outcome	Sample space	Event
Roll a die and record the number facing upwards	2	$S = \{1, 2, 3, 4, 5, 6\}$	The number facing upwards is odd
Flip two coins and record the sides which are facing upwards	Heads Tails	$S = \{HH, HT, TH, TT\}$	The sides facing upwards are the same
Interview three consumers and record their choice of product A or product B	A B B	$S = \{AAA, AAB, ABB, ABA, BAA, BAB, BBA, BBB\}$	The consumers all choose the same product
Select a call-centre operative from a utilities company and record their gender	M	$S = \{M, F\}$	The call-centre operative is male

However, it should be noted that this selection represents just some of the examples that could be devised:

- There are many other experiments that could be carried out based on rolling a die, flipping coins, interviewing consumers and observing shoppers; in the first example, we could have decided to roll two dice and record the sum of the upward facing numbers.
- The second column lists an outcome from one trial of the experiment; we could have chosen 3 or 6, but not 9, for the first example.
- For each experiment that we have chosen in the table, the sample space is the only sample space that could be defined; there are no alternative lists that could be substituted in this column.
- There are several possible events that could be defined for each experiment in our table; for the die rolling, we could have defined the example event as 'the number facing upwards is greater than 4'.

Approaches to Probability

In this section, we introduce three different approaches that can be used to determine the probability of an event: classical, empirical and subjective.

CLASSICAL APPROACH

The **classical approach** to probability can be applied to situations where the probability of every possible outcome of an experiment is the same. In this case, we say that the experiment has **equally likely outcomes**. We measure the proportion of times that an event will occur, and so the probability of an event is calculated as follows:

$$\text{probability of an event} = \frac{\text{number of ways the event can occur}}{\text{number of possible outcomes}}$$

It is not necessary to actually perform the experiment when using the classical approach because the probability of an event is determined by understanding the nature of the experiment and by counting relevant outcomes in the sample space. We can use the classical approach to choose a specific sample from a larger group of elements because, as we discussed in Chapter 2, every possible sample of a specified size has an equal chance of being selected in simple random sampling.

EXAMPLES – CLASSICAL APPROACH

1. Experiment: roll a die and record the number facing upwards
   Event: 'the number facing upwards is less than 5'
   Sample space: $S = \{1, 2, 3, 4, 5, 6\}$

   P(number on a die is less than 5)

   $$= \frac{\text{number of elements in the sample space that are less than 5}}{\text{number of elements in the sample space}}$$

   There are four elements in the sample space that belong to this event $\{1, 2, 3, 4\}$, so:

   $$P(\text{number on a die is less than 5}) = \frac{4}{6}$$

2. Experiment: randomly select two members of a sales team (Matt, Jane, Alex, Emma and Nick) to meet with a client
   Event: 'Jane is selected to attend the meeting'
   Sample space: $S = \{$Matt/Jane, Matt/Alex, Matt/Emma, Matt/Nick, Jane/Alex, Jane/Emma, Jane/Nick, Alex/Emma, Alex/Nick, Emma/Nick$\}$

   $$P(\text{Jane is selected}) = \frac{\text{number of elements in the sample space that include Jane}}{\text{number of elements in the sample space}}$$

   There are four elements in the sample space that include Jane, $\{$Matt/Jane, Jane/Alex, Jane/Emma, Jane/Nick$\}$, so:

   $$P(\text{Jane is selected}) = \frac{4}{10}$$

EMPIRICAL APPROACH

We can apply the **empirical approach** to determine the probability of an event when our experiment does not have equally likely outcomes. Given a set of collected data, the relative frequency of an event is used to estimate the probability for that event:

$$\text{probability of an event} = \frac{\text{number of times the event is observed}}{\text{total number of observations}}$$

We have two choices for the data source in this approach – we can use an existing set of data or we can repeatedly perform the experiment to collect a new data set.

Using the empirical approach, we obtain an approximate probability rather than an exact probability because there will be different relative frequencies for an event in each set of data or each repeatedly performed experiment. As the number of observations increases, the estimate becomes numerically closer to the actual probability of the event.

Because it is based on relative frequencies, the empirical approach is sometimes known as relative frequency probability.

EXAMPLES – EMPIRICAL APPROACH

1. A supermarket employees 300 people; 180 of the employees work part-time and 120 are full-time workers. If an employee is selected at random, we can use the empirical approach to estimate the probability that they work part-time as follows:

$$P(\text{part-time}) = \frac{\text{number of part-time workers}}{\text{total number of employees}} = \frac{120}{300}$$

2. In a customer satisfaction survey, 250 supermarket customers were asked to state their primary reason for shopping in the store. The results of the survey are shown below:

Reason for shopping	Frequency
low prices	110
locally sourced produce	12
flexible opening hours	32
large car park	65
friendliness of staff	31

If a customer is selected at random, we can use relative frequencies to estimate the probability that low prices are the primary reason for shopping in the store:

$$P(\text{low prices}) = \frac{\text{number of customers who answer 'low prices' in the survey}}{\text{number of customers who participated in the survey}} = \frac{110}{250}$$

SUBJECTIVE APPROACH

There are many situations in which our experiment does not have equally likely outcomes and cannot be performed repeatedly. We would be unable to use the classical or empirical approach in this case but we may apply the subjective approach instead.

This approach is based on the personal experience and judgement of the individual who is determining the probability of the event. There is no formula – the probability is assigned arbitrarily depending on the likelihood with which the individual believes the event will happen.

EXAMPLE – SUBJECTIVE APPROACH

On behalf of an online clothing company, a market researcher invites ten shoppers to join a focus group to discuss the customer service offered by the company.

During the focus group meeting, he plans to make a telephone call to the customer service department and record the number of minutes it takes for him to talk to a representative of the company. He would like to investigate the probability that he will wait more than 5 minutes before speaking to a customer service representative.

Once the telephone call has been made, it would not be possible to repeat the experiment again with exactly the same set of circumstances. There may be a different number of customer service representatives 'on call' when the next telephone call is made, or more shoppers may be telephoning at the same time, or there may be some very complex issues being resolved that take considerable time.

As this is not a repeatable experiment and it does not have equally likely outcomes, we could apply the subjective probability approach and ask each of the ten members of the focus group to assign a probability to the event. In this case, it is likely that we would obtain several, maybe ten, different probabilities for this event, depending on the knowledge and experience of the shoppers. For example, someone in the group who had previously remained in an automated queue for 20 minutes would have a very different opinion about the probability compared to someone who had spoken immediately to a customer service representative in their last three telephone calls.

Basic Properties

Regardless of the approach that we use to determine the probability of an event, all probabilities are defined by the two properties described below.

PROPERTY 1

We express the probability of an event using a numerical value within the range of zero to one, inclusive. The probability of an event cannot be a value that is less than zero or greater than one, so probabilities such as −0.65 or 2.7 are not possible. For a specific event A, we can express this property using mathematical notation as follows:

$$0 \leq P(A) \leq 1$$

Assigning a probability of zero indicates that the event will not occur; this event is known as an **impossible event**. An event with a probability equal to exactly one will be certain to occur and is called a **certain event**. If an event A is an impossible event, then $P(A) = 0$; if $P(B) = 1$, then event B is a certain event. Most often, we determine the probability of an event to be between zero and one, rather than exactly zero or exactly one. A probability close to zero would indicate that an event is very unlikely to occur; similarly, an event with probability very close to one would be very likely to occur.

The diagram below gives a visual representation of this property.

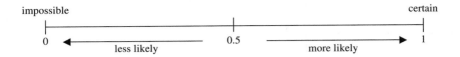

PROPERTY 2

In our earlier section on terminology, we defined a simple event as an event consisting of a single element in the sample space.

When the probabilities of all simple events for an experiment are added together, the sum must be equal to 1. So, if the sample space is defined as $S = \{e_1, e_2, e_3, \ldots, e_n\}$, then

$$\sum P(e_i) = P(e_1) + P(e_2) + P(e_3) + \cdots + P(e_n) = 1$$

Returning to our tabulated examples, this property shows us:

Experiment	Sample space	
Roll a die and record the number facing upwards	$S = \{1, 2, 3, 4, 5, 6\}$	$P(1) + P(2) + P(3) + P(4)$ $+ P(5) + P(6) = 1$
Flip two coins and record the sides which are facing upwards	$S = \{\text{HH, HT, TH, TT}\}$	$P(\text{HH}) + P(\text{HT}) + P(\text{TH}) + P(\text{TT}) = 1$
Interview three consumers and record their choice of product A or product B	$S = \{\text{AAA, AAB,}$ ABB, ABA, BAA, $\text{BAB, BBA, BBB}\}$	$P(\text{AAA}) + P(\text{AAB}) + P(\text{ABB})$ $+P(\text{ABA}) + P(\text{BAA}) + P(\text{BAB})$ $+P(\text{BBA}) + P(\text{BBB}) = 1$
Select a call centre operative from a utilities company and record their gender	$S = \{\text{M, F}\}$	$P(\text{M}) + P(\text{F}) = 1$

Probability Model

A probability model can be constructed by assigning a probability to every element in the sample space for an experiment. A probability model is valid only if the probabilities assigned can be defined by the two properties described in the previous section.

EXAMPLES – PROBABILITY MODEL

Returning to two of our earlier examples:

1. Experiment: randomly select two members of a sales team (Matt, Jane, Alex, Emma and Nick) to meet with a client

Sample space: S = {Matt/Jane, Matt/Alex, Matt/Emma, Matt/Nick, Jane/Alex, Jane/Emma, Jane/Nick, Alex/Emma, Alex/Nick, Emma/Nick}

The table below shows each pair of sales team members that could be selected, and their probability of being selected. It is a valid probability model because:

- every probability is greater than zero and less than one, inclusive;
- the sum of the probabilities is equal to 1.

Pair of sales team members	Probability
Matt/Jane	0.1
Matt/Alex	0.1
Matt/Emma	0.1
Matt/Nick	0.1
Jane/Alex	0.1
Jane/Emma	0.1
Jane/Nick	0.1
Alex/Emma	0.1
Alex/Nick	0.1
Emma/Nick	0.1

2. In a customer satisfaction survey, 250 supermarket customers were asked to state their primary reason for shopping in the store. Assigning probabilities based on the relative frequencies gives:

Reason for shopping	Frequency	Probability
low prices	110	0.440
locally sourced produce	12	0.048
flexible opening hours	32	0.128
large car park	65	0.260
friendliness of staff	31	0.124

Both of the basic properties apply to the probabilities and so we can conclude that this is a valid probability model.

Venn Diagrams

A Venn diagram, named after John Venn (1834–1923), can be used to provide a visual interpretation of an experiment and associated events. The sample space of the experiment is represented by a rectangle and each event is shown as a circle or an ellipse within the rectangle.

In its simplest form, a Venn diagram can be drawn to display a single event. In the diagram below, the event A is represented by the shaded area inside the ellipse.

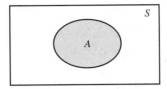

Venn diagrams are particularly useful for showing the relationships between two or more events and we will use them in the remainder of this chapter as new concepts are introduced.

Mutually Exclusive Events

Events that cannot occur at the same time are known as **mutually exclusive events**; they have no common elements. Each time an experiment is repeated, no more than one of a collection of mutually exclusive events will occur.

The Venn diagram below provides a visual representation of two mutually exclusive events, A and B.

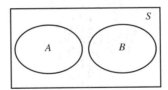

Suppose we conducted an experiment that involved rolling a die and recording the number facing upwards.

Defining two events, A: 'the number facing upwards is odd', and B: 'the number facing upwards is even', we can see that the events A and B are mutually exclusive because they cannot occur at the same time: the number facing upwards on a die cannot be odd **and** even. There are no shared elements in events A and B: $A = \{1, 3, 5\}$, whereas $B = \{2, 4, 6\}$.

Independent Events

Two events are called **independent events** if the occurrence of one event in an experiment does not have any effect on the occurrence of the other event.

Suppose we conducted an experiment that involved rolling a die, recording the number facing upwards and flipping a coin, recording the side facing upwards. Defining two events, A: 'the number facing upwards is odd', and B: 'the side facing upwards is a head', we can see that the events A and B are independent because the probability of getting an odd number facing upwards on the die does not influence the probability of the coin side being a 'head'.

Complement Rule

If we identify an event A, then we can define a **complement event** which consists of all of the elements in the sample space that are not in A. The complement of A is denoted as A^c or A', and is read as 'not A'; it can be represented as the shaded area on a Venn diagram as follows:

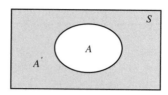

The events A and A' are mutually exclusive because the occurrence of event A means that event A' does not occur and vice versa.

Earlier in this chapter, we showed that when the probabilities for every element in the sample space for an experiment are added together, the sum must be equal to one. The two events A and A' together include every element in the sample space and therefore the sum of their probabilities must also be equal to one: $P(A) + P(A') = 1$. So, if we know the probability of an event, we can calculate the probability of its complement, and vice versa.

Rearranging the equation gives us the complement rule, which states that

$$P(A) = 1 - P(A') \quad \text{and} \quad P(A') = 1 - P(A)$$

EXAMPLES – COMPLEMENT RULE

1. In an earlier example, we considered an experiment in which a die was rolled and the number facing upwards was recorded. Using the classical approach to probability, we found that

$$P(\text{number on a die is less than 5}) = \frac{4}{6}$$

   Applying the complement rule gives

$$P(\text{number on a die is greater than or equal to 5})$$

$$= 1 - P(\text{number on a die is less than 5}) = 1 - \frac{4}{6} = \frac{2}{6}$$

   We can verify that this result is correct by referring to the sample space for the experiment; there are two elements in the sample space that are greater than or equal to 5: {5, 6}.

2. After the polling stations closed for local elections, 650 adults were asked if they had voted; 390 adults said they had chosen to vote, whereas 260 adults had abstained. If one of the 650 adults is selected at random, we can use relative frequencies to estimate that

$$P(\text{the adult selected did vote}) = \frac{390}{650} = 0.6$$

Suppose we use A to denote the event 'the adult selected did vote', then A' would represent the event 'the adult selected did not vote'. The complement rule states that $P(A') = 1 - P(A)$, so

$$P(A') = 1 - \frac{390}{650} = 0.4$$

Intersection and Union

If we define events A and B, then the **intersection** of these two events is the collection of elements in the sample space that are common to both event A and event B. Using probability notation, we denote this intersection as $A \cap B$, read as 'A and B'. The intersection $A \cap B$ occurs if and only if events A and B both occur.

The collection of all elements in the sample space that belong to at least one of these events is known as the **union** of A and B. It is denoted as $A \cup B$, read as 'A or B'. The occurrence of the union means that either A or B or both events occur.

The shaded area on a Venn diagram can be used to describe intersection and union.

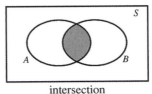

intersection
$A \cap B$
A and B
events A and B both occur

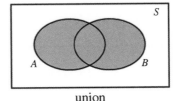

union
$A \cup B$
A or B
either A or B or both events occur

EXAMPLES – INTERSECTION AND UNION

1. Experiment: roll a die and record the number facing upwards
   Based on this experiment, we can define two events, A: 'the number facing upwards is odd', and B: 'the number facing upwards is a multiple of 3'. The elements $\{1, 3, 5\}$ belong to A and $\{3, 6\}$ belong to B.
   The intersection, $A \cap B$, consists of all elements that are common to both event A and event B. In this case, there is only one element $\{3\}$ which belongs to both events.

In the union, $A \cup B$, we include all the elements in the sample space that belong in either A or B or both events. For this experiment, the set of elements in the union is $\{1, 3, 5, 6\}$.

2. Experiment: randomly select an employee, and record whether they have a company pension and whether they have a company car.
   Event A: 'the employee has a company pension'
   Event B: 'the employee has a company car'
   For this example, the intersection of events A and B represents all of the employees who have both a company pension and a company car. It is all of the employees who answered 'yes' when asked 'do you have a company pension?' and 'yes' when asked 'do you have a company car?'.
   In the union of A and B, we would include all of the employees who:
   - just have a company pension;
   - just have a company car;
   - have both a company pension and a company car.

   It is all those employees who are included in either event A, or event B, or in both events.

Addition Rule

The **addition rule** provides us with a way of calculating the probability of the union of two events. If two events, A and B, are not mutually exclusive, recall that a visual representation of their union is as shown in the diagram:

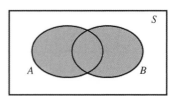

We could calculate the probability of the shaded area by adding together the probability of each individual event. However, as we can see from the diagram, this would mean that the central section, or intersection of the two events, would be accounted for twice. Therefore, we must subtract the probability of the intersection from the sum of the individual probabilities. This procedure results in the addition rule for the union of two events:

$$P(A \cup B) = P(A) + P(B) - P(A \cap B)$$

If our two events, A and B, are mutually exclusive, then there are no elements in the sample space which belong to both event A and event B. The intersection is therefore an impossible event and its probability is zero. So, for two events, A and B, that are mutually exclusive, the addition rule becomes

$$P(A \cup B) = P(A) + P(B)$$

In either case, the addition rule can be extended to the calculation of the union of more than two events.

EXAMPLES – ADDITION RULE

1. A supermarket employees 200 people; 40 of the employees work part-time, 60 of the employees are male, and 15 are female and work part-time. Defining the following events: event F: 'a randomly selected employee is female' and event PT: 'a randomly selected employee works part-time', we can deduce that

$$P(F) = 1 - P(F') = 1 - \frac{60}{200} = \frac{140}{200} \quad P(PT) = \frac{40}{200} \quad P(F \cap PT) = \frac{15}{200}$$

Using the addition rule, we can calculate the probability of the union of the two events:

$$P(F \cup PT) = P(F) + P(PT) - P(F \cap PT) = \frac{140}{200} + \frac{40}{200} - \frac{15}{200} = \frac{165}{200}$$

2. In an online survey, 60 home owners were asked whether they would like to have solar panels fitted to their property roof. The collected responses are shown in the table below.

Response	Home owners
yes	20
no	5
maybe	35

Selecting a home owner at random, we can define three events:

Y = the home owner wants solar panels,

N = the home owner does not want solar panels,

M = the home owner is undecided about solar panels.

The events Y and N are mutually exclusive because they cannot occur at the same time: a home owner cannot answer 'yes' and 'no' to the question about solar panels. Therefore, we can calculate the probability that a randomly selected home owner has made a decision about solar panels as follows:

$$P(Y \cup N) = P(Y) + P(N) = \frac{20}{60} + \frac{5}{60} = \frac{25}{60}$$

3. The following table shows the views of 500 teenagers about their preferred method for buying clothing:

Purchasing method	Males	Females	Totals
online	55	90	145
in-store	20	175	195
no preference	110	50	160
totals	185	315	500

Using the frequencies and totals in the table, and the addition rule, we can calculate probabilities according to our area of interest. The total number of females is 315, so

$$P(\text{a randomly chosen teenager is female}) = \frac{315}{500} = 0.63$$

The total number of teenagers who prefer to shop in-store is 195, so

$$P(\text{a randomly chosen teenager prefers to shop in-store}) = \frac{195}{500} = 0.39$$

Preferring to shop online and having no preference are mutually exclusive events, so

$$P(\text{a randomly chosen teenager prefers shopping on-line or has no preference})$$
$$= P(\text{online}) + P(\text{no preference}) = \frac{145}{500} + \frac{160}{500} = 0.61$$

Preferring to shop in-store and being male are not mutually exclusive events, so

$$P(\text{a randomly chosen teenager prefers shopping in-store or is male})$$
$$= P(\text{in-store}) + P(\text{male}) - P(\text{in-store and male}) = \frac{195}{500} + \frac{185}{500} - \frac{20}{500} = 0.72$$

Conditional Probability

The conditional probability of an event is the probability that the event occurs, given the knowledge that another event has already occurred.

For example, the conditional probability of an event B is the probability that event B occurs, given that we know that event A has already occurred. It is denoted as $P(B|A)$, read as 'the probability of B given A'.

To calculate conditional probability, we use the following formulae:

$$P(B|A) = \frac{P(B \cap A)}{P(A)} \quad \text{and} \quad P(A|B) = \frac{P(A \cap B)}{P(B)}$$

Whenever the occurrence of event A does not have any effect on the occurrence of event B, we say that the events A and B are independent and the conditional probability, $P(B|A)$, is equal to the probability of event B: it is unchanged by the occurrence of event A. So, for two independent events:

$$P(B|A) = P(B) \quad \text{and} \quad P(A|B) = P(A)$$

EXAMPLES – CONDITIONAL PROBABILITY

1. A restaurant owner carried out a survey to understand the preferences of its customers on a Saturday evening. After finishing their meal, 37% of customers said they would like coffee and 24% said they would like both a dessert and coffee.

We can define the following events: event C: 'the customer would like coffee' and event D: 'the customer would like a dessert'. So

$$P(C) = 0.37 \quad \text{and} \quad P(D \cap C) = 0.24$$

Randomly selecting a customer in the restaurant, we can calculate the probability that they would like dessert, given that they would like coffee, as follows:

$$P(D \mid C) = \frac{P(D \cap C)}{P(C)} = \frac{0.24}{0.37} = 0.649$$

2. The supervisor at an airline company records the arrival and departure details for 100 flights from the UK. He finds that 56 of the flights depart on time and 18 of the flights depart on time and arrive on time. Defining the following events: event D: 'a randomly selected flight departs on time' and event A: 'a randomly selected flight arrives on time', we can deduce the following probabilities:

$$P(D) = 0.56 \quad \text{and} \quad P(D \cap A) = P(A \cap D) = 0.18$$

Therefore, using the formula for conditional probability, we can calculate the probability that a randomly selected flight which leaves on time will arrive on time:

$$P(A \mid D) = \frac{P(A \cap D)}{P(D)} = \frac{0.18}{0.56} = 0.321$$

Multiplication Rule

Rearranging the formulae for conditional probability gives the **multiplication rule**, which can be used can be used to calculate the probability of the intersection of two events as follows:

$$P(A \cap B) = P(B \mid A)P(A)$$

Recalling that $P(A \cap B)$ is the same as $P(B \cap A)$, we can derive the equivalent formula:

$$P(A \cap B) = P(A \mid B)P(B)$$

As the multiplication rule is a rearrangement of the formulae for conditional probability, we can use this rule to calculate the intersection of two events or the conditional probability for two events. For two independent events, our knowledge of conditional probability shows that $P(A \mid B) = P(A)$, and so the multiplication rule becomes

$$P(A \cap B) = P(A)P(B)$$

EXAMPLES – MULTIPLICATION RULE

1. Suppose we returned to our earlier experiment that involved rolling a die, recording the number facing upwards, and flipping a coin, recording the side facing upwards. We defined two events, A: 'the number facing upwards is odd' and B: 'the side facing upwards is a head', and we found that A and B were independent.
As $P(A) = \frac{1}{2}$ and $P(B) = \frac{1}{2}$, we can find the probability of their intersection using the multiplication rule:

$$P(A \cap B) = P(A)P(B) = \frac{1}{2} \times \frac{1}{2} = \frac{1}{4}$$

2. From all of the houses within the same postal district, we select one at random. The probability that the house has a conservatory is 0.4 and the probability that the house has a garage, given that it has a conservatory, is 0.8.
Using the multiplication rule, and defining the events $C =$ 'the house has a conservatory' and $G =$ 'the house has a garage', we can calculate the probability that the selected house has a conservatory and a garage as follows:

$$P(C \cap G) = P(G|C)P(C) = 0.8 \times 0.4 = 0.32$$

3. In a group of 20 trainee accountants, there are 8 females and 12 males. At random, an auditor chooses the work of two trainees to check for mistakes.
Using F to represent 'female' and M to represent 'male', we can identify the first and second trainee selected using subscripts. For example, F_1M_2 will mean that first a female is selected, followed by a male.
If we are interested in the probability that the auditor will choose the work of two females, we need to use the multiplication rule as follows:

$$P(F_1 \cap F_2) = P(F_2|F_1)P(F_1)$$

From the information given, we know that the probability of choosing a female first, $P(F_1)$, is $\frac{8}{20}$.
For $P(F_2|F_1)$, we can consider the number of females and the total number of trainees that remain in the group given that a female is chosen first.
When a female is chosen, there are 19 trainee accountants remaining, 7 of whom are female, so $P(F_2|F_1) = \frac{7}{19}$.
Returning to our multiplication rule, we can calculate:

$$P(F_1 \cap F_2) = P(F_2|F_1)P(F_1) = \frac{7}{19} \times \frac{8}{20} = 0.147$$

HINTS AND TIPS

INTERSECTION AND UNION FOR THREE EVENTS

Earlier in this chapter, we have discussed intersection and union in terms of two events. However, it is possible to extend these concepts to three events, A, B and C.

The intersection, denoted as $A \cap B \cap C$, is the collection of elements in the sample space that are common to all three events; it can be represented on a Venn diagram as follows:

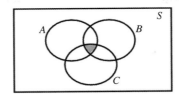

The Venn diagram below represents the union of events A, B and C, denoted as $A \cup B \cup C$. It is the collection of elements in the sample space that belong to at least one of A, B and C.

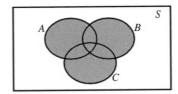

EXPRESSING PROBABILITIES

The probability of an event can be expressed as a fraction, a decimal or a percentage; for an event A, we could say $P(A) = 0.4$ or $P(A) = \frac{2}{5}$ or $P(A) = 40\%$.

EQUIVALENCE IN INTERSECTIONS AND UNIONS

Because 'both event A and event B occurring' is the same as 'both event B and event A occurring', we can say that $A \cap B$ is the same as $B \cap A$. Similarly, as shown in the Venn diagram below, it can be seen that $A \cup B$ is the same as $B \cup A$.

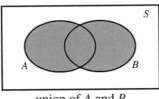

union of A and B
$A \cup B$

Practice Exercises

1   A survey given to a sample of 140 supermarket customers showed that 62 of them used a store loyalty card to collect points during their last visit. If two customers were randomly selected from the sample, find the probability that both of those customers used a store loyalty card.

2   The sample space for an experiment is $S = \{1, 2, 3, 4, 5, 6, 7, 8\}$ and each element is equally likely. Events are defined as follows: $A = \{3, 4, 5, 6\}$, $B = \{1, 2, 3, 4\}$, $C = \{7, 8\}$.
(a) Are events A and C mutually exclusive? Give a reason for your answer.
(b) Are events A and B mutually exclusive? Give a reason for your answer.
(c) List the elements in $B \cup C$. Write down $P(B \cup C)$.
(d) List the elements in A'.

3   For each experiment listed below, define the sample space using appropriate notation.
(a) flip three coins and record the sides which are facing upwards
(b) select a train from a rail journey schedule and record whether it was early, late or on-time when it reached its final destination
(c) choose an undergraduate student at a university and record their year of study

4   The probability that a member of a political party is male is 0.74 and the probability that a member is male and has children is 0.20. The conditional probability that a randomly selected party member has children, given that he is male:
(a) equals 0.27
(b) is greater than 1
(c) cannot be calculated

5   In a survey conducted about hot drink preference, it is found that the probability that a randomly selected female prefers tea is 0.34 and the probability that a randomly selected female prefers coffee is 0.59. If a female is randomly selected from the respondents:
(a) What is the probability that she does not prefer coffee?
(b) What is the probability that she prefers tea or prefers coffee?
(c) Is it possible for the probability that she prefers hot chocolate to be 0.21?

6   The following table show the category of magazines that are available for subscription with a company that provides an online ordering service.

Magazine category	Frequency
computers and technology	61
crafts	88
food and home	109
science and nature	18
sport	134

(*Continued*)

Magazine category	Frequency
travel	38
lifestyle	52
total	500

Use this data set to construct a probability model for magazine categories.

7 For each of the following, draw a Venn diagram using a shaded area to represent the event:
(a) not *A*
(b) *A* ∪ *B*
(c) *A* and *B* and *C*

8 The sales records at a supermarket show that during a three-month period, 65% of shoppers spent over £100 in one transaction. If the probability that a shopper spent over £100 in one transaction and paid with a credit card is 0.28, calculate the probability that a shopper paid with a credit card given that they spent over £100 in one transaction.

9 A research project involved interviewing 340 children who attended the same school. It was found that 289 of them had at least one sibling. If a child is randomly selected from this group, what is the probability that they have at least one sibling?

10 The probability that a teacher in a school has a degree in the subject in which they teach is 0.72. Suppose we select two teachers at random from this school. Calculate the probability that both teachers have a degree in the subject in which they teach.

11 If we randomly select an adult living in the UK, the probability that they are a home owner is 0.64 and the probability that they are a car owner is 0.75. Do we have enough information to calculate the probability that a randomly selected adult living in the UK owns a home or owns a car? Explain your response.

12 Explain what is meant by the classical approach to probability.

13 For a research project investigating the relationship between gender and exercise, 200 adults were asked if they have been a member of a gym. The results are shown below:

	Female	Male	Total
Has been a gym member	24	65	89
Has not been a gym member	80	31	111
Total	104	96	200

If we choose one adult at random from the 200 respondents, find the probability that this adult:
(a) has been a gym member
(b) is female
(c) is male, given that they have been a gym member
(d) has not been a gym member, given that they are female

14 Given that A and B are independent events, find $P(A \cap B)$ when $P(A) = 0.34$ and $P(B) = 0.41$.

15 In a floral display at a garden centre, there are 200 flowers; 60 flowers are pink, 80 are yellow, 40 are white and the remaining flowers are purple. If a flower is picked at random from the floral display, find the following probabilities:
(a) $P(\text{yellow})$
(b) $P(\text{purple})$
(c) $P(\text{red})$

16 If A and B are mutually exclusive events, work out the probability of the union of A and B for the following experiments:
(a) $P(A) = 0.36$ and $P(B) = 0.11$
(b) $P(A) = 0.22$ and $P(B) = 0.69$

17 In words and notation, describe the meaning of the shaded area on the Venn diagram shown below.

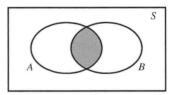

18 Which of the following numerical values cannot be the probability of an event? Give a reason for your response.
(a) 0.265
(b) 0
(c) –0.921
(d) $\frac{4}{5}$
(e) 2.164
(f) 1

19 The table below shows the number of part-time and full-time workers at a company, also categorised by gender.

	Part-time	Full-time	Total
Male	72	103	175
Female	161	64	225
Total	233	167	400

Find the probability that a randomly selected worker:
(a) is female or works part-time
(b) works full-time or is male

20 The editor of a business-focused magazine asked 350 companies if they made a profit last year; 203 companies said that they did make a profit. If one of the companies is selected at random, use the empirical approach to find the probability that the company did not make a profit.

21 Which approach to probability can be applied to situations where the probability of every possible outcome of an experiment is the same?
(a) subjective
(b) classical
(c) empirical

22 In the context of probability, briefly explain what is meant by the terms experiment, outcome, sample space and event.

23 Each of the following tables shows a possible probability model for the distribution of six varieties when a sample of doughnuts is chosen for inspection at a bakery. Decide if the numerical values in each table provide a valid probability model. Give reasons for your responses.

(a)

Doughnut variety	Probability
apple pie	0.16
chocolate iced	0.31
original glazed	0.27
raspberry jam	0.09
strawberry gloss	0.05
rainbow sprinkles	0.12

(b)

Doughnut variety	Probability
apple pie	0.26
chocolate iced	0.17
original glazed	0.42
raspberry jam	0.74
strawberry gloss	0.09
rainbow sprinkles	0.14

(c)

Doughnut variety	Probability
apple pie	0.23
chocolate iced	0.24
original glazed	0.09
raspberry jam	0.35
strawberry gloss	0.17
rainbow sprinkles	−0.08

24 Find $P(A \cap B)$ when:
(a) $P(A) = 0.67$ and $P(B|A) = 0.29$
(b) $P(B) = 0.14$ and $P(A|B) = 0.23$

25 When a survey is conducted of all of the houses in the same postcode area, it is found that 65% of the houses have a garage, 22% have a conservatory, and 6% have both. What is the probability that a randomly selected house in this postcode area has a garage or a conservatory or both?

26 Data were collected from television viewers by an advertising company. The company wanted to investigate any differences in the effectiveness of advertising between male and female viewers. The table below shows the number of viewers, by gender, who purchased the product shown in an advertisement, and the number of viewers who did not make a purchase.

	Made a purchase	Did not make a purchase	Total
Male	128	304	432
Female	256	312	568
Total	384	616	1000

If we randomly selected one of these television viewers, find:
(a) P(female and did not make a purchase)
(b) P(male and made a purchase)

27 Given that $P(B) = 0.39$ and $P(A \cap B) = 0.36$, find the conditional probability that event A occurs given that event B has already occurred.

28 Decide whether the classical, empirical or subjective approach to probability is being used in each of the following scenarios.
(a) As sales have increased each month throughout the last year, the sales manager at a domestic appliance manufacturer thinks that the probability of sales increasing in the coming month is 0.92.

(b) A travel agent records the type of holiday booked by a sample of 500 customers. If a customer is selected at random from the sample, she wishes to calculate the probability that they have booked a sports holiday.

29 If an event A has a probability of 0.4 of occurring, is this the same as writing $P(A) = \frac{2}{5}$?

30 Given that $P(A) = 0.23$ and $P(B|A) = 0.61$, find the probability of the intersection of events A and B.

31 Fill in the blank spaces in the following statements about probability.
   (a) An _____ event has a probability of zero.
   (b) An event with a probability equal to exactly _____ will be certain to occur.
   (c) Events that cannot occur at the same time are known as _____ _____.
   (d) Two events are called independent if the occurrence of one event in an experiment does not have any _____ on the occurrence of the other event.

32 For an experiment that involves rolling a die and recording the number facing upwards, we can define two events, A: 'the number facing upwards is less than 5' and B: 'the number facing upwards is an even number'. Which is the set of elements that represents the intersection of A and B?
   (a) {2, 4, 6}
   (b) {1, 2, 3, 4, 6}
   (c) {2, 4}

33 Library customers are allowed to borrow a maximum of six books at a time. The table below shows the probability model for the number of books borrowed from a library during one week.

Number of books borrowed	Probability
1	0.11
2	0.09
3	0.25
4	0.34
5	0.06
6	0.15

   (a) Is this a valid probability model? Give a reason for your answer.
   (b) What is the probability that a randomly selected customer borrowed 3 or 4 books?
   (c) What is the probability that a randomly selected customer borrowed fewer than 5 books?

34 On the platform at a train station, the information board shows that the 07:14 train will depart on time. However, a regular traveller who takes the 07:14 train each morning to work knows that this train has been late on the previous two days. He thinks the probability of the train departing on time is 0.25. Which probability approach is the regular traveller using?

35 Five friends eat in an Italian restaurant on a Saturday night in May. Their names are Kate, Sally, Olivia, Alison and Mary. The restaurant owner decides to give free dessert to two people on each table in the restaurant and he draws names from a hat to make the selection process fair.
(a) Define the sample space for this experiment.
(b) What is the probability that Mary and Sally will receive free dessert?
(c) What is the probability that Kate does not receive free dessert?
(d) What is the probability that Alison receives free dessert?

36 In an online survey, women with children were asked whether they ever worked at weekends. Permitted responses were 'always', 'sometimes' and 'never'. Decide whether the probabilities for the three responses could be as follows:

$$P(\text{always}) = 0.36 \quad P(\text{sometimes}) = 0.71 \quad P(\text{never}) = 0.19$$

Give a reason for your answer.

37 Decide whether the following statements are TRUE or FALSE. Explain your response for any FALSE statements.
(a) The addition rule is the same, regardless of whether two events are mutually exclusive or not mutually exclusive.
(b) The events A and A' are mutually exclusive because the occurrence of event A means that event A' does not occur and vice versa.
(c) $P(A \cap B)$ is not equal to $P(B \cap A)$.
(d) The probability of an event can be expressed as a fraction, a decimal or a percentage.

38 An estate agent works out that 67.4% of the houses he has marketed are sold below the advertised sale price. If a house is randomly selected from this group, what is the probability that it will have sold below the advertised sale price?

39 Given that $P(A) = 0.43$, $P(A \cup B) = 0.67$ and $P(A \cap B) = 0.12$, calculate $P(B)$.

40 Given that $P(A) = 0.63$ and $P(B) = 0.28$, find the probabilities of the following:
(a) $P(A \cup B)$ if A and B are mutually exclusive
(b) $P(B')$
(c) $P(A \cup B)$ if $P(A \cap B) = 0.05$
(d) $P(A \cap B)$ if A and B are mutually exclusive

Solutions to Practice Exercises

1. The probability that both customers used a loyalty card is $\frac{62}{140} \times \frac{61}{139} = 0.1943$

2. (a) Events A and C are mutually exclusive because they do not have any common elements.
   (b) Events A and B are not mutually exclusive because $A \cap B = \{3, 4\}$.
   (c) $B \cup C = \{1, 2, 3, 4, 7, 8\}$ and so $P(B \cup C) = \frac{6}{8} = 0.75$
   (d) $A' = \{1, 2, 7, 8\}$

3. (a) $S = \{HHH, HHT, HTH, HTT, THH, THT, TTH, TTT\}$
   (b) $S = \{E, L, OT\}$
   (c) $S = \{1st, 2nd, 3rd, 4th\}$

4. Option (a). $P(\text{has children} \mid \text{is male}) = \frac{0.20}{0.74} = 0.27$

5. (a) $P(\text{does not prefer coffee}) = 1 - 0.59 = 0.41$
   (b) $P(\text{prefers tea or prefers coffee}) = 0.34 + 0.59 = 0.93$
   (c) It is not possible for the probability that she prefers hot chocolate to be 0.21, because then $P(\text{prefers tea or prefers coffee or prefers hot chocolate})$ would be $0.34 + 0.59 + 0.21$, which is greater than 1.

6. Probability model for magazine categories

Magazine category	Frequency
computers and technology	61/500 = 0.122
crafts	0.176
food and home	0.218
science and nature	0.036
sport	0.268
travel	0.076
lifestyle	0.104

7. (a)

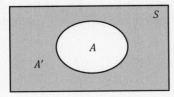

(b)

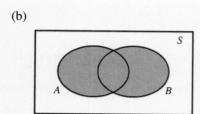

(c)

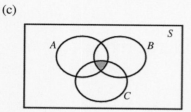

8 $P(\text{paid with credit card} \mid \text{spent over} \pounds100) = \dfrac{0.28}{0.65} = 0.431$

9 $P(\text{at least one sibling}) = \dfrac{289}{340} = 0.85$

10 $P(\text{both teachers have a degree in their subject}) = 0.72 \times 0.72 = 0.5184$

11 We do not have enough information to calculate the probability that a randomly selected adult living in the UK owns a home or owns a car. Some adults will own a house and a car, and we would need to know this proportion to calculate the union of our two events.

12 The classical approach to probability can be applied to situations where the probability of every possible outcome of an experiment is the same. In this case, we say that the experiment has equally likely outcomes. We measure the proportion of times that an event will occur, and so the probability of an event is calculated as follows:

$$\text{probability of an event} = \frac{\text{number of ways the event can occur}}{\text{number of possible outcomes}}$$

It is not necessary to actually perform the experiment when using the classical approach because the probability of an event is determined by understanding the nature of the experiment and by counting relevant outcomes in the sample space.

13 (a) $P(\text{has been a gym member}) = \dfrac{24 + 65}{200} = 0.445$

(b) $P(\text{is female}) = \dfrac{24 + 80}{200} = 0.52$

(c) $P(\text{is male} \mid \text{has been a gym member}) = \dfrac{65}{200} \div \dfrac{89}{200} = \dfrac{65}{89}$

(d) $P(\text{has not been a gym member} \mid \text{is female}) = \dfrac{80}{200} \div \dfrac{104}{200} = \dfrac{80}{104}$

14 If A and B are independent events, $P(A \cap B) = P(A) \times P(B) = 0.34 \times 0.41 = 0.1394$

15

(a) $P(\text{yellow}) = \dfrac{80}{200} = 0.4$

(b) $P(\text{purple}) = \dfrac{20}{200} = 0.1$

(c) $P(\text{red}) = 0$ because there are no red flowers in the floral display.

16 (a) If A and B are mutually exclusive, $P(A \cup B) = P(A) + P(B) = 0.36 + 0.11 = 0.47$
(b) If A and B are mutually exclusive, $P(A \cup B) = P(A) + P(B) = 0.22 + 0.69 = 0.91$

17 In words, the shaded area on the Venn diagram is described as the intersection of event A and event B. Using appropriate notation, we state $A \cap B$.

18 (c) and (e) because the probability of an event cannot be a value that is less than zero or greater than one.

19

(a) $P(F \cup PT) = P(F) + P(PT) - P(F \cap PT) = \dfrac{225}{400} + \dfrac{233}{400} - \dfrac{161}{400} = 0.7425$

(b) $P(M \cup FT) = P(M) + P(FT) - P(M \cap FT) = \dfrac{175}{400} + \dfrac{167}{400} - \dfrac{103}{400} = 0.5975$

20 $P(\text{no profit}) = 1 - \dfrac{203}{350} = 0.42$

21 Option (b). The classical approach to probability can be applied to situations where the probability of every possible outcome of an experiment is the same. In this case, we say that the experiment has equally likely outcomes.

22 Experiment
    An experiment is any action or process that can be repeated.
Outcome
    An outcome is simply the result of an experiment.
Sample space
    The sample space is the set of all possible outcomes of an experiment.
Event
    An event is a collection of one or more outcomes of an experiment.

23 (a) Yes – this is a valid probability model because each probability is between zero and one inclusive, and the sum of the probabilities is one.
(b) No – this is not a valid probability model because the sum of the probabilities is more than one.
(c) No – this is not a valid probability model because $P(\text{rainbow sprinkles})$ is less than zero.

24 (a) $P(A \cap B) = P(B|A) \times P(A) = 0.29 \times 0.67 = 0.1943$

(b) $P(A \cap B) = P(A|B) \times P(B) = 0.23 \times 0.14 = 0.0322$

25 $P(\text{garage or conservatory or both}) = 0.65 + 0.22 - 0.06 = 0.81$

26 (a) $P(\text{female and did not make a purchase}) = \dfrac{312}{1000} = 0.312$

(b) $P(\text{male and made a purchase}) = \dfrac{128}{1000} = 0.128$

27 $P(A|B) = \dfrac{P(A \cap B)}{P(B)} = \dfrac{0.36}{0.39} = 0.923$

28 (a) For the domestic appliance manufacturer, the subjective approach is being used because the probability is based on the personal experience and judgement of the sales manager.

(b) The travel agent would use the empirical approach to probability because this experiment does not have equally likely outcomes. The sample data can be used to calculate the probability based on relative frequencies.

29 Yes, because the probability of an event can be expressed as an equivalent fraction, decimal or percentage.

30 $P(A \cap B) = P(B|A) \times P(A) = 0.23 \times 0.61 = 0.1403$

31 (a) impossible

(b) one

(c) mutually exclusive

(d) effect

32 Option (c). The elements $\{1, 2, 3, 4\}$ belong to event A and $\{2, 4, 6\}$ belong to B. The intersection, $A \cap B$, consists of all elements that are common to both event A and event B. In this case, there are two elements $\{2, 4\}$ which belong to both events.

33 (a) This is a valid probability model because each probability is between zero and one inclusive, and the sum of the probabilities is one.

(b) $P(\text{3 books or 4 books}) = 0.25 + 0.34 = 0.59$

(c) $P(\text{less than 5 books}) = 0.11 + 0.09 + 0.25 + 0.34 = 0.79$

34 The regular traveller is using the subjective approach because his estimate of the probability of the 07:14 train departing on time is based on his personal experience.

35 (a) $S = \{\text{KS, KO, KA, KM, SO, SA, SM, OA, OM, AM}\}$

(b) $P(\text{Mary and Sally}) = \dfrac{1}{10} = 0.1$

(c) $P(\text{not Kate}) = \dfrac{6}{10} = 0.6$

(d) $P(\text{Alison}) = \dfrac{4}{10} = 0.4$

36 No – the assigned probabilities are not possible because their sum is greater than one.

37 (a) FALSE

The general addition rule for the union of two events is

$$P(A \cup B) = P(A) + P(B) - P(A \cap B)$$

However, if the two events are mutually exclusive, then the probability of the intersection is is zero and so the addition rule becomes

$$P(A \cup B) = P(A) + P(B)$$

(b) TRUE

(c) FALSE

Because 'both event A and event B occurring' is the same as 'both event B and event A occurring', we can say that $P(A \cap B)$ is the same as $P(B \cap A)$.

(d) TRUE

38 Converting the percentage into a decimal, the probability that it will have sold below the advertised sale price is 0.674.

39 Rearranging the addition rule,

$$P(B) = P(A \cup B) + P(A \cap B) - P(A) = 0.67 + 0.12 - 0.43 = 0.36$$

40 (a) If A and B are mutually exclusive, $P(A \cup B) = P(A) + P(B) = 0.63 + 0.28 = 0.91$

(b) $P(B') = 1 - P(B) = 1 - 0.28 = 0.72$

(c) If $P(A \cap B) = 0.05$, $P(A \cup B) = P(A) + P(B) - P(A \cap B) = 0.63 + 0.28 - 0.05 = 0.86$

(d) If A and B are mutually exclusive, then $P(A \cap B) = 0$

Introducing Statistical Inference

This chapter explains how to:

- distinguish between discrete and continuous random variables
- describe the properties of a normal distribution
- understand the importance of the standard normal distribution
- calculate and interpret the area under the standard normal curve
  - to the left of a z-score
  - to the right of a z-score
  - between two specified z-scores
- interpret the sampling distribution of a sample statistic and use this knowledge to calculate an interval estimate for the population mean

central limit theorem	normal distribution	sampling distribution
confidence interval	point estimate	standard error
confidence level	population parameter	standard normal curve
continuous random variable	probability density function	standard normal distribution
discrete random variable	probability distribution	z-score
interval estimate	random variable	
normal curve	sample statistic	

Introduction

We begin this chapter with an introduction to random variables and then provide an explanation of the importance of a normal distribution, describing its properties and parameters. Methods are presented for using statistical tables to calculate the area under the standard normal curve for a range of different situations, including when it is necessary to standardise the random variable.

Statistical inference involves using sample statistics to help us reach conclusions about the population from which the sample was selected. It is necessary to use sample data because it can be expensive, impractical and sometimes impossible to collect information from every member of a population. Building on our understanding of random variables and normal distributions, we will focus on the sample mean and explore its sampling distribution. Finally, we develop a procedure for constructing an interval estimate of the population mean when the population standard deviation is known.

Random Variables

At the start of Chapter 9, we introduced the idea of a probability experiment and its outcomes. Extending these concepts, we can now define a **random variable**: it is a variable whose possible values are the numerical outcomes of a random experiment. Uppercase and lowercase letters are used to distinguish between a random variable and its outcomes. We use an uppercase letter, usually X, to represent a random variable and then the corresponding lowercase letter, x, when we need to describe the outcomes of the experiment.

EXAMPLE – RANDOM VARIABLE

Suppose we decide to flip two coins and record the sides which are facing upwards. We already know that the sample space for this experiment is $S = \{HH, HT, TH, TT\}$. If we let X represent the number of tails recorded each time we conduct the experiment, then X is a random variable. The possible values of X are $x = 0$, $x = 1$, or $x = 2$ where we would record no tails, one tails or two tails in the outcome of the experiment.

Discrete and Continuous Random Variables

There are two types of random variables: discrete and continuous. For a **discrete random variable**, all of its possible values can be listed, usually as a result of counting rather than measuring; most discrete random variables have a finite number of possible outcomes. If our experiment involves measurements, then we would define a **continuous random variable** whose outcome can be any numerical value within a given interval; in this case, there are an infinite number of possible outcomes which cannot all be listed.

EXAMPLE – DISCRETE RANDOM VARIABLE

Experiment: randomly select an employee who works in a hospital and record how many times they have visited their doctor in the past month. If the random variable X represents the number of visits to the doctor by the selected employee, then X is a discrete random variable because the outcomes of the experiment are countable. The possible values are $x = 0, 1, 2, 3, \ldots$.

EXAMPLE – CONTINUOUS RANDOM VARIABLE

Experiment: randomly choose a 200 ml bottle of shampoo from a production line and measure the actual amount of shampoo in the bottle. If X denotes the amount of shampoo in the randomly selected bottle, then X can be any value within a certain range. In terms of accuracy, the amount of shampoo might be measured as 196 ml, or 196.37 ml, or 196.372618 ml. Therefore X is a continuous random variable because we cannot list all of the possible outcomes for the experiment.

Probability Distributions

The **probability distribution** of a random variable provides information about the possible values that the variable can assume, and the probabilities associated with those values. Depending on the nature of the random variable, a probability distribution can be presented as a table, an equation or a graph.

PROBABILITY DISTRIBUTION FOR DISCRETE RANDOM VARIABLES

For a discrete random variable, its probability distribution is most often provided as a table which lists all of the possible values of the variable and the probability associated with each value. As explained in the previous chapter, we can apply the empirical approach to determine probabilities by using the relative frequencies obtained from an existing set of data or an experiment. The probability distribution of a discrete random variable must satisfy two characteristics:

- The probability associated with each value of the variable lies between 0 and 1 inclusive.
- The sum of the probabilities associated with all possible values of the variable is equal to 1.

We can use a probability distribution table to identify the probability for an individual value of the random variable and also to calculate cumulative probabilities.

EXAMPLES – PROBABILITY DISTRIBUTION FOR DISCRETE RANDOM VARIABLE

1. Returning to our earlier experiment which involved flipping two coins and recording the sides which are facing upwards, recall that X represents the number of tails recorded each time we conduct the experiment and the possible values of X are $x = 0$, $x = 1$, or $x = 2$. Using the sample space $S = \{HH, HT, TH, TT\}$, we can construct the probability distribution for the discrete random variable X as shown below.

Number of tails x	Probability $P(x)$
0	0.25
1	0.50
2	0.25

In addition to using the table to identify $P(X = 1)$ as 0.5, we can also calculate:

$$P(X < 2) = P(X = 0) + P(X = 1) = 0.25 + 0.50 = 0.75$$

2. The table below shows the number of bedrooms in each house on the same street in the residential area of a city.

Number of bedrooms	Frequency	Relative frequency
1	9	0.09
2	12	0.12
3	42	0.42
4	21	0.21
5	13	0.13
total	100	1.00

If X is the number of bedrooms in a house randomly selected from the street, we can use the relative frequencies to construct the probability distribution for the random variable X. Assigning probabilities based on the relative frequencies gives:

Number of bedrooms x	Probability $P(x)$
1	0.09
2	0.12
3	0.42
4	0.21
5	0.13

We can see that, for a randomly selected house, $P(X = 1) = 0.09$ and $P(X > 3) = 0.34$.

PROBABILITY DISTRIBUTION FOR CONTINUOUS RANDOM VARIABLES

It is not possible to use a table to represent the probability distribution of a continuous random variable because there are an infinite number of possible values for the variable which cannot all be listed. For continuous random variables we use a mathematical equation instead; it is known as a **probability density function**.

The probability density function of a continuous random variable must satisfy two characteristics:

- The probability density function is never negative.
- The total area under the curve of the function is equal to one.

We use the curve of a probability density function to provide the probabilities for a continuous random variable over an interval of values rather than for an individual value, because the probability of obtaining a specific value is actually zero.

The area under the curve for an interval represents the probability that a continuous random variable assumes a value within that interval. A visual representation of this idea is shown below: the probability that the value of a variable X lies between a and b is given by the area under the curve between those two points.

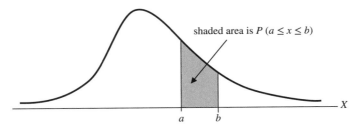

shaded area is $P\,(a \leq x \leq b)$

Normal Distribution

For real-world data, many continuous random variables have a similarly shaped probability distribution. The shape that occurs most often is known as a **normal distribution**. If a variable is normally distributed it means that many of the data values will be clustered around a central value, with fewer values occurring as the distance from the central value increases.

As an example, consider the time it takes an employee to commute by car from home to work each weekday morning over a period of one month. The journey time will be very similar on most days, but occasionally it may take a much shorter time or a much longer time to commute. Perhaps the local schools will be closed for a day and so the journey time will be considerably reduced due to fewer people travelling at that time. On another occasion, long delays may be caused by a road closure due to a burst water pipe. We would say that the probability density function has the shape of a **normal curve**.

The following variables may also be normally distributed:

- maximum daily temperature;
- weight of packages in a manufacturing process;
- time taken to complete a project;
- annual cost of car insurance.

A normal curve is shown in the diagram below. You can see that it has a clearly defined shape: it is bell-shaped with a single peak and symmetry about the central value.

PROPERTIES OF A NORMAL DISTRIBUTION

Normal distributions have the following properties:

Property	Additional information
The total area under the normal curve is equal to 1	The area under the curve represents probabilities and the total of all probabilities is equal to 1
It is a symmetrical distribution about the mean	The left-hand side of the curve is a mirror-image of the right-hand side; on each side of the mean, the area under the curve is 0.5
It has a single, central peak at the mean value	Most of the values are clustered around the mean, with fewer values occurring as the distance from the mean increases
The curve is asymptotic along the horizontal axis	On each side of the distribution, the tails of the curve extend indefinitely without touching the x-axis

The parameters of a normal distribution are the mean, μ, and the standard deviation, σ. Each unique combination of values for μ and σ will produce a different normal curve.

The mean determines the location of the centre of a curve on the x-axis; increasing the mean of a distribution will move the curve to the right, but its overall shape will remain unchanged. This is illustrated in the diagram below, which shows two normal curves with the same standard deviation but different mean values.

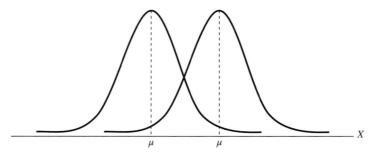

The following diagram shows how the standard deviation affects the spread of the curve when the mean value remains the same. Increasing the standard deviation will result in a flatter, wider curve with a larger spread, whereas a smaller standard deviation will produce a taller, narrower curve.

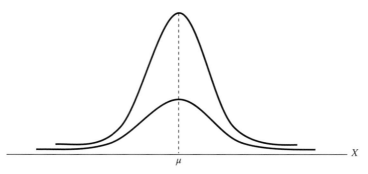

For all normal distributions, it is possible to state the percentage of data values that lie within a certain distance of the mean as follows:

- approximately 68% of the data values lie within one standard deviation of the mean, between $\mu - \sigma$ and $\mu + \sigma$;
- approximately 95% of the data values lie within two standard deviations of the mean, between $\mu - 2\sigma$ and $\mu + 2\sigma$;
- approximately 99.7% of the data values lie within three standard deviations of the mean, between $\mu - 3\sigma$ and $\mu + 3\sigma$.

A visual representation of this characteristic is given below.

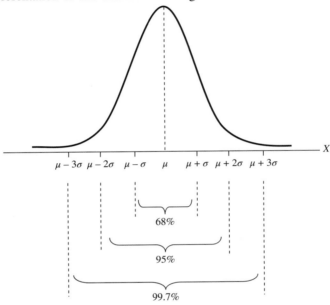

The Standard Normal Distribution

We noted earlier that the area under the curve for an interval represents the probability that a continuous random variable assumes a value within that interval. Calculating the area under a normal curve would involve working with a complex mathematical function, which would be time-consuming and difficult; as an alternative method, we rely on the use of statistical tables to provide the required probabilities. It would be unrealistic to create a table for every normal curve with a unique combination of mean and standard deviation, and so instead we identify a specific normal distribution with $\mu = 0$ and $\sigma = 1$; this is known as the **standard normal distribution** and is shown in the diagram below.

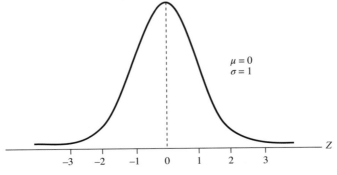

The horizontal axis is now labelled Z because the standard normal random variable represented by this distribution is always denoted by Z to distinguish it from other random variables.

For the **standard normal curve**, a specific value of z represents the distance between the mean and that point expressed in terms of the standard deviation; a value to the right of the mean is positive, whereas all values to the left of the mean are negative. A specific value of z, marked on the horizontal axis, is also known as a **z-score**.

USING STANDARD NORMAL DISTRIBUTION TABLES

The statistical table associated with the standard normal distribution provides the cumulative probability to the left of a range of positive and negative z-scores; in terms of notation, this would be expressed as $P(Z \leq z)$, and it is equivalent to the area under the standard normal curve that lies to the left of the specific value of z. The standard normal table in the Appendix can be used for z-values between -3.09 and 3.09.

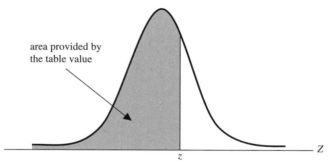

area provided by the table value

The following example illustrates the steps required for using the table to find the area under the standard normal curve to the left of a z-score.

1. Split the z-score into two parts:

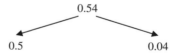

0.54

0.5   0.04

2. Find the table row that corresponds to the first part of the z-score and the table column for the second part of the z-score:

z	0.00	0.01	0.02	0.03	0.04	0.05	...
...							
0.2					0.5948		
0.3					0.6331		
0.4					0.6700		
0.5	0.6915	0.6950	0.6985	0.7019	0.7054	0.7088	
0.6					0.7389		
0.7					0.7704		
...							

3. The table value located at the intersection of the relevant row and column provides the area under the standard normal curve to the left of the z-score. In this example, we can say that:
   - $P(Z \leq 0.54) = 0.7054$.
   - The area under the standard normal curve to the **left** of $z = 0.54$ is 0.7054.
   - The probability that the continuous random variable Z assumes a value that is *less than* 0.54 is 0.7054.

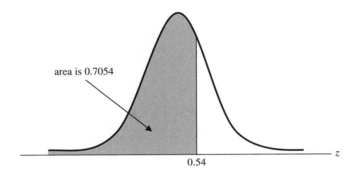

Because we know that the total area under a normal curve is equal to one, we can use the table values to calculate the area of other regions as well as the area to the left of a z-score. The area to the right of a specific z-score is found by subtracting the area to the left of the z-score from 1.

For example, if we wanted to find the area to the right of $z = 0.54$ then we would subtract the table value for the z-score from 1, as follows:

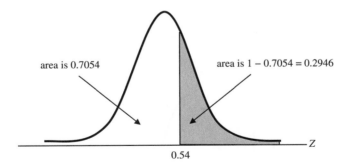

Here we can say that:

- $P(Z \geq 0.54) = 0.2946$.
- The area under the standard normal curve to the **right** of $z = 0.54$ is 0.2946.
- The probability that the continuous random variable Z assumes a value that is *greater than* 0.54 is 0.2946.

We can also find the area under the normal curve between two specific z-scores. This is achieved by subtracting the area to the left of the smallest z-score from the area to the left of the largest z-score. In practice, we simply look up both probabilities in the table and subtract the smallest from the largest.

For example, if we wanted to find the area under the curve between $z_1 = -1.85$ and $z_2 = -0.54$, then we would use the table to find each probability and calculate the required area by subtraction.

z	0.00	0.01	0.02	0.03	0.04	0.05	...
...							
– 1.9						0.0256	
– 1.8	0.0359	0.0351	0.0344	0.0336	0.0329	0.0322	
– 1.7						0.0401	
– 1.6						0.0495	
– 1.5						0.0606	
– 1.4						0.0735	
...							
– 0.9					0.1736		
– 0.8					0.2005		
– 0.7					0.2296		
– 0.6					0.2611		
– 0.5	0.3085	0.3050	0.3015	0.2981	0.2946	0.2912	0.2877
– 0.4					0.3300		
...							

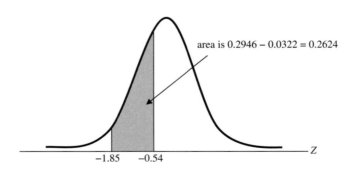

area is 0.2946 – 0.0322 = 0.2624

In this case, we can say that:

- $P(-1.85 \leq Z \leq -0.54) = 0.2624$.
- The area under the standard normal curve **between** $z_1 = -1.85$ and $z_2 = -0.54$ is 0.2624.
- The probability that the continuous random variable Z assumes a value *in the interval* -1.85 to -0.54 is 0.2624.

Alternatively, we can reverse our processes and use the table values to find the z-score associated with a specified area under the standard normal curve.

The following example illustrates the steps required for using the table to find the z-score that has an area of 0.6217 to its left under the standard normal curve.

1. Find the table value that is equal to the known area:

z	0.00	0.01	0.02	0.03	0.04	0.05	...
...							
0.2		0.5832					
0.3	0.6179	0.6217	0.6255	0.6293	0.6331	0.6368	
0.4		0.6591					
0.5		0.6950					
0.6		0.7291					
0.7		0.7611					
...							

2. Combine the relevant row heading and column heading to work out the required z-score:

0.3

0.01

0.31

We can say that the z-score that has an area of 0.6217 to its left under the standard normal curve is 0.31.

STANDARDISING NORMALLY DISTRIBUTED VARIABLES

The procedures described in the previous subsection apply only to situations in which the starting point is the standard normal distribution. However, it is more likely that we will be working with a continuous random variable X that is normally distributed with a mean which is not zero and a standard deviation which differs from 1.

When X is a normally distributed random variable with mean μ and standard deviation σ, it can be converted into the standard normal distribution using the following formula:

$$Z = \frac{X - \mu}{\sigma}$$

Once we have carried out this process, known as **standardising**, we can then use the table for the standard normal distribution to work out an area under the normal curve for a z-score associated with a specified area.

If our x-value is less than the mean of the distribution, then the corresponding z-score will be **negative**; standardised x-values that are greater than the mean of the distribution will result in **positive** z-scores.

EXAMPLE – STANDARDISING NORMALLY DISTRIBUTED VARIABLES

Suppose X is a continuous random variable that is normally distributed with $\mu = 22$ and $\sigma = 5$. We can convert any specific x-value into its corresponding z-value. For $x = 34$,

$$z = \frac{x - \mu}{\sigma} = \frac{34 - 22}{5} = 2.4$$

Using the table for the standard normal distribution gives $P(Z \leq 2.4) = 0.9918$ and so we can also say that $P(X \leq 34) = 0.9918$.
For $x = 16$,

$$z = \frac{x - \mu}{\sigma} = \frac{16 - 22}{5} = -1.2$$

Finding the area under the normal curve to the left of $z = -1.2$ gives $P(Z \leq -1.2) = 0.1151$ and so we can also say that $P(X \leq 16) = 0.1151$.

EXAMPLE – NORMAL DISTRIBUTIONS

From historical information, a leading manufacturer of household products knows that the dispensing lifetimes of its air fresheners are approximately normally distributed with a mean of 30 days and a standard deviation of 4 days.

Selecting an air freshener at random, we can calculate the probability that it lasts between 25 and 28 days; this is the same as stating the percentage of air fresheners that will last for this period of time.

Let X represent the lifetime of an air freshener, measured in days; $\mu = 30$ and $\sigma = 4$. We can convert our x-values into z-scores using the standardising formula.
For $x = 25$,

$$z = \frac{x - \mu}{\sigma} = \frac{25 - 30}{4} = -1.25$$

For $x = 28$,

$$z = \frac{x - \mu}{\sigma} = \frac{28 - 30}{4} = -0.5$$

Using the standard normal distribution table to find the area to the left of each z-value, we find that $P(Z \leq -1.25) = 0.1057$ and $P(Z \leq -0.5) = 0.3085$, so the probability that an air freshener lasts between 25 and 28 days is $0.3085 - 0.1057 = 0.2028$.

We can conclude that approximately 20.28% of air fresheners manufactured will last between 25 and 28 days.

Population Parameters and Sample Statistics

To distinguish between working with an entire population and using data collected from a sample, we have different terminology and notation for our values of interest.

A **population parameter** is a quantity measured for a population; it is generally an unknown value which is fixed. When we have collected sample data, we use the term **sample statistic** to refer to a quantity measured for the sample; a sample statistic can be calculated for any sample and its value will vary according to the members of the population selected for inclusion in the sample.

In the remainder of this chapter, we will focus the most commonly used population parameters and sample statistics:

Quantity	Parameter or statistic	Notation
population mean	parameter	μ
population standard deviation	parameter	σ
sample mean	statistic	$\bar{x}$
sample standard deviation	statistic	s

SAMPLING DISTRIBUTION

If we are interested in the value of a parameter for an entire population, we may decide to collect data from a sample and then calculate the corresponding sample statistic. Repeatedly selecting samples of the same size from a population will mean that we calculate many sample statistics which are all likely to be slightly different in value.

As an example, consider the role of the quality control department in a company that produces cereal. The quality controller will choose a sample of cereal packets and weigh each of them to calculate the mean packet weight for that sample. If this process was repeated daily for 5 days, it would result in the calculation of five sample means; each sample mean might be unique, or some of them may be the same. The table below shows a possible set of results for 500 g packets of cereal.

Day	Sample size	Sample mean
1	50	501.3
2	50	499.6
3	50	502.6
4	50	506.2
5	50	499.6

As the numerical value of a sample statistic varies and is the result of a random experiment, we can state that a sample statistic is actually a random variable with a probability distribution that provides information about the possible values that the sample statistic can assume for a given sample size. The probability distribution of a sample statistic is known as its **sampling distribution**; it can be used to make inferences about a population parameter.

SAMPLING DISTRIBUTION OF $\bar{x}$

The sampling distribution of $\bar{x}$ shows us how the sample statistic varies for different samples of size n. For the sampling distribution of $\bar{x}$, we denote the mean as $\mu_{\bar{x}}$ and the standard deviation as $\sigma_{\bar{x}}$. The sampling distribution of $\bar{x}$ has several important properties which are listed below.

Property	Notation	Additional information
The mean of the sampling distribution of $\bar{x}$ is equal to population mean	$\mu_{\bar{x}} = \mu$	• This is simply the mean of all the sample means for sample size n that could possibly be calculated for a population • The mean of an individual sample could be smaller or larger than the fixed population mean
The standard deviation of the sampling distribution of $\bar{x}$ is equal to the standard deviation of the population divided by the square root of the sample size	$\sigma_{\bar{x}} = \dfrac{\sigma}{\sqrt{n}}$	• The **standard error** of the sample mean is an alternative name given to the standard deviation of the sampling distribution of $\bar{x}$ • The value of $\sigma_{\bar{x}}$ becomes smaller as the sample size increases: there is less variation in a larger sample and the sample mean is closer to the population parameter μ
If the population of interest is normally distributed, then the sampling distribution of $\bar{x}$ will also be normally distributed regardless of sample size		• The population of interest has parameter mean μ and standard deviation σ
For large sample sizes ($n \geq 30$), the sampling distribution of $\bar{x}$ will be approximately normally distributed regardless of the distribution of the original population		• This property is called the **central limit theorem** • The sample size required varies depending on the distribution of the population, but generally it should be at least 30 • The approximation to a normal distribution becomes more accurate as the sample size increases

Earlier in this chapter we discussed how the area under a normal curve for an interval represents the probability that a continuous random variable assumes a value within that interval. We can now apply these methods to the sample mean $\bar{x}$, using z-scores to calculate probabilities associated with $\bar{x}$ with the following formula:

$$z = \frac{\bar{x} - \mu}{\sigma_{\bar{x}}}$$

EXAMPLE – SAMPLING DISTRIBUTION OF $\bar{x}$

Returning to our earlier example involving a company that produces cereal, the quality controller knows that the weights of all packets of cereals produced are normally distributed. This knowledge is based on historical records which have shown that the parameters for the normal distribution are $\mu = 500.64$ g and $\sigma = 29.7$ g.

For a random sample of 50 cereal packets, we can find the probability that the mean weight $\bar{x}$ will be less than 505 grams. Because the population is normally distributed, we know that the sampling distribution of $\bar{x}$ will also be normally distributed. The parameters for the sampling distribution of $\bar{x}$ are:

$$\mu_{\bar{x}} = \mu = 500.64$$

$$\sigma_{\bar{x}} = \frac{\sigma}{\sqrt{n}} = \frac{29.7}{\sqrt{50}} = 4.20$$

We are interested in $P(\bar{x} \leq 505)$ and so converting the $\bar{x}$-value to a z-score using the standardising formula gives,
For $\bar{x} = 505$,

$$z = \frac{\bar{x} - \mu}{\sigma_{\bar{x}}} = \frac{505 - 500.64}{4.20} = 1.04$$

Using the standard normal distribution table, we find that the area under the standard normal curve to the left of $z = 1.04$ is 0.8508. Here we can conclude that the probability that the sample mean will be less than 505 grams is 0.8508.

Point and Interval Estimates

A **point estimate** or an **interval estimate** can be used to assign a value to a population parameter based on a sample statistic that we have calculated.

For a point estimate, we would collect data from a sample and then calculate a sample statistic such as the sample mean. This single value, or point, could be used as an estimate of the population mean. However, as each sample would provide a different sample statistic, there would be variability between the point estimate and the true population parameter.

Rather than use a single value to estimate a population parameter, we could construct an interval around a point estimate giving a range of values which we would expect to contain the unknown population parameter. If we also provide a statement about our level of confidence that the interval contains the corresponding population parameter, we have constructed a **confidence interval**.

For example, if we construct a 90% confidence interval, we are stating that there is a 90% chance that the interval will contain the true value of the population parameter. This means that if we repeatedly take samples (each of the same size *n*) from the population and construct a 90% confidence interval for each sample, we expect that:

- 90% of the calculated confidence intervals will contain the true population parameter;
- 10% of the calculated confidence intervals will **not** contain the true population parameter.

The diagram below presents this interpretation visually.

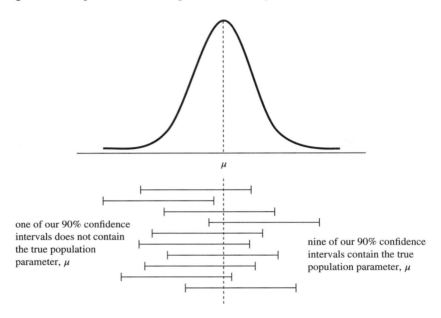

one of our 90% confidence intervals does not contain the true population parameter, μ

nine of our 90% confidence intervals contain the true population parameter, μ

Although any confidence level can be used for constructing the interval, we generally use 90%, 95% and 99%.

We write a confidence interval as a pair of values which are the lower and upper limits of our range; the values are enclosed in brackets to show that they belong together as a pair, and the lower limit is always stated as the first value.

CONFIDENCE INTERVAL FOR POPULATION MEAN

When the population standard deviation σ is known, we construct a confidence interval for the population mean μ using

$$\bar{x} \pm z \frac{\sigma}{\sqrt{n}}$$

The value for z in the formula depends on the confidence level being used, and it is found by applying the procedures described earlier in this chapter. The diagram below shows a visual representation of finding the z-value 1.96 for a 95% confidence interval using the standard normal distribution table.

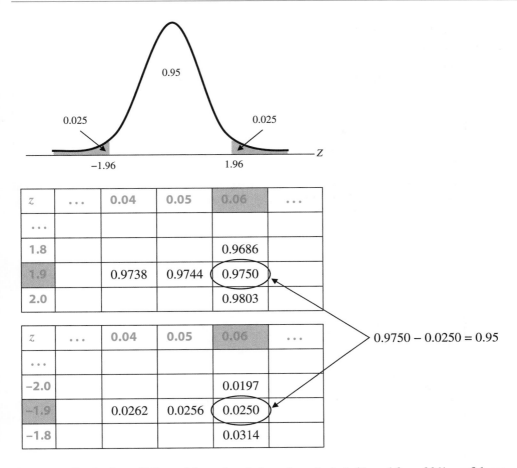

Correspondingly, for a 90% confidence level, the value of z is 1.64, and for a 99% confidence interval we would use 2.58.

EXAMPLE – CONFIDENCE INTERVAL FOR POPULATION MEAN

From historical information, a supermarket chain knows that the times spent in a check-out queue by its customers are approximately normally distributed with a population standard deviation of 4 minutes. Selecting a random sample of 35 customers provides us with a sample statistic $\bar{x} = 18$; this is a point estimate of the population mean μ.

We can construct a 99% confidence interval for the mean queuing time of all customers using the z-value of 2.58, as follows:

$$\bar{x} \pm z \frac{\sigma}{\sqrt{n}} = 18 \pm 2.58 \times \frac{4}{\sqrt{35}} = 18 \pm 1.74$$

So our 99% confidence interval for the population mean μ is (16.256, 19.744), and we can conclude that there is a 99% chance that the interval will contain the mean queuing time of all customers.

HINTS AND TIPS

NON-EXACT TABLE VALUES

When using the standard normal table to identify the z-score associated with a specified area under the standard normal curve, you may find that the known area is not actually a value in the table. In this situation, you should choose the table value that is numerically closest to the known area and then proceed as usual, combining the row and column headings to obtain the z-score.

For example, suppose we wanted to find the z-score that has an area of 0.80 to its left under the standard normal curve. The closest table value to 0.80 is 0.7995, so we would conclude that the z-score with an area of 0.80 to its left under the standard normal curve is approximately 0.84.

z	0.00	0.01	0.02	0.03	0.04	0.05	...
...							
0.6					0.7389		
0.7					0.7704		
0.8	0.7881	0.7910	0.7939	0.7967	0.7995	0.8023	
0.9					0.8264		
1.0					0.8508		
1.1					0.8729		
...							

MISINTERPRETING CONFIDENCE INTERVALS

Take care when you are interpreting a confidence interval that you have constructed. The probability represents the likelihood that the interval contains the population parameter and so the confidence level should be associated with the interval, not the sample statistic or the population parameter.

It is therefore incorrect to say: 'There is a 95% chance that the interval will contain the sample mean'; the confidence interval will *definitely* contain the sample mean because the interval is constructed with the sample mean at the centre of the range of values.

VARIATIONS IN STANDARD NORMAL DISTRIBUTION TABLES

When you use a standard normal distribution table, always check that you understand the diagram or instructions that are provided with the table. In this chapter, all of the table values used in the examples are taken from a table which provides the area under the standard normal curve that lies to the *left* of the specific value of z. However, some tables provide the area that lies to the *right* of the z-value instead and the methods described in this chapter must be adjusted accordingly.

Practice Exercises

1   In the context of estimating a population parameter, explain the difference between a point estimate and an interval estimate.

2   The results of a research project show that the project completion times for a London-based consultancy are normally distributed with a mean of 45 days and a standard deviation of 7 days. For samples of size 10, determine the mean and standard deviation for the sampling distribution of the sample mean.

3   State whether each random variable is discrete or continuous.
(a) number of train tickets sold in three hours
(b) time spent browsing a website
(c) number of customers in a supermarket check-out queue

4   Find the area under the standard normal curve that lies to the **left** of:
(a) $z = 2.35$
(b) $z = -1.87$

5   Decide whether the following statements about the parameters of a normal distribution are TRUE or FALSE. Explain your response for any FALSE statements.
(a) The parameters of a normal distribution are the mean, μ, and the standard deviation, σ.
(b) Every normal distribution has a mean of 1 and a standard deviation of 0.
(c) For normal distributions with the same mean, their curve always looks exactly the same.

6   Give a definition of the sampling distribution of $\bar{x}$.

7   The continuous random variable X, represents the length of a film (in minutes) shown at a cinema; it is approximately normally distributed with $\mu = 195$ and $\sigma = 26$. If a film is randomly selected, determine the probability that this film will be:
(a) more than 201 minutes in length
(b) less than 194.5 minutes in length

8   Find the z-score for each of the following values of $\bar{x}$ where the population has $\mu = 39$ and $\sigma = 7.6$ and the sample size is $n = 140$.
(a) $\bar{x} = 40.7$
(b) $\bar{x} = 38.1$

9   What is the purpose of a probability distribution for a discrete random variable?

10 If we constructed one hundred 90% confidence intervals for a population with mean μ, the approximate number of intervals that would contain the true value of μ is:
(a) 90
(b) 10
(c) none of the intervals

11 Explain briefly what is meant by the term 'random variable'.

12 Find the area under the standard normal curve that lies to the **right** of:
(a) $z = -1.94$
(b) $z = 2.23$

13 Explain the difference between a discrete random variable and a continuous random variable. Give an example of each type to support your explanation.

14 The distribution of monthly mortgage payments for home owners is approximately normally distributed with $\mu = £1857.54$ and $\sigma = £94.15$. Given that $\bar{x}$ is the average monthly mortgage payment for a random sample of 22 home owners, fully describe the sampling distribution of $\bar{x}$.

15 When the population standard deviation σ is known, constructing a confidence interval for the population mean μ requires the use of the formula

$$\bar{x} \pm z \frac{\sigma}{\sqrt{n}}$$

Explaining your method, determine the value of z for a 99% confidence level.

16 Fill in the blank spaces in the following statements about the properties of the sampling distribution of $\bar{x}$.
(a) The mean of an individual sample could be smaller or larger than the fixed _____ mean.
(b) The value of $\sigma_{\bar{x}}$ becomes _____ as the sample size increases.
(c) The _____ of the sampling distribution of $\bar{x}$ is equal to population mean.
(d) The _____ _____ of the sample mean is an alternative name given to the standard deviation of the sampling distribution of $\bar{x}$.

17 Each of the following lists provides a value for the sample mean $\bar{x}$, the sample size n and the population standard deviation σ. Using $z = 1.64$, construct a 90% confidence interval for each list.
(a) $\bar{x} = 62$, $n = 31$ and $\sigma = 16$
(b) $\bar{x} = 8.64$, $n = 100$ and $\sigma = 0.77$

18 (a) Describe what is meant by a population parameter and a sample statistic.
(b) State the notation used to identify the population mean and a sample mean.

19 A population is non-normally distributed with a mean of 63 and a standard deviation of 9. The probability that the sample mean for a random sample of size $n = 87$ will be greater than 62 is:
(a) -1.04
(b) 0.1492
(c) 0.8508

20 Given that $P(Z \leq -0.31) = 0.3783$, calculate $P(Z > 0.31)$ without using the standard normal distribution table. Explain how you derived your answer.

21 Let X be a continuous random variable that is normally distributed with $\mu = 16$ and $\sigma = 3.4$. Find:
(a) $P(X \geq 14)$
(b) $P(X \leq 19)$
(c) $P(15.5 \leq X \leq 16.5)$

22 For all normal distributions, state the percentage of data values that lie within the following distances of the mean:
- approximately ___% of the data values lie within one standard deviation of the mean.
- approximately ___% of the data values lie within two standard deviations of the mean.
- approximately ___% of the data values lie within three standard deviations of the mean.

23 Each of the tables below provides all possible values for a random variable X with their associated probabilities. Decide if the numerical values in each table represent a valid probability distribution. Give reasons for your responses.
(a)

x	$P(x)$
0	0.34
1	0.96
2	0.12
3	0.07

(b)

x	$P(x)$
0	0.21
1	0.05
2	0.48
3	0.26

(c)

x	$P(x)$
0	0.31
1	0.16
2	−0.41
3	0.12

24 Find the area under the standard normal curve that lies **between**:
(a) $z = -0.72$ and $z = -1.25$
(b) $z = 1.95$ and $z = 2.34$

25 From historical information, a corporate events organiser knows that the times spent organising a team-building day are approximately normally distributed with a population standard deviation of 0.25 days.
Selecting a random sample of 46 events provides us with a sample statistic $\bar{x} = 8$ days and a 95% confidence interval for the mean organising time of all events is $(7.928, 8.072)$. Write a statement to interpret this confidence interval.

26 A physiotherapy centre can offer patients an appointment in the morning, afternoon or evening. On a particular day, four patients telephone the centre to make an appointment. If X is the number of patients from among these four who choose an evening appointment, list the possible values that X can assume.

27 With the aid of an example, explain the steps that are needed to use the standard normal distribution table to find the z-score that has a specified area to its left under the standard normal curve. Assume that the table provides the cumulative probability to the left of a range of positive and negative z-scores and that the specified area is a value listed in the table.

28 Find the z-score for each of the following values of x for a normal distribution that has $\mu = 117$ and $\sigma = 14.9$.
(a) $x = 150$
(b) $x = 91$

29 For the weights of packages delivered by an international courier company, the mean is 3.44 kg and the standard deviation is 0.27 kg.
(a) Describe the sampling distribution of the sample mean weight for samples of 200 packages.
(b) If we know that the distribution of package weights is not normally distributed, does this affect your answer to part (a). Give a reason for your answer.

30 For a population known to be normally distributed, the standard deviation is 68.7. A random sample of size 17 taken from this population provides a sample mean of 251.4. Construct confidence intervals for the population mean using 90%, 95% and 99% confidence levels.

31 The probability distribution of a discrete random variable must satisfy the following two characteristics:
(a) The probability associated with each value of the variable lies between _____ and _____ inclusive.
(b) The _____ of the probabilities associated with all possible values of the variable is equal to 1.

32 A random sample of 180 apartments for rent with a letting agent gave the mean monthly rental as £726. The population standard deviation for all monthly rentals with the letting agent is £46.
(a) What is the value of the point estimate for the population mean monthly rental of all apartments?
(b) Construct a 95% confidence interval for the mean monthly rental of all apartments.

33 A large population has parameters $\mu = 17$ and $\sigma = 3$.
(a) Define the sampling distribution of $\bar{x}$ for samples of size $n = 100$.
(b) Did you make any assumptions when you answered part (a)? Explain your response.
(c) Can you define the sampling distribution of $\bar{x}$ for samples of size $n = 4$ without any further information?

34 (a) Explain how the curve of a normal distribution is affected when the value of the mean is increased.
(b) Explain how the curve of a normal distribution is affected when the value of the standard deviation is decreased.

35 A population is normally distributed with a mean of 138 and a standard deviation of 21. Using the standard normal table, determine the probability that the sample mean for a random sample of size $n = 25$ will be:
(a) less than 128
(b) greater than 128

36 Given that $P(Z < 1.21) = 0.8869$, calculate $P(Z \geq 1.21)$ without using the standard normal distribution table. Explain how you derived your answer.

37 Decide whether the following statements are TRUE or FALSE. Explain your response for any FALSE statements.
(a) A sampling distribution is the probability distribution of a population parameter.
(b) It is often quicker and more efficient to conduct a census rather than choosing a sample for data collection.
(c) A sample statistic is a random variable.

38 Explain what is wrong with the following statement which provides an incorrect interpretation of a 99% confidence interval: 'There is a 99% chance that the interval will contain the sample mean.'

39 Fill in the blank spaces in the following statements about the properties of a normal distribution.
(a) The total _____ under the normal curve is equal to 1.
(b) It is a symmetrical distribution about the _____.
(c) The left-hand side of the curve is a mirror-image of the _____ side; on each side of the mean, the area under the curve is equal to _____.
(d) The curve is asymptotic along the _____ axis.

40 The table below shows the probability distribution for the number of times a machine stops working over a three-month period at a manufacturing facility. Decide whether this is a valid probability distribution and explain your response.

Number of machine breakdowns	Probability
0	0.1359
1	0.3441
2	0.0593
3	0.2982
4	0.0417
5	0.1208

Solutions to Practice Exercises

1   A point estimate of a population parameter is a single value of a sample statistic. An interval estimate is a range of values which we would expect to contain the population parameter.

2   For the sampling distribution of the sample mean, the mean is 45 days and the standard deviation is 2.214 days.

3   (a) discrete random variable
   (b) continuous random variable
   (c) discrete random variable

4   Using the standard normal distribution table:
   (a) The area under the standard normal curve to the **left** of $z = 2.35$ is 0.9906.
   (b) The area under the standard normal curve to the **left** of $z = -1.87$ is 0.0307.

5   (a) TRUE
   (b) FALSE
        Each unique normal distribution has its own mean and standard deviation values. Only the standard normal distribution has a mean of 1 and a standard deviation of 0.
   (c) FALSE
        For normal distributions with the same mean, the location of the centre of their curve on the x-axis will be the same, but the value of the standard deviation will affect the spread of the curve; increasing the standard deviation will result in a flatter, wider curve with a larger spread, whereas a smaller standard deviation will produce a taller, narrower curve.

6   The sampling distribution of $\bar{x}$ is the probability distribution of all possible values of the $\bar{x}$ calculated from samples of size n from a population.

7   (a) Converting the x-value into its corresponding z-value gives,
        for $x = 201$,

$$z = \frac{x - \mu}{\sigma} = \frac{201 - 195}{26} = 0.23$$

   Using the table for the standard normal distribution,

$$P(Z > 0.23) = 1 - 0.5910 = 0.4090$$

   and so
$$P(X > 201) = 0.4090$$

   (b) Converting the x-value into its corresponding z-value gives,
        for $x = 194.5$,

$$z = \frac{x - \mu}{\sigma} = \frac{194.5 - 195}{26} = -0.02$$

Using the table for the standard normal distribution,

$$P(Z < -0.02) = 0.4920$$

and so

$$P(X < 194.5) = 0.4920$$

[8] Because the sample size is large, irrespective of the distribution of the population:

$$\mu_{\bar{x}} = \mu = 39$$

$$\sigma_{\bar{x}} = \frac{\sigma}{\sqrt{n}} = \frac{7.6}{\sqrt{140}} = 0.642$$

(a) Converting the $\bar{x}$-value to a z-score using the standardising formula gives, for $\bar{x} = 40.7$,

$$z = \frac{\bar{x} - \mu}{\sigma_{\bar{x}}} = \frac{40.7 - 39}{0.642} = 2.65$$

(b) Converting the $\bar{x}$-value to a z-score using the standardising formula gives, for $\bar{x} = 38.1$,

$$z = \frac{\bar{x} - \mu}{\sigma_{\bar{x}}} = \frac{38.1 - 39}{0.642} = -1.40$$

[9] The probability distribution for a discrete random variable provides information about the possible values that the variable can assume, and the probabilities associated with those values.

[10] Option (a). Approximately 90 intervals would contain the true value of μ if we constructed one hundred 90% confidence intervals for a population with mean μ.

[11] A random variable is a variable whose possible values are the numerical outcomes of a random experiment.

[12] Using the standard normal distribution table:
(a) The area under the standard normal curve to the **left** of $z = -1.94$ is 0.0262, so the required area is $1 - 0.0262 = 0.9738$.
(b) The area under the standard normal curve to the **left** of $z = 2.23$ is 0.9871, so the required area is $1 - 0.9871 = 0.0129$.

[13] For a discrete random variable, all of its possible values can be listed, usually as a result of counting rather than measuring; most discrete random variables have a finite number of possible outcomes. Example: the number of customer complaints received in an hour.

If our experiment involves measurements, then we would define a continuous random variable whose outcomes can be any numerical value within a given interval; in this case, there are an infinite number of possible outcomes, which cannot all be listed. Example: time taken to commute from home to work each day.

14   The sampling distribution of $\bar{x}$ is normally distributed.
The mean of the sampling distribution of $\bar{x}$ is equal to the population mean, £1857.54.
The standard deviation of the sampling distribution of $\bar{x}$ is

$$\sigma_{\bar{x}} = \frac{\sigma}{\sqrt{n}} = \frac{94.15}{\sqrt{22}} = £20.07$$

15   For a 99% confidence level, we need to find the z-scores that have an area under the standard normal curve between them of 0.99.
Using the table for the standard normal distribution gives z-scores of -2.58 and 2.58 and so our value of z in the formula is 2.58.

16   (a) population
(b) smaller
(c) mean
(d) standard, error

17   (a) A 90% confidence interval using the z-value of 1.64 is

$$\bar{x} \pm z\frac{\sigma}{\sqrt{n}} = 62 \pm 1.64 \times \frac{16}{\sqrt{31}} = 62 \pm 4.713$$

which is (57.287, 66.713).
(b) A 90% confidence interval using the z-value of 1.64 is

$$\bar{x} \pm z\frac{\sigma}{\sqrt{n}} = 8.64 \pm 1.64 \times \frac{0.77}{\sqrt{100}} = 8.64 \pm 0.126$$

which is (8.514, 8.766).

18   (a) A population parameter is a quantity measured for a population; it is generally an unknown value which is fixed. A sample statistic is a quantity measured for a sample taken from a population; it can be calculated for any sample and its value will vary according to the members of the population selected for inclusion in the sample.
(b) The population mean is denoted by μ and a sample mean is denoted by $\bar{x}$.

19   Option (c). The corresponding z-score is -1.04 and the area under the standard normal curve to the left of this value is 0.1492, so the probability that the sample mean for a random sample of size $n = 87$ will be greater than 62 is $1 - 0.1492 = 0.8508$.

20   Because the standard normal is symmetrical about the mean, $P(Z > 0.31)$ is the same as $P(Z \leq -0.31)$, so $P(Z > 0.31) = 0.3783$.

21 (a) Converting the x value into its corresponding z value gives, for $x = 14$,

$$z = \frac{x - \mu}{\sigma} = \frac{14 - 16}{3.4} = -0.59$$

Using the table for the standard normal distribution,

$$P(Z \geq -0.59) = 0.7224$$

and so

$$P(X \geq 14) = 0.7224$$

(b) Converting the x value into its corresponding z value gives, for $x = 19$,

$$z = \frac{x - \mu}{\sigma} = \frac{19 - 16}{3.4} = 0.88$$

Using the table for the standard normal distribution,

$$P(Z \leq 0.88) = 0.8106$$

and so

$$P(X \leq 19) = 0.8106$$

(c) Converting the x values into their corresponding z values gives, for $x = 15.5$,

$$z = \frac{x - \mu}{\sigma} = \frac{15.5 - 16}{3.4} = -0.15$$

and for $x = 16.5$,

$$z = \frac{x - \mu}{\sigma} = \frac{16.5 - 16}{3.4} = 0.15$$

Using the table for the standard normal distribution,

$$P(Z \leq -0.15) = 0.4404 \quad \text{and} \quad P(Z \leq 0.15) = 0.5596$$

therefore

$$P(-0.15 \leq Z \leq 0.15) = 0.5596 - 0.4404 = 0.1192$$

and so

$$P(15.5 \leq X \leq 16.5) = 0.1192$$

22 68, 95, 99.7

23 (a) No – this is not a valid probability distribution because the sum of the probabilities is more than one.

(b) Yes – this is a valid probability distribution because each probability is between zero and one inclusive, and the sum of the probabilities is one.

(c) No – this is not a valid probability distribution because one of the probabilities is stated as less than zero.

24 Using the standard normal distribution table:

(a) Under the standard normal curve, the area to the left of $z = -0.72$ is 0.2358 and the area to the left of $z = -1.25$ is 0.1057. So the required area is $0.2358 - 0.1057 = 0.1301$.

(b) Under the standard normal curve, the area to the left of $z = 1.95$ is 0.9744 and the area to the left of $z = 2.34$ is 0.9904. So the required area is $0.9904 - 0.9744 = 0.0160$.

25 We can conclude that there is a 95% chance that the interval (7.928, 8.072) will contain the mean organising time of all events.

26 X can assume the values 0, 1, 2, 3 or 4.

27 The following example illustrates the steps required for using the standard normal distribution table to find the z-score that has an area of 0.6217 to its left under the standard normal curve, assuming that the table provides the cumulative probability to the left of a range of positive and negative z-scores.

1. Find the table value that is equal to the known area:

z	0.00	0.01	0.02	0.03	0.04	0.05	...
...							
0.2		0.5832					
0.3	0.6179	0.6217	0.6255	0.6293	0.6331	0.6368	
0.4		0.6591					
0.5		0.6950					
0.6		0.7291					
0.7		0.7611					
...							

2. Combine the relevant row heading and column heading to work out the required z-score:

0.3   0.01

0.31

Therefore the z-score that has an area of 0.6217 to its left under the standard normal curve is 0.31.

28 (a) Converting the x-value to a z-score using the standardising formula gives, for $x = 150$,

$$z = \frac{x - \mu}{\sigma} = \frac{150 - 117}{14.9} = 2.21$$

(b) Converting the x-value to a z-score using the standardising formula gives, for $x = 91$,

$$z = \frac{x - \mu}{\sigma} = \frac{91 - 117}{14.9} = -1.74$$

29 (a) The sampling distribution of the sample mean weight for samples of 200 packages is normally distributed with a mean of 3.44 kg and a standard deviation of 0.019 kg.

(b) No – the answer to part (a) is not affected because the sample size is large ($n \geq 30$) and so the sampling distribution will be approximately normally distributed regardless of the distribution of the original population.

30 A 90% confidence interval is

$$\bar{x} \pm z \frac{\sigma}{\sqrt{n}} = 251.4 \pm 1.64 \times \frac{68.7}{\sqrt{17}} = 251.4 \pm 27.326$$

which is (224.074, 278.726).

A 95% confidence interval is

$$\bar{x} \pm z \frac{\sigma}{\sqrt{n}} = 251.4 \pm 1.96 \times \frac{68.7}{\sqrt{17}} = 251.4 \pm 32.658$$

which is (218.742, 284.058).

A 99% confidence interval is

$$\bar{x} \pm z \frac{\sigma}{\sqrt{n}} = 251.4 \pm 2.58 \times \frac{68.7}{\sqrt{17}} = 251.4 \pm 42.988$$

which is (208.412, 294.388).

31 (a) 0, 1

(b) sum

32 (a) The point estimate for the population mean monthly rental of all apartments is equal to the sample mean which is £726.

(b) A 95% confidence interval for the mean monthly rental of all apartments is

$$\bar{x} \pm z \frac{\sigma}{\sqrt{n}} = 726 \pm 1.96 \times \frac{46}{\sqrt{180}} = 726 \pm 6.72$$

which is (719.28, 732.72).

33 (a) The sampling distribution of $\bar{x}$ for samples of size $n = 100$ would be approximately normally distributed with parameters $\mu = 17$ and $\sigma = 0.3$.

(b) No – it was not necessary to make any assumptions because the sample size is more than 30 and so the sampling distribution of $\bar{x}$ will be approximately normally distributed regardless of the distribution of the original population.

(c) No – we would need to know if the population of interest is normally distributed to be able to define the sampling distribution of $\bar{x}$ for samples of size $n = 4$ because the sample size is small.

34 (a) The mean determines the location of the centre of a normal distribution curve on the x-axis. Increasing the mean of a distribution will move the curve to the right but its overall shape will remain unchanged.

(b) The standard deviation of a normal distribution affects the spread of the curve. Decreasing the standard deviation will result in a taller, narrower curve, but the centre of location of the curve will remain the same.

35 Because the population is normally distributed,

$$\mu_{\bar{x}} = \mu = 138$$

$$\sigma_{\bar{x}} = \frac{\sigma}{\sqrt{n}} = \frac{21}{\sqrt{25}} = 4.2$$

(a) Converting the $\bar{x}$-value to a z-score using the standardising formula gives, for $\bar{x} = 128$,

$$z = \frac{\bar{x} - \mu}{\sigma_{\bar{x}}} = \frac{128 - 138}{4.2} = -2.38$$

Using the standard normal distribution table, the area under the standard normal curve to the left of $z = -2.38$ is 0.0087. The probability that the sample mean for a random sample of size $n = 25$ will be less than 128 is 0.0087.

(b) Because the total area under the standard normal curve is equal to 1, the probability that the sample mean for a random sample of size $n = 25$ will be greater than 128 is $1 - P(X < 128) = 1 - 0.0087 = 0.9913$.

36 Because the total area under the standard normal curve equals 1, $P(Z \geq 1.21) = 1 - P(Z < 1.21) = 1 - 0.8869 = 0.1131$.

37 (a) FALSE

A sampling distribution is the probability distribution of a sample statistic.

(b) FALSE

It is usually less time-consuming and less costly to collect data using a sample rather than collecting data about every member of the population.

(c) TRUE

38 The confidence interval will definitely contain the sample mean because the interval is constructed with the sample mean at the centre of the range of values. Therefore, there is a 100% chance that the interval will contain the sample mean.

39 (a) area
(b) mean
(c) right, 0.5
(d) horizontal

40 Yes – this is a valid probability distribution because each probability is between 0 and 1 inclusive, and the sum of the probabilities is 1.

Appendix: The Standard Normal Distribution

The table values represent the area under the standard normal curve to the left of each z-score. Follow the instructions in the example in Chapter 10, which illustrates the steps required for using this table.

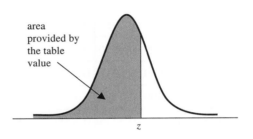

area provided by the table value

z	0.00	0.01	0.02	0.03	0.04	0.05	0.06	0.07	0.08	0.09
−3.0	0.0013	0.0013	0.0013	0.0012	0.0012	0.0011	0.0011	0.0011	0.0010	0.0010
−2.9	0.0019	0.0018	0.0018	0.0017	0.0016	0.0016	0.0015	0.0015	0.0014	0.0014
−2.8	0.0026	0.0025	0.0024	0.0023	0.0023	0.0022	0.0021	0.0021	0.0020	0.0019
−2.7	0.0035	0.0034	0.0033	0.0032	0.0031	0.0030	0.0029	0.0028	0.0027	0.0026
−2.6	0.0047	0.0045	0.0044	0.0043	0.0041	0.0040	0.0039	0.0038	0.0037	0.0036
−2.5	0.0062	0.0060	0.0059	0.0057	0.0055	0.0054	0.0052	0.0051	0.0049	0.0048
−2.4	0.0082	0.0080	0.0078	0.0075	0.0073	0.0071	0.0069	0.0068	0.0066	0.0064
−2.3	0.0107	0.0104	0.0102	0.0099	0.0096	0.0094	0.0091	0.0089	0.0087	0.0084
−2.2	0.0139	0.0136	0.0132	0.0129	0.0125	0.0122	0.0119	0.0116	0.0113	0.0110
−2.1	0.0179	0.0174	0.0170	0.0166	0.0162	0.0158	0.0154	0.0150	0.0146	0.0143
−2.0	0.0228	0.0222	0.0217	0.0212	0.0207	0.0202	0.0197	0.0192	0.0188	0.0183
−1.9	0.0287	0.0281	0.0274	0.0268	0.0262	0.0256	0.0250	0.0244	0.0239	0.0233
−1.8	0.0359	0.0351	0.0344	0.0336	0.0329	0.0322	0.0314	0.0307	0.0301	0.0294
−1.7	0.0446	0.0436	0.0427	0.0418	0.0409	0.0401	0.0392	0.0384	0.0375	0.0367
−1.6	0.0548	0.0537	0.0526	0.0516	0.0505	0.0495	0.0485	0.0475	0.0465	0.0455
−1.5	0.0668	0.0655	0.0643	0.0630	0.0618	0.0606	0.0594	0.0582	0.0571	0.0559
−1.4	0.0808	0.0793	0.0778	0.0764	0.0749	0.0735	0.0721	0.0708	0.0694	0.0681

(Continued)

z	0.00	0.01	0.02	0.03	0.04	0.05	0.06	0.07	0.08	0.09
−1.3	0.0968	0.0951	0.0934	0.0918	0.0901	0.0885	0.0869	0.0853	0.0838	0.0823
−1.2	0.1151	0.1131	0.1112	0.1093	0.1075	0.1056	0.1038	0.1020	0.1003	0.0985
−1.1	0.1357	0.1335	0.1314	0.1292	0.1271	0.1251	0.1230	0.1210	0.1190	0.1170
−1.0	0.1587	0.1562	0.1539	0.1515	0.1492	0.1469	0.1446	0.1423	0.1401	0.1379
−0.9	0.1841	0.1814	0.1788	0.1762	0.1736	0.1711	0.1685	0.1660	0.1635	0.1611
−0.8	0.2119	0.2090	0.2061	0.2033	0.2005	0.1977	0.1949	0.1922	0.1894	0.1867
−0.7	0.2420	0.2389	0.2358	0.2327	0.2296	0.2266	0.2236	0.2206	0.2177	0.2148
−0.6	0.2743	0.2709	0.2676	0.2643	0.2611	0.2578	0.2546	0.2514	0.2483	0.2451
−0.5	0.3085	0.3050	0.3015	0.2981	0.2946	0.2912	0.2877	0.2843	0.2810	0.2776
−0.4	0.3446	0.3409	0.3372	0.3336	0.3300	0.3264	0.3228	0.3192	0.3156	0.3121
−0.3	0.3821	0.3783	0.3745	0.3707	0.3669	0.3632	0.3594	0.3557	0.3520	0.3483
−0.2	0.4207	0.4168	0.4129	0.4090	0.4052	0.4013	0.3974	0.3936	0.3897	0.3859
−0.1	0.4602	0.4562	0.4522	0.4483	0.4443	0.4404	0.4364	0.4325	0.4286	0.4247
−0.0	0.5000	0.4960	0.4920	0.4880	0.4840	0.4801	0.4761	0.4721	0.4681	0.4641

z	0.00	0.01	0.02	0.03	0.04	0.05	0.06	0.07	0.08	0.09
0.0	0.5000	0.5040	0.5080	0.5120	0.5160	0.5199	0.5239	0.5279	0.5319	0.5359
0.1	0.5398	0.5438	0.5478	0.5517	0.5557	0.5596	0.5636	0.5675	0.5714	0.5753
0.2	0.5793	0.5832	0.5871	0.5910	0.5948	0.5987	0.6026	0.6064	0.6103	0.6141
0.3	0.6179	0.6217	0.6255	0.6293	0.6331	0.6368	0.6406	0.6443	0.6480	0.6517
0.4	0.6554	0.6591	0.6628	0.6664	0.6700	0.6736	0.6772	0.6808	0.6844	0.6879
0.5	0.6915	0.6950	0.6985	0.7019	0.7054	0.7088	0.7123	0.7157	0.7190	0.7224
0.6	0.7257	0.7291	0.7324	0.7357	0.7389	0.7422	0.7454	0.7486	0.7517	0.7549
0.7	0.7580	0.7611	0.7642	0.7673	0.7704	0.7734	0.7764	0.7794	0.7823	0.7852
0.8	0.7881	0.7910	0.7939	0.7967	0.7995	0.8023	0.8051	0.8078	0.8106	0.8133
0.9	0.8159	0.8186	0.8212	0.8238	0.8264	0.8289	0.8315	0.8340	0.8365	0.8389
1.0	0.8413	0.8438	0.8461	0.8485	0.8508	0.8531	0.8554	0.8577	0.8599	0.8621
1.1	0.8643	0.8665	0.8686	0.8708	0.8729	0.8749	0.8770	0.8790	0.8810	0.8830

(Continued)

z	0.00	0.01	0.02	0.03	0.04	0.05	0.06	0.07	0.08	0.09
1.2	0.8849	0.8869	0.8888	0.8907	0.8925	0.8944	0.8962	0.8980	0.8997	0.9015
1.3	0.9032	0.9049	0.9066	0.9082	0.9099	0.9115	0.9131	0.9147	0.9162	0.9177
1.4	0.9192	0.9207	0.9222	0.9236	0.9251	0.9265	0.9279	0.9292	0.9306	0.9319
1.5	0.9332	0.9345	0.9357	0.9370	0.9382	0.9394	0.9406	0.9418	0.9429	0.9441
1.6	0.9452	0.9463	0.9474	0.9484	0.9495	0.9505	0.9515	0.9525	0.9535	0.9545
1.7	0.9554	0.9564	0.9573	0.9582	0.9591	0.9599	0.9608	0.9616	0.9625	0.9633
1.8	0.9641	0.9649	0.9656	0.9664	0.9671	0.9678	0.9686	0.9693	0.9699	0.9706
1.9	0.9713	0.9719	0.9726	0.9732	0.9738	0.9744	0.9750	0.9756	0.9761	0.9767
2.0	0.9772	0.9778	0.9783	0.9788	0.9793	0.9798	0.9803	0.9808	0.9812	0.9817
2.1	0.9821	0.9826	0.9830	0.9834	0.9838	0.9842	0.9846	0.9850	0.9854	0.9857
2.2	0.9861	0.9864	0.9868	0.9871	0.9875	0.9878	0.9881	0.9884	0.9887	0.9890
2.3	0.9893	0.9896	0.9898	0.9901	0.9904	0.9906	0.9909	0.9911	0.9913	0.9916
2.4	0.9918	0.9920	0.9922	0.9925	0.9927	0.9929	0.9931	0.9932	0.9934	0.9936
2.5	0.9938	0.9940	0.9941	0.9943	0.9945	0.9946	0.9948	0.9949	0.9951	0.9952
2.6	0.9953	0.9955	0.9956	0.9957	0.9959	0.9960	0.9961	0.9962	0.9963	0.9964
2.7	0.9965	0.9966	0.9967	0.9968	0.9969	0.9970	0.9971	0.9972	0.9973	0.9974
2.8	0.9974	0.9975	0.9976	0.9977	0.9977	0.9978	0.9979	0.9979	0.9980	0.9981
2.9	0.9981	0.9982	0.9982	0.9983	0.9984	0.9984	0.9985	0.9985	0.9986	0.9986
3.0	0.9987	0.9987	0.9987	0.9988	0.9988	0.9989	0.9989	0.9989	0.9990	0.9990

The values in this table were generated using the NORMSDIST function in MS Excel.

Glossary

addition rule   A method used to calculate the probability of the union of two events.

arithmetic mean   A more precise way of referring to the mean.

average   A typical value that is representative of a data set.

bar chart   A diagram in which the frequency of data values in a category is represented by the height of a rectangular bar.

bimodal   A data set in which two modes can be identified.

bivariate data   Data that involves the measurements or observations of two variables.

box plot   A diagram that provides a visual representation of a five-number summary.

box-and-whisker plot   An alternative name for a box plot.

cause-and-effect relationship   An association between two variables in which a change in one variable causes a change in the other variable.

census   Data is collected from every member of a population.

central limit theorem   A mathematical theorem which states that, for large sample sizes, the sampling distribution of the mean will be approximately normal, regardless of the distribution of the original population.

certain event   An event with a probability equal to exactly 1 that will be certain to occur.

class   Groups into which data are categorised using a grouped frequency distribution.

class boundary   The half-way point between a specified class and the previous class, or the next class.

class limit   The end-points of a class when it is included in the table for a grouped frequency distribution.

class mid-point   The half-way point between the upper class boundary and the lower class boundary of a specified class.

class width   The numerical difference between the upper class boundary and the lower class boundary of a specified class.

classical approach   A method used to determine the probability of an event when an experiment has equally likely outcomes.

closed question   A question with a fixed number of possible answers from which a respondent must choose.

cluster sampling   A sampling method which involves dividing a population into groups, known as clusters. All members of one or more randomly selected clusters are included in the sample.

coefficient of variation The standard deviation expressed as a percentage of the mean.

combined mean The arithmetic means of more than one data set, combined into a single value.

complement event The set of elements in the sample space that are not in an event.

compound event An event that consists of more than one element in the sample space.

conditional probability The probability that an event occurs, given the knowledge that another event has already occurred.

confidence interval A method used to describe the level of confidence that a range of values contains a population parameter.

confidence level The probability that a confidence interval contains a population parameter.

continuous Continuous data can take any numerical value within a specific range.

continuous random variable A variable whose outcomes can be any numerical value within a given interval.

convenience sampling A sampling method which involves choosing members of a population that are conveniently available to be included in the sample.

correlation coefficient A measure of the strength and direction of the linear relationship between two quantitative variables.

cumulative frequency The number of values in a data set that are less than or equal to a specific value.

cumulative relative frequency The cumulative frequency of a specified value, expressed as a percentage.

data Information that is observed or measured; it is used for analysis and presentation.

data set A collection of related data.

dependent variable A variable that can be predicted by the value of an independent variable.

descriptive statistics Processing and summarising data using tabular, graphical and numerical methods.

deviation The difference between each value in a data set and the mean of the values.

discrete Discrete data can take only a finite number of possible numerical values.

discrete random variable A variable for which all of the possible values can be listed.

empirical approach A method used to determine the probability of an event when an experiment does not have equally likely outcomes.

equally likely outcomes A situation in which the probability of every possible outcome of an experiment is the same.

event A collection of one or more outcomes of an experiment.

experiment Any action or process that can be repeated for which we can identify all of the outcomes that could possibly occur.

explanatory variable An alternative name for an independent variable.

extrapolation Use of a mathematical model to predict a value outside the range of the data set on which the model is based.

first quartile An alternative name for the lower quartile.

five-number summary A way of describing a data set using the minimum, lower quartile, median, upper quartile and maximum values.

frequency distribution A table that shows the frequency with which each value occurs in a data set.

gradient A measure of the direction and steepness of a line.

grouped frequency distribution A table in which values are formed into groups and the number of occurrences in each group from a data set is recorded.

histogram A diagram in which the frequency of data values in a class is represented by the area of a rectangular bar.

impossible event An event with a probability equal to exactly 0 that will never occur.

independent events Two events are independent if the occurrence of one event in an experiment does not have any effect on the occurrence of the other event.

independent variable A variable that can be used to predict the value of a dependent variable.

inferential statistics Using sample data to make generalisations about the population from which the sample was taken.

interpolation Use of a mathematical model to predict a value within the range of the data set on which the model is based.

interquartile range The difference between the upper quartile and the lower quartile.

intersection For two events, the set of elements in the sample space that are common to both of the events.

interval estimate A range of values which we would expect to contain a population parameter.

interview A conversation in which a set of questions is used to gather information from an interviewee.

interviewee The person who is being interviewed.

least squares method A mathematical technique used to identify the line of best fit for a data set.

line of best fit The line that provides the best prediction for a dependent variable based on an independent variable.

linear equation An equation that describes a straight line on a graph.

linear relationship An association between two variables which are directly proportional to each other.

lower class boundary The half-way point between the upper class limit of the previous class and the lower class limit of the specified class.

lower class limit The smallest end-point of a class when it is included in the table for a grouped frequency distribution.

lower quartile The value which separates the smallest 25% of the values from the remaining data set.

lurking variable An additional variable which may account for a cause-and-effect relationship between two variables.

mean The average of a set of numbers, calculated as the sum of the data values divided by the number of values in the set.

measure of central tendency A way of describing a data set by identifying a typical value that is representative of its values.

median The middle value which divides an ordered data set into two halves.

mode The value which occurs most frequently in a data set.

modified box plot A diagram that provides a visual representation of a five-number summary and includes outliers.

multimodal A data set in which more than two modes can be identified.

multiplication rule A method used to calculate the probability of the intersection of two events.

mutually exclusive events Events that cannot occur at the same time.

negative correlation A relationship between two variables in which the values of one variable increase whilst the values of the other variable decrease.

non-response bias When non-responders have different characteristics and opinions than the respondents and the interviewees.

normal curve A curve on a graph that describes a normal distribution.

normal distribution A distribution in which many of the data values are clustered around a central value with fewer values occurring as the distance from the central value increases.

observation The value of a variable for a specific member in the group that is of interest.

open question A question that allows a respondent to compose their own answer.

outcome The result of an experiment.

outlier An extreme value in a data set.

pie chart A circular diagram divided into segments, each one representing a category as a proportion of the whole data set.

pilot study A small-scale study to test the quality of the questions designed for a questionnaire or an interview.

point estimate A single value used as an estimate of a population parameter.

population The entire group in which we are interested.

population parameter A quantity measured for a population.

positive correlation A relationship between two variables in which the values of both variables increase or decrease together.

primary data Data that is collected by a researcher for a specific purpose.

probability A measure of the likelihood that an event will occur.

probability density function A mathematical function used to describe the probability distribution of a continuous random variable.

probability distribution A table, an equation or a graph that provides information about the possible values that a variable can assume.

probability model Use of a mathematical representation in which a probability is assigned to every element in the sample space for an experiment.

proportional allocation In stratified sampling, when the number of members taken from each stratum is in proportion to the relative size of the group within the population.

qualitative data Data that cannot be described using a numerical value.

qualitative variable A variable that describes qualitative data.

quantitative data Data can be counted or measured on a numerical scale.

quantitative variable A variable that describes quantitative data.

quartiles The three values that divide an ordered data set into four equal parts.

questionnaire A set of written questions designed to gather information from a respondent.

quota sampling A sampling method which involves categorising the members of a population using a particular characteristic. The sample includes a specified number of members from each category.

random variable A variable whose possible values are the numerical outcomes of a random experiment.

range The difference between the largest value and the smallest value in a data set.

raw data Data values that are recorded in the order in which they are collected.

regression line An alternative name for a line of best fit.

relative frequency The frequency with which each value occurs in a data set, expressed as a proportion of all the data values.

relative frequency probability An alternative name for the empirical approach to probability.

representative When the characteristics of the sample members reflect as closely as possible the characteristics of the population from which the sample was taken.

residual The vertical difference between a data point and the line of best fit on a graph.

resistant A statistic is resistant if it is not substantially influenced by extreme data values that occur in the data set.

respondent The person who completes a written questionnaire.

response bias When the answers given by a respondent or an interviewee do not reflect the true facts and/or their opinions.

response variable An alternative name for a dependent variable.

sample A subset of members selected from the population of interest.

sample space The set of all possible outcomes of an experiment.

sample statistic A quantity measured for a sample.

sampling distribution The probability distribution of a sample statistic.

sampling frame A list that includes information about every member of a population.

scatter diagram A diagram for displaying the values of two quantitative variables so that any potential relationship between them can be observed.

secondary data Data that is used, but not collected, by a researcher.

simple event An event that consists of a single element in the sample space.

simple linear regression   Use of a mathematical model to investigate the relationship between the two variables by determining how a change in the value of one variable affects the value of the other variable.

simple random sampling   A sampling method in which every possible sample of a specified size has an equal chance of being selected.

standard deviation   The positive square root of the variance.

standard error   The standard deviation of the sampling distribution of a statistic.

standard normal curve   The curve on a graph that describes a standard normal distribution.

standard normal distribution   A normal distribution with parameters $\mu = 0$ and $\sigma = 1$.

stem and leaf diagram   A diagram in which the digits of each quantitative data value are separated into a stem and a leaf.

stratified sampling   A sampling method which involves dividing a population into groups, known as strata. Simple random sampling is used on every stratum to select members for the sample.

subjective approach   A method used to determine the probability of an event based on the personal experience and judgement of an individual.

systematic sampling   A sampling method which involves choosing a starting point at random in a list of all members of a population, and then systematically selecting each member that occurs in the list at a specific interval.

third quartile   An alternative name for the upper quartile.

time series plot   A diagram used to display quantitative data collected at specific time intervals.

union   For two events, the set of elements in the sample space that belongs to at least one of the events.

upper class boundary   The half-way point between the upper class limit of the specified class and the lower class limit of the next class.

upper class limit   The largest end-point of a class when it is included in the table for a grouped frequency distribution.

upper quartile   The value which separates the smallest 75% of the values from the remaining data set.

variable   A characteristic or an attribute that can have different values.

variance   The average squared difference between each value in a data set and the mean of the values.

Venn diagram   A diagram that can be used to provide a visual representation of an experiment and associated events.

weighted mean   An arithmetic mean where some data values contribute more weight than others.

y-intercept   The point on a graph where a straight line crosses the y-axis.

z-score   For the standard normal curve, the distance between the mean and a point on the horizontal axis, expressed in terms of the standard deviation.

Index

Note: Page numbers in *italics* relate to illustrations